LITERARY CRITICISM
AND BIBLICAL HERMENEUTICS

American Academy of Religion
Academy Series

Edited by
Carl A. Raschke

Number 48

LITERARY CRITICISM AND BIBLICAL HERMENEUTICS:
A CRITIQUE OF FORMALIST APPROACHES

by
Lynn M. Poland

Lynn M. Poland

LITERARY CRITICISM AND BIBLICAL HERMENEUTICS: A CRITIQUE OF FORMALIST APPROACHES

Scholars Press
Chico, California

LITERARY CRITICISM
AND BIBLICAL HERMENEUTICS

by
Lynn M. Poland

© 1985
American Academy of Religion

BS
500
.P59
1985

Library of Congress Cataloging in Publication Data

Poland, Lynn M., 1949-
  Literary criticism and biblical hermeneutics.

  (American Academy of Religion academy series ; 48)
  Originally presented as the author's thesis (Ph.D.—
University of Chicago, 1981).
  Bibliography: p.
  Includes Index.
  1. Bible—Criticism,   interpretation,   etc.—History—
20th century. 2. Bible—Hermeneutics. I. Title. II. Series
BS500.P59   1985   220.6'6'01   85-2477
ISBN 0–89130–825–3 (alk. paper)
ISBN 0–89130–836–9 (pbk. : alk. paper)

Printed in the United States of America
on acid-free paper

TABLE OF CONTENTS

ACKNOWLEDGEMENTS

To advise well is to enable. It has been my good fortune to have had such an advisor in Anthony C. Yu. For his good counsel, and for the generosity of my readers, David L. Bartlett, Hans Dieter Betz, and David Tracy, I am most grateful.

INTRODUCTION

Although certain kinds of literary theory have always exerted an influence on interpreters of Scripture, an increasing number of biblical scholars have begun to appropriate the theories and practices of modern, secular criticism in a self-conscious and systematic way./1/ In New Testament studies, which is my focus here, primary attention has been given to the parables and the synoptic gospels./2/ While their work shows variety in method and purpose, these scholars share a conviction that the historical-critical method which has dominated modern biblical criticism requires revision. As Norman Petersen has remarked, for example, "Today the historical critical paradigm is in a process of potentially revolutionary change. . . . The future of the historical critical paradigm is a lively question."/3/ These contemporary scholars argue that while the methods of source, form, and redaction criticism are all varieties of literary criticism, these approaches do not give sufficient consideration to the specifically literary aspects of the biblical texts. As a consequence, they wish to reserve the term *literary criticism* for their own recent perspective. Petersen also writes, for example:

> It should be noted that for most historical critics, 'literary criticism' refers to *source* criticism! Otherwise the adjective 'literary' is used principally in connection with the notion of literary history, which refers to the history of the form and style of the material used in the composition of the biblical writings. As a result of this usage, biblical critics until recently have lacked an understanding of literature like that found among literary critics./4/

In addition to their challenge to the hegemony of historical criticism, many of these scholars express impatience with the dominant modern hermeneutic tradition, as it is represented in particular by Rudolf Bultmann. In the interest of retrieving or restating the theological message of Scripture threatened by destructive historical criticism, they argue, the Bultmannian hermeneutic abstracts the subject matter of a text from its form, thus violating the integrity of the biblical writings. William A. Beardslee, for example, writes of Bultmann's method of existential interpretation: "Just as it relegates ideas to a secondary position, . . . it also thrusts literary form into the background as secondary and separable from the existential stance which the form expresses."/5/

In contrast to the presuppositions of both historical criticism and Bultmannian demythologizing, our contemporary scholars insist that the *meaning* of a text is inseparable from the forms in which it is expressed. The meaning of the biblical writings is not to be found behind the texts in the events to which they ostensively refer, nor in the cultural and religious situation which produced them. Nor is the meaning of the texts to be located in some set of moral or philosophical truths abstracted from the cohesive unity of the literary work. Instead, they call for a new approach to biblical studies, one which views the meaning of the biblical writings as inseparable from the internal form and structure of a text. The first requirement, they argue, is to "understand the text as text."

To assert that the form and content of a work are inextricably related, and thus that the meaning of a text is in some sense "in" the structure of the work itself, is to adopt two of the main tenets of modern formalist literary criticism, particularly that phase of American literary criticism, the New Criticism, represented by scholars such as Cleanth Brooks, John Crowe Ransom, René Wellek, and Austin Warren. As many biblical scholars have noted, their own recent challenge to historical criticism and Bultmannian interpretation parallels the intentions of the New Critics earlier in this century: the New Criticism arose, in part, as a legitimate reaction to the hegemony of literary history. A century ago, literary scholars were engaged in projects not very different from those which continue to occupy traditional biblical critics at present. Committed to the rigorous application of the tools of scientific research, philologists scrutinized *Piers Plowman*, editors looked for apocryphal passages in Chaucer and Shakespeare, while others sought to reconstruct the original *ur*-form of *Sir Gawain and the Green Knight*./6/

The New Critics' dissatisfaction with this kind of literary history sprang in part from its excesses: it yielded an abundance of unrelated facts and minute details from the lives and quarrels of authors. The chief source of their dissatisfacton, however, was the literary historian's presupposition that the meaning of a literary work is located in its causes—in the artistic personality, or in its casual antecedents in the political, social, or economic spheres.

As the second chapter of this study will spell out in detail, the New Critics were reacting to other cultural forces as well as to the procedures of literary history—including the developing tendency toward scientism in the modern period, with its growing claim to be arbiter of what constitutes true knowledge. The New Critics stressed the inseparability of form and content and asserted that the meaning of a literary work is an affair of its total structure in order to defend the peculiarly aesthetic being of literature as a mode of knowledge distinct from the abstract propositional truths of science and philosophy.

This project explores the consequences of this kind of literary theory for the larger task of biblical hermeneutics. Two assumptions guiding my inquiry can be stated at the outset. First, it is assumed that the kind of attention to the forms of religious expression in the biblical documents which literary criticism of this kind makes possible is a significant and positive contribution to the process of biblical interpretation. The growing number of studies from this perspective have already significantly enriched our understanding of biblical texts, and of the ways in which particular literary forms, such as narrative, parable, or psalm, are linked to a particular religious or theological content. Among the central values of this literary turn are the possibilities it offers for encouraging dialogue between the too often estranged disciplines of theology and biblical studies. An investigation of New Testament narrative, for example, is an important source for renewed theological reflection on classical problems such as the ground of biblical authority, on the interrelation of theological concepts and symbolic discourse, and on the relation between the character of disclosure belonging to literary texts and the concept of revelation./7/

Second, the larger task of biblical hermeneutics is assumed to include that of rendering the biblical writings meaningful for contemporary communities of faith This is not to prescribe a particular interpretive method, but to affirm the traditional formal aim of biblical interpretation—to show that the meaning of Scripture extends, as St. Bernard stated, *hodie usque ad nos*, "even to us today." Together these assumptions define the normative question underlying my investigation: a way must be found to integrate the important literary critical investigations of

the design and structure of the biblical writings with a hermeneutic theory which is equally concerned with the meaning and
significance of the texts for the present./8/

It is not the aim of this study to construct such a biblical
hermeneutic, however. My goal is a considerably more modest
one: to explore the specific problems which the introduction of
literary criticism poses for the task of biblical interpretation. It is
my conviction that the critical assumptions of modern formalist
literary criticism are in many respects at odds with, or at least
insufficient for, the full task of biblical interpretation. The second chapter of my project, therefore, undertakes to examine the
basic tenets and underlying presuppositions of this kind of criticism, by looking at both the theoretical statements of the literary
critics themselves, and at the historical context in which this
criticism emerged. An historical perspective is essential for
understanding the New Criticism, in my view, because the critical principles they espoused were developed, at least in part, in
response to several different currents within both literary scholarship and the larger cultural situation. Because they wish to
defend literature on a number of different fronts, I will argue,
the New Critical program exhibits a central internal inconsis-
tency. While on the one hand they wish to uphold the autonomy
and self-sufficiency of literary art, and to maintain its discontinuity with extrinsic spheres of meaning, on the other hand they
argue that literature provides a kind of "experiential" knowledge
which can extend and transform our perceptions of human experience in the world—surely an extrinsic aim.

As a number of contemporary literary theorists have pointed
out, this kind of criticism tends to eliminate the historical
dimension from both the text and its interpretation./9/ By
severing the literary work's ties to its origins in human experience, and by suppressing a text's claim to disclose something
about the world, formalist criticism de-historicizes and de-
contextualizes the works it studies. Furthermore, these critics
tend to view their enterprise as an entirely "disinterested" procedure; a formal analysis of a text's internal structure is often spoken of as an "objective criticism" unaffected by the interpreter's
presuppositions and particular perspective. Its weaknesses as a
program for literary study, whether we refer here to secular
literature or to the biblical writings, then, are that it ignores the
historical dimensions of interpretation and fails to explicate that

complex process by which texts can transform our experience of the world and our structures of belief. Furthermore, in giving exclusive attention to the inner dynamics of a literary work, formalism neglects the particular truths a text may disclose or illumine. Since each of these aspects of the literary situation are of crucial importance for biblical interpretation, whatever hermeneutic model one wishes to propose, these limitations must indeed be considered and reckoned with.

This chapter focuses on the specific strategies proposed by the American New Criticism, since the majority of biblical scholars who have employed literary criticism, at least in the initial phases of this movement, have turned to the writings of the New Critics. A growing number of biblical scholars have also adopted varieties of structuralist methods. While it is beyond the scope of my project to examine these methods in detail, my analysis of the limits of the New Criticism could be extended to other varieties of formalist criticism, including structuralism, as well. Among literary scholars, it is not uncommon to use the term *formalism* as a catch word for literary theories which focus on the intrinsic or internal structure of the literary work, rather than on the text's author, genetic context, referent, or reader. As many literary scholars have noted, structuralism can be viewed as a radicalizing extension of the basic formalist tendencies inherent in the New Critical program./10/ The dilemmas which the New Criticism poses for biblical interpretation are therefore considered here as representative of the limitations of formalist literary criticism in general.

Just what the task of biblical interpretation entails is the focus of the first chapter of my study. Here, Bultmann's hermeneutical program is examined within the larger contexts of pre-critical and modern biblical interpretation. Bultmann's interpretation theory is exemplary for this study for several reasons. Bultmann astutely perceived the central issues with which a specifically modern program for biblical interpretation must wrestle: the alien character of the world views represented in the biblical writings for twentieth-century readers; the complex relation between the kerygmatic subject matter or intention of the texts and the forms in which it is expressed; and, perhaps most importantly, the historical nature of understanding as such. Bultmann recognized that the pre-understanding of the historically situated interpreter is a necessary pre-condition for understanding, so that no purely "scientific," presuppositionless understanding is possible. Whether or not one accepts Bultmann's specific responses to these problems, the issues themselves must be addressed before any modern model for biblical interpretation can be accepted as adequate.

The specific strengths and weaknesses of Bultmann's proposals make him an exemplary figure in a further sense. The majority of scholars who advocate a literary approach to biblical interpretation—and the three scholars considered in Chapter III are representative in this regard—each attempt, in their own way, to go "beyond Bultmann," charging him with an insensitivity to the distinctive capacities of literary structure and poetic language. While this is in many respects an accurate judgment, close attention to the whole of Bultmann's program enables us to see why a literary analysis of the form and structure of the biblical writings is not, in itself, an adequate alternative to the Bultmannian hermeneutic. Bultmann's constructive proposals were, after all, theologically motivated: his demythologizing program was founded on the central theological conviction that the biblical texts witness to the kerygma—both a permanent scandal for comprehension and a material norm for Scripture. While the New Testament texts, unlike literature in the broad sense, intend to speak of the kerygma, they may do so more or less adequately. A critique of the content of the New Testament witnesses is thus, in Bultmann's view, demanded by the character of the writings themselves—in fact, Bultmann argues, this critical processs has already begun within the canon in the writings of Paul and John. While Bultmann's "translation" of the biblical writings into the categories of existentialist philosophy may indeed do violence to the integrity of the texts as literary wholes, to dismiss Bultmann too hastily is to fail to see the complexity of the interpretive issues involved here. To argue that form and content are inseparable in a literary work does not begin to address the question of the nature of the content or intention of the biblical texts as religious documents. To attend to the specific strengths and weaknesses of Bultmann's program, then, is to view him as a significant resource for evaluating the contributions of recent New Testament criticism and for developing a contemporary biblical hermeneutic.

A final sense in which Bultmann is important for this study becomes apparent in the three case studies presented in Chapter III. My project concerns those scholars who have appropriated formalist literary criticism with the intention of serving the larger aim of interpreting the biblical texts for contemporary communities of faith. Unlike scholars who are content to treat the Bible *as* literature, that is, they wish to maintain the scriptural status of the biblical writings. In pursuing this aim, these scholars have thus attempted—sometimes self-consciously, more often implicitly—to integrate the critical assumptions of formalism with other theological and interpretive presuppositions. The latter, furthermore, are often those of Bultmann or of the post-Bultmannian "New Hermeneutic." Because a consistently formalist biblical criticism and a Bultmannian hermeneutic method are, as I have indicated, in several respects logically exclusive enterprises, attempts to join both programs inevitably run into difficulties.

The purpose of Chapter III is to examine how these two programs are interwoven in the projects of John Dominic Crossan, Hans W. Frei, and Dan Otto Via, Jr. The underlying aim of this chapter is to clarify the possibilities for, and the difficulties of, successfully integrating literary criticism within the larger framework of biblical interpretation, by locating the specific points at which problems appear in the writings of these three scholars.

One clear conclusion to be drawn from this study is that the methodological difficulties entailed by joining a formalist program for literary analysis with a hermeneutic theory adequate for biblical interpretation demand a thorough re-thinking of the basic critical assumptions underlying both. The last chapter of my study therefore presents a case study of a different kind: the philosopher Paul Ricoeur has undertaken a project of this scope. Ricoeur has developed a hermeneutic theory which aims to modify and integrate formalist literary criticism (structuralism in particular) and existentialist interpretation. In addition, Ricoeur has addressed the peculiar problems belonging to biblical interpretation by considering the relation between theological and general hermeneutics, by reflecting on the notions of 'revelation' and 'testimony' with regard to the biblical writings, and through his own analysis of the New Testament parables./11/ The final chapter of my study will therefore introduce those aspects of Ricoeur's work which, in my view, begin to lay the foundation for a biblical hermeneutic that can include the contributions and perspectives of formalist literary criticism.

8   Literary Criticism and Biblical Hermeneutics

NOTES

/1/   Since at least the eighteenth century, biblical scholarship has tended to reflect the theories and practices of secular literary criticism as they were developed in a particular historical period. Early modern examples of the use of literary criticism in biblical scholarship are numerous. Among them, Bishop Löwth's study of the parallelism and other technical features of Hebrew poetry, *De Sacra Poesi Hebraeorum* (1753), was a pioneer in realizing the peculiar nature of Hebrew poetry. Löwth was followed by such studies as Herder's *Vom Geist der Ebräischen Poesie* (1782–83), and the influential theories of Julius Wellhausen in *Die Composition des Hexateuchs* (1876–77) and *Prolegomena zur Geschichte Israels* (1883). Useful overviews of these developments can be found in *The Interpreter's Dictionary*, rev. ed. (1962), s.v. "Biblical Criticism, History of," by S. J. DeVries; and s.v. "Interpretation, History and Principles of," by K. Grobel.

/2/   In addition to the work of the three scholars considered in Chapter III, see the Selected Bibliography for other studies of New Testament texts from this perspective. See also the journals *Semeia* and *Linguistica Biblica* for contemporary experiments in literary criticism of biblical texts.

/3/   Norman Petersen, *Literary Criticism for New Testament Critics* (Philadelphia: Fortress Press, 1978), p. 10.

/4/   Ibid.

/5/   William A. Beardslee, *Literary Criticism of the New Testament* (Philadelphia: Fortress Press, 1970), p. 2.

/6/   See the editors' excellent review of the developments of modern biblical and literary criticism in *The Bible and Its Literary Milieu*, ed. John Maier and Vincent Tollers (Grand Rapids: William B. Eerdmans Co., 1979), pp. 1–23. See also Roland Mushat Frye, "Literary Criticism and Gospel Criticism," *Theology Today* 36 (1979): 207–19.

/7/   George W. Stroup assesses the importance of narrative studies for theology in "A Bibliographic Critique," *Theology Today* 32 (1975): 133–43. See also Paul Ricoeur's reflections on the significance of studies of symbolic discourse for theology in "From Existentialism to the Philosophy of Language," in *The Philosophy of Paul Ricoeur*, ed. Charles E. Reagan and David Stewart (Boston: Beacon Press, 1978), p. 92. (The latter is cited hereafter as *Philosophy*.)

/8/   Edgar V. McKnight proposes a "narrative hermeneutics" which seeks to integrate structuralist literary criticism with Dilthey's hermeneutic theory in *Meaning in Texts* (Philadelphia: Fortress Press, 1978).

/9/   Studies and critiques of the New Critical movement are numerous. Among the most perceptive are those of Gerald Graff, *Poetic Statement and Critical Dogma* (Evanston: Northwestern University Press, 1970), and *Literature Against Itself* (Chicago: University of Chicago Press, 1979), pp. 129–49.

/10/   Among the scholars who use the term *formalism* in the broad sense that I do here, and who have reflected on the relationship between the varieties of formalist criticism, several excellent studies are: David Couzens Hoy, *The Critical Circle* (Berkeley: University of California Press, 1978); Jerome Mazzeo, *Varieties of Interpretation* (Notre Dame: University of Notre Dame Press, 1978); and Geoffrey Hartman, *Beyond Formalism: Literary Essays, 1958–1970* (New Haven: Yale University Press, 1970). See also Paul de Man, "The Crisis of Contemporary Criticism," *Arion* 6 (Spring, 1967): 38–57.

/11/   For references to the pertinent writings of Paul Ricoeur, see the notes to Chapter IV.

CHAPTER I
BULTMANN IN RETROSPECT

The striking sense of urgency in Bultmann's programmatic essay of 1941, "New Testament and Mythology," can be misleading, for Bultmann certainly recognized that the proper understanding and appropriation of the New Testament message is a question as old as the Gospel itself. Plato's moral and metaphysical criticisms of the Homeric poetry had, of course, already established reflection on the relation between myth and truth within the tradition of Western thought, so that the problem of demythologizing belonged to scriptural interpretation from its beginnings. By calling attention to the issue, then, Bultmann's aim was not to outline a new concern, but to situate those interpretive practices which have necessarily always taken place within the context of comprehensive hermeneutical reflection./1/ Bultmann's urgency, nevertheless, betrays his conviction that a sufficiently comprehensive New Testament hermeneutic must address the distinctively modern exegetical difficulties created by the development of historical consciousness./2/ The task for hermeneutical reflection, in Bultmann's view, is to chart a conflict: while the Christian Church professes the New Testament writings, as Scripture, to be of abiding religious significance, modern exegetes necessarily view the New Testament texts as documents originating in, and addressed to, an autonomous world, culturally and temporally alien from our own. The problems of myth and truth, and of the meaning of the New Testament writings, are thus now irrevocably annexed to, and transformed by, the question of the nature of historical understanding. Bultmann's hermeneutical program is an attempt to reckon with this network of issues precisely in their interrelation./3/

The Hermeneutical Task

Bultmann's hermeneutic program has a practical aim: to conceive the task of demythologization as one ultimately "in the supreme service of faith" is to accept a place within the long tradition of Christian exegesis. The interpretations of the biblical texts which the exegetical tradition has produced, beginning with the interpretation of the Hebrew Scriptures within the New Testament itself, are notoriously varied and often contradictory. Nearly as various are the hermeneutical principles assembled to provide methodological warrant for these interpretations: what the texts say, how they say it, and how one determines that meaning are three interdependent issues continually rearranged in varying theoretical configurations throughout the tradition. The formal aim of interpretations has remained constant, however. Scriptural interpretation seeks to preserve or recover the abiding significance of the canonical texts for the believing community wherever, and whenever, it exists. Christians claim that as Scripture, the biblical texts must speak *hodie usque ad nos*, "even to us today."

In one sense, of course, this interpretive aim, together with the exegetical crisis which makes interpretation necessary, is not unique to scriptural hermeneutics. In the Western tradition, the interpretation of all culturally normative texts, beginning with the Homeric poetry, has been provoked by similar crises: whenever exegetes confront those texts assumed to bear some authoritative claim to truth with a reflective awareness of "modern" knowledge and other languages for truth, the mediating function of interpretation becomes a necessity./4/ The interpretive methods applied to the scriptural texts are also shared with the larger Western literary tradition: allegorical, typological, rationalist, historical-critical, and even existentialist interpretive techniques have been typical of the exegesis of the classics of Western literature as well as of the Christian "classics," its Scriptures./5/

It is important to note that throughout the history of both traditions the condition for the possibility of interpretation has been located in the nature of language. The frequent use of the distinction between "letter" and "spirit" among interpreters of Scripture points to an assumption concerning linguistic meaning that was generally accepted in the western tradition at least until the Reformation, and which is still very much debated at present: language is polysemous; its meaning or content is not necessarily, or only, what it apparently seems to say on its literal or formal level. Language's form and its content are not identical./6/ To go "beyond" the letter, either by substituting another meaning for the literal or by moving through the literal to other levels of meaning that depend upon it, has been a perpetual temptation for exegetes, both pre-critical and modern, and it has been justified in a variety of ways.

For some interpreters, one moves beyond the literal because the author of a text or the text itself seems to *intend* such a move. Both the allegorical interpreters of Homer and a host of scriptural exegetes have argued in this way. According to Heraclitus, for example, Homer should be interpreted allegorically because he intended his writings to be allegories; for Augustine and other biblical exegetes, it is the Divine Author who intended Scripture to be polysemous. As Augustine wrote: "For what could God have more generously and abundantly provided in the divine writings than that the same words might be understood in various ways."/7/

As will become clear throughout this study, the question of intentionality is a complex issue in the interpretation of texts, for even those modern scholars who insist that the author's intention is not normative for interpretation still tend to argue that the *text* is intentionally open to other interpretations. In Bultmann's program, as we shall see, the argument from intention is also central: the New Testament's mythological statements, he maintains, intend to express a sense of the transcendent ground and limit of human existence, despite their literal objectification of the transcendent in worldly terms.

This argument was often extended by biblical interpreters to explain why the Divine Author intended there to be multiple and hidden meanings in the biblical texts. He did so, argue Origen, Augustine and others, in order to stimulate and educate Scripture's more intelligent readers. "What is discovered with more difficulty is discovered with more pleasure," noted Augustine; the "useful and healthful obscurity" in much of Scripture is "for the purpose of exercising and sharpening, as it were, the minds of the readers and of destroying fastidiousness and stimulating the desire to learn."/8/ God intends that Scripture contain multiple meanings, furthermore, in order to accommodate himself to the varying intellectual capacities of his readers. While the hidden, spiritual meanings of the divine writings will be recognized by the educated or privileged, they will remain hidden from those for whom a fuller glimpse of the truth might prove harmful. As Origen suggested, God does not cast his pearls before swine, and this is for the protection of both./9/

Platonic moral interpretations of classical texts, on the other hand, were justified on ideological grounds: since the literal meanings of the texts were offensive to readers, it was argued that the texts must really mean something else. For both biblical and Homeric interpreters, much of what the texts appeared to say conflicted with what was held to be rational or *theoprepres*, "befitting the divine." As Philo commented on the Genesis accounts of creation, for example, "That which is said here is mythical. For how could anyone accept that a woman, or any human being at all, came out of a man's side?" And "To suppose that [God] planted vines, and olive or apple or pomegranate or other trees, would be sheer silliness which it would be hard to cure."/10/ This argument is also operative in Bultmann's program, for it is the offensiveness of New Testament mythology for modern thought, together with his perception of the text's own intention, which makes demythologization possible and necessary.

For pre-critical biblical exegetes even this ideological argument is grounded in the Divine Author's intention, however. If the forms in which the biblical writings were expressed were in some places inadequate to the divine truth which was their content, the truth of the content itself was guaranteed by its author. And since the content of Scripture was believed to be the one revealed and final truth concerning the physical and human worlds, past and present, any "criticism" of the adequacy of specific biblical passages on the formal or literal level was conceived to be an internal, rather than an external, criticism of the texts. One could apply to the texts an encyclopediac knowledge of "words" and "things," "numbers" and "music," as Augustine recommended, with the understanding that from the perspective of eternal truth the truth in all of culture's instruments belongs within the picture of reality set out in Scripture. As Augustine wrote, "Every good and true Christian should understand that wherever he finds the truth, it is the Lord's."/11/ According to the Platonic scheme of much pre-critical exegesis, to see through the literal, even to criticize it, is to perceive the text from an ever larger perspective, increasingly closer to that of God's eternal point of view: through the interpretive process our minds conform, or "come up to," an ever greater understanding of Truth. The Bible, in Augustine's metaphor, is the

"Good Physician"—both the medicine and the cure—since through the rigors of of learning to see what is hidden there, one is made capable of true sight./12/

Christian hermeneutics was, of course, first concerned with the relation between Jesus Christ and the Hebrew Scriptures, and subsequently with the relation between the New and Old Testaments. It was also concerned with the relation between Scripture and reality itself. Both of these concerns can be found in Paul: not only are the Hebrew Scriptures to be understood with reference to Christ, but to our lives as well. Just as Christ's death and resurrection have become the spiritual meaning of the Old Testament, so do our lives acquire a new spiritual meaning when interpreted in light of the event of Christ. As he writes, "For in dying as he died, he died to sin, once for all, and in living as he lives, he lives to God. In the same way you must regard yourselves to be dead to sin and alive to God, in union with Christ Jesus" (Rom. 6:10-11)./13/

If a condition for the possibility of these kinds of interpretive procedures lies in the polysemy of language, and if scriptural hermeneutics receives its impetus and final aim from the authority of the texts, the result of such exegesis was, and continues to be, the preservation and creation of tradition. For in each case—the interpretation of the Christ event in the categories of Hebraic and Hellenistic culture, the christological reading of the Hebrew Scriptures, and the actualization of the meaning of Scripture in the present reality of its readers—there is a process of mutual decipherment at work. A new event, context, or situation becomes meaningful as it enters into relation with a prior network of intelligibility. To interpret the new in terms of the preexisting, in turn, is itself to present a new understanding of the relations which constitute the original horizon of meaning. If Christ's identity and significance first become intelligible in relation to the Hebrew Scriptures, at the same time it can be said that the Christ event "opened" those Scriptures and disclosed a new meaning there./14/ If the events of our lives take on a particular pattern as they are interpreted in relation to the biblical writings, so Christ's death and resurrection receive new meaning when understood, with Paul, as an exegesis of human existence. T. S. Eliot nicely described this process of mutual decipherment with regard to literary tradition:

> What happens when a new work of art is created is
> something that happens simultaneously to all the works
> of art which preceded it. The existing monuments form
> an ideal order among themselves, which is modified by
> the introduction of the new . . . work of art among
> them. Whoever has approved this idea of order . . . will
> not find it preposterous that the past should be altered
> by the present as much as the present is directed by the
> past./15/

Christianity has never been a "religion of the book" in a
strict sense, then. It is not strictly the written text itself, but its
content, which has been held to be sacred: Scripture can thus be
translated into any vernacular, bound, and carried into any
unholy place, without violating its sacred character./16/ Before
the modern period, the authority of Scripture rested on the
belief that the biblical writings were in some manner inspired by
God through the Holy Spirit, and that they revealed God's will
for all of reality and humankind, past and present. The aim of
exegesis, then, was ultimately to seek the Divine Author's intention, which was identical with the content and abiding significance of Scripture. For this reason we see a kind of contradiction
apparent throughout the pre-critical tradition of Christian exegesis. While Origen, for example, devoted great energy to textual
scholarship, he seemed to make relatively little use of it in his
exposition of the meaning of the biblical writings. What was of
ultimate significance was the revealed content of Scripture, and
this, he could sometimes go so far as to say, could be preserved
in material falsehood. Where attempts at harmonizing the biblical accounts failed, Origen could argue that the factual truth of
the "letter" is not always of importance for grasping its eternal
and revealed content./17/

To appeal to the religious content of Scripture over against
its literal form is clearly a circular procedure, since the meaning
of the whole can only be grasped through its parts, and the parts
from the whole. For pre-critical interpreters, the unity of the
whole was presumed, if problematic, so that the hermeneutic
task was to grasp the author's intention, the unifying principle of
the whole, and to interpret individual passages in the light of
Scripture's highest intention. Even in the New Testament, for
example, we see the figure of Jesus interpreting individual passages of the Hebrew Scriptures in light of what he takes to be

the texts' own highest utterances, and in terms of those principles he conceives to be keys to the meaning of the whole—love of God and neighbor, and the fulfillment of scriptural prophecy in his mission and person.

The hermeneutical problem, of course, is how to determine the intention of the whole. Each interpreter appealed to some formulation of Scripture's "highest utterances" as the guiding principle for other "dark" passages. For Paul, and later for Luther, for example, the governing principle of exegesis is that the meaning of all passages is finally determined with reference to Christ. Luther writes: "This is to be the true touchstone by which all books are to be judged, when one sees whether they urge Christ or not, as all Scripture shows forth Christ."/18/ For Augustine, the principle of *caritas* is the ultimate norm:

> Whoever, therefore, thinks that he understands the divine Scriptures or any part of them so that it does not build the double love of God and of our neighbor does not understand it at all. Whoever finds a lesson there useful to the building of charity, even though he has not said what the author may be shown to have intended in that place, has not been deceived, nor is he lying in any way./19/

If determining the content of Scripture is a circular procedure, discerning which interpretation of the text's highest utterances is valid is equally problematic. While the writers of the New Testament and other early Christian exegetes appealed to their own inspiration as warrant for the validity of their interpretations, as will Luther in part, Irenaeus and Tertullian in the late second and early third centuries added to this the argument which was to hold final authority for orthodox Christianity until the Reformation: the ultimate standard for correct interpretation is the *rule of faith*, "that which has been believed everywhere by everyone," as preserved in the Church and apostolic succession./20/ The meaning of Scripture is regulated by institutionalized tradition—an external authority in the sense that God and the Gospel brought the Church into existence, an internal authority in that interpretation is established by the shared cultural, historical and religious perspectives of those "insiders" who claim possession of the text.

A third kind of appeal, a supplement to the above, was typical of the Alexandrian allegorical tradition—one appealed to what is self-evidently rational. The highest purpose of Scripture, for this Platonic tradition, is the revelation of philosophical truths, for the new gnosis given by Christ the Logos contains the highest truths of religion. Scripture, like nature and history, is a system of symbolic correspondences; since it is inspired by God, each word and letter refers to the spiritual realm. While this appeal to reason did not prevent interpreters from recognizing the capacity of symbolic and poetic statement to give insight, the spiritual realities pointed to by the text's symbolic language are nevertheless held to be the same truths expressed in another way by philosophy. The symbolic discourse in the biblical writings is therefore a constant source for reflection on transcendent reality; interpretation is never complete./21/

While the Reformers remained very much a part of the medieval world in many respects, they introduced some decisive changes in scriptural hermeneutics. Luther's principle of *sola scriptura was not new in its assertion of biblical* authority, but in its rejection of the authority of the Pope and the Councils as the authoritative interpreters of Scripture. The Catholic argument, as we have seen, was put forward to guarantee the validity of scriptural interpretations: if the meaning of the Bible is not simply identical with its literal form, differing interpretations may result. If Scripture is to be an infallible revelation, they reasoned, God must have ensured the revelatory quality of the texts by establishing an inerrant interpreter. The Pope can declare the truth, it was argued, both because he is the custodian of the tradition, and because he is guarded from error by the Holy Spirit./22/

Luther rejected the authority of the Church as interpreter of Scripture for a number of reasons. First, he argued that Scripture is sufficiently clear that there is no need for an authoritative office for its interpretation. As he wrote, Scripture is "of itself most certain, easy to understand, and reliable, interpreting itself, and so proving, judging, and explaining all other writings in everything."/23/ This is a significant shift: for Luther, the historical and theological content of Scripture was held to be identical with its literal sense. The "awkward and foolish fables" of four-fold exegesis were thus rejected, at least in principle, since polysemy was rejected—there is only one genuine meaning in Scripture. "The Holy Spirit," he wrote, "is the simplest writer and advisor in heaven and on earth. That is why his words can have no more than the one simplest meaning, which we call the written one, or the literal meaning of the tongue."/24/ As a number of Luther's interpreters have pointed out, with this hermeneutical principle Luther laid the foundation for historical criticism and other secular modes of formal analysis, including philological, grammatical, and literary critical studies./25/ While varieties of historical and textual criticism were not absent from exegesis before Luther, they were not prompted by the kind of logical necessity which Luther's notion of scriptural clarity implies. Unlike earlier interpreters who separated the human and temporal elements of Scripture from its divine and eternal content, in Luther's hermeneutic to grasp the form is to grasp the content of the biblical writings. Attention to the particularity of the forms of the text is thus necessary in principle.

For Luther, the distinction between letter and spirit lies not between the literal and spiritual senses of Scripture, between form and content, but instead concerns the whole substance or content of Scripture as it ceases to be a merely alien, external letter and becomes spirit, something alive in the heart of the reader. The proper spiritual understanding of Scripture concerns not only the "outer clarity" of the theological content gained from exegesis, but the "inner clarity" of the reader's heart—the experience of grace and salvation given by the Holy Spirit through the external words of Scripture./26/

The true and single content of Scripture and the material principle of interpretation for Luther is Christ, or the Gospel proclaiming Christ. Here Luther makes a decisive shift from medieval uses of Scripture, and rethinks the character of the Bible itself, redefining the nature of the text in terms of its central subject matter, the Gospel. Scripture is not strictly the Word of God, then, but the words in which God's Word, Christ, is presented. Scripture is the "manger" in which Christ lies; Christ is "swaddled" in Scripture./27/ This permits Luther to introduce a new kind of theological criticism, or *Sachkritik*. Scripture's authority is derived from the Gospel, which both constitutes and judges Scripture. Rather than criticizing the changing forms of Scripture like the allegorical interpreters, Luther measures the books of the Bible in terms of their content, and the test is whether they present the Gospel of Christ as saviour: "That which does not preach Christ is not apostolic, though it be the work of Peter or Paul and conversely that which does teach Christ is apostolic even though it be written by Judas, Annas, Pilate or Herod."/28/

While historical, philological, and other modes of analysis of the text's forms are necessary to understand the content of Scripture, Christ, they are therefore not sufficient for the full task of interpretation—a theological verdict is required as well. Thus Luther chooses as his canon within the canon those texts which in his reading most clearly proclaim the Gospel, or the tension between Law and Gospel, while assigning other books a lower status. Indeed, Luther leaves Hebrews, James, Jude and Revelation unnumbered in the Table of Contents of his New Testament, and caustically remarks that he would willingly use "Jimmy" to light his fire.

While Luther also retains the traditional view that the authority of Scripture rests on its inspired character—the words of Scripture are the words of the Holy Spirit—his elevation of the authority of the Gospel over Scripture itself is Luther's central contribution to biblical hermeneutics. How does he know that his canon within the canon is the key to Scripture? Luther assumed that since Scripture is clear and "self-interpreting," all exegetes would agree that this is where the kernel of Christianity lies. Furthermore, for Luther the Gospel is fundamentally a spoken, a preached word:

> The Gospel is nothing else than the preaching and proclamation of the grace and mercy of God which Jesus Christ earned and gained for us through his death. It is properly not something written down with letters in a book but more an oral proclamation and a living word./29/

The Word of God is first an event, God's act in Christ, and then the proclamation of that event by the apostles, and finally the event in which that Word elicits and enacts faith in the hearts of its auditors. Thus the test of which biblical passages preach Christ, and the locus of biblical revelation, lie in part in the experience of faith with which the words are received. This receptiveness to the Word is grace, and is beyond the auditor's own power: "God must say to you in your heart, this is God's word."/30/

While Luther's hermeneutic principles preserve the earlier emphasis on the author's intention—now with an added stress on the unity of form and content or intention—at the same time he affirms the centrality of the reader's appropriation of the text in the interpretive process. For the Word of God has become a sacramental word: proclamation of the Gospel is not so much the transmission of information as the vehicle of grace. Just as the Gospel proclaims the glory and power of God concealed within the shame and weakness of the Cross, so faithfully to appropriate the Bible is to receive the glory and power of God's Word hidden within the outer words of Scripture from those without the eyes of faith which grace provides. The understanding of Scripture cannot in this sense be preserved and passed on—a further reason for Luther's rejection of the authority of church tradition. To understand the text spiritually is an event which must occur and reoccur in the present lives of the faithful.

Bultmann conceives his own hermeneutical program as a "radicalization" of Luther's doctrine of justification by faith, and a continuation of the principle of *Sachkritik* established by Luther. While it is beyond the scope of this essay to outline the numerous ways in which Bultmann's hermeneutical and theological principles are related to those of Luther, one point deserves restatement. Luther asserts that exegesis of the "letter" is the direct means to grasp the substance and content of Scripture, so that secular modes of analysis are in principle essential and appropriate for interpretation. On the other hand, what is religiously significant about Scripture—the Word of God as original revelation, which becomes through grace an event of revelation anew in the hearts of the faithful—is now in a sense only ambiguously related to the form-content of the biblical texts themselves. Against the "enthusiasts," Luther insists incontrovertibly that "it must be firmly maintained that God gives no one His Spirit or His grace except through or with the outward word which precedes it."/31/ Nevertheless, the kernel of revelation, for Luther, is the Word of God, Christ, distinct from Scripture, and truly to apprehend this revelation requires not just erudition, but grace as well. This clear distinction between Scripture and Word of God is typical of Bultmann as well as of a number of other twentieth-century Protestant theologians. It needs to be kept in view, because it points to a central limitation of all formalist analyses of the biblical writings for interpreters working within the framework of this theological tradition. Even if one upholds an inextricable relation between Scripture's form and content, analyses of the text's form are not sufficient for interpretation. If the central locus of revelation is held to be the event of Christ distinct from Scripture, to understand what the texts say is not yet to have actualized their religious significance in and for the present.

The Problem

It is a long way from Luther to Bultmann, however, for Bultmann's hermeneutic is prompted by the distinctively modern exegetical difficulties created by the development of modern historical consciousness. In dealing with Scripture Luther presupposed the self-evident validity of the biblical picture of the world and of history. He could therefore ignore the cultural distance separating him from the world of the biblical writings, projecting himself into the experiences of the biblical characters, and interspersing references to the events of his own day throughout his commentaries on the texts. As Roland Bainton remarks, "The men of Luther's circle moved in a perpetual passion play."/32/ Luther could also readily identify his own doctrine with the content of the scriptural writings, asserting their "clarity" without suspecting that his conceptual framework differed in any essential respects from that of the biblical writers. While the point at which modernity begins is much debated, two cardinal principles represent the difficulties with which the modern hermeneutical tradition has been concerned./33/ In Bultmann's formulation, they are, first, "The interpretation of the biblical writings is not subject to conditions different from those applying to all other kinds of literature," and, second, "Modern thought as we have inherited it brings with it criticism of the New Testament view of the world."/34/ Bultmann's first principle simply restates a position first systematically articulated by Schleiermacher and generally accepted by the mainstream of biblical criticism throughout the nineteenth century. When Schleiermacher collapsed the distinction between *hermeneutica sacra* and *hermeneutica profana*, he aimed to elevate hermeneutical principles from the practical "rules of thumb" collected by interpreters of special classes of texts to philosophical status; he desired hermeneutic rules that were systematic and universal./35/ His formulation of "general" hermeneutics as the theory of understanding was his attempt to meet these requirements.

The process of understanding a text, sacred or secular, is always the same, he argued, because the human mind and the way it determines meaning through language is everywhere the same. Before Schleiermacher all hermeneutical reflection on both the Bible and on classical texts had been confind within given assumptions about their normative character. For Schleiermacher, in contrast, any "special hermeneutics" is simply a special application of the general rules pertaining to the understanding of all texts, and is justified only on the basis of a text's distinctive use of language: "We could manage quite well with the general alone."/36/ As a consequence, all dogmatic assumptions about the normative status of biblical texts are suspended, and concern with the biblical texts as Scripture is therefore isolated from the task of interpreting or understanding them./37/

To thus subsume sacred and profane hermeneutics under a general theory of understanding is of course itself a reflection of the change from pre-critical to modern assumptions. For to deny the validity of a *hermeneutica sacra* is to deny that there is any philosophically justifiable way in which biblical texts can be distinguished absolutely from other texts, and therefore to call into question the philosophical foundation on which the scriptural hermeneutic had rested./38/ The special status Christians ascribed to the biblical texts throughout the long pre-critical tradition rested on belief in their ontological uniqueness, an assumption founded upon a supernaturalist metaphysics. But to view the biblical texts as texts among other texts is to lose the immediate conviction that they have unconditional authority. To ascribe authority to the biblical world is henceforth to *choose* among a number of potential authorities. In the relativistic context of historicism there can be no self-evidently valid perspective on the world. One must confer authority on a chosen world view, so that one is inevitably in a position of authority higher than that to which one submits./39/

Bultmann's second principle points to a related difficulty—the consequences of an awareness of the historical and cultural distance separating modern consciousness from that of the ancients. As Troeltsch astutely stated the problem, the difficulty historical criticism posed for believers lay not so much in its conclusions as in the presuppositions underlying the historical method itself: "Once the historical method is applied to biblical science and church history," he wrote, "it is a leaven that alters everything, and, finally, bursts apart the entire structure of theological methods employed until the present."/40/ The historical method "alters everything," first, because it presupposes the modern naturalistic and scientific world view, which flatly contradicts the mythological picture of the world represented in the biblical writings. The scientific historian inevitably criticizes the content of the biblical picture of reality. In addition, following the Reformation tendency to seek the original intention of the first apostolic preaching, historical criticism attempts to recover the meaning of the biblical texts in their original situation. But with an awareness of the distance between the texts and the present, together with the presuppositions governing scientific inquiry, the biblical texts become objects situated wholly in the past, divorced from the personal and cultural standpoint of the interpreter. To understand the meaning of the biblical texts for their own time requires the scientist to exclude his or her own subjective perspectives and responses. Alienation of the texts from the interpreter becomes both a cultural fact and a methodological principle./41/

The chief consequence of both principles is the distinctive problematic of modern scriptural hermeneutics: an interpreter of the biblical texts who aims to preserve their abiding religious significance must be at once an insider and an outsider, negotiating between the critical perspectives of the modern sciences and the recovery of meaning for faith./42/ Whether and how these two perspectives can be maintained without compromising one or the other is the burden of the modern exegetical tradition.

Of crucial importance for the development of modern biblical interpretation is the way the perspective of outsider was first defined: to approach the biblical writings as an outsider meant to apply the critical-historical method. The question of the rational, and then historical, veracity of the events narrated in the biblical texts, particularly in the Gospel narratives, was of immediate critical concern for obvious reasons. The narrative portions of the biblical writings are characterized by what Hans Frei has called "history-likeness": the biblical narratives certainly seem to refer to historical events, and their historical referentiality had, of course, been traditionally assumed./43/ To demonstrate the divine organization of the texts through exegesis had been assumed to constitute proof of their historicity as well./44/ Furthermore, since Christianity claims to be founded on the entrance of God in the historical events of Jesus' life and death, the historical referentiality of the Gospel narratives is of immediate theological consequence.

As Van Harvey points out, the conflicts between outsider and insider, critic and authority, that marked the first attempts to apply historical criticism to the Bible quickly became what was essentially a conflict concerning freedom of inquiry, with orthodox believers hoping to preserve Scripture's special status from the ungodly criticism by either rejecting it outright or using it selectively./45/ The critics, of course, gradually triumphed, largely through the efforts of Protestant liberal theologians, whose consistent and rigorous application of historical criticism not only established the historical method as the paradigmatic model of investigation, but also, in Harvey's phrase, served to "save Protestantism from obscuritantism."/46/ With what Bultmann describes as "ruthless honesty and absolute clarity," the historical critics aimed to discover "what really happened," to look behind the New Testament texts as they appear without the blinders of dogmatic bias, and to subject the writings' putative claims of fact to scrutiny according to historical science's rigorous ideals of description, objectivity, and disinterest. The chief contribution of the liberals, in Bultmann's view, was their insistence that Christian faith cannot demand a suspension of what Harvey calls the "morality of knowledge" operative in daily life and intellectual inquiry./47/ In hermeneutic terms, they maintained that the meaning of the biblical writings for faith must not contradict the legitimate investigation of the text's meaning by historical science./48/

Certain assumptions operative in the early application of the historical-critical paradigm have been most crucial in setting the terms of modern discussion. When liberal critics undertook the task of establishing the exact nature of the New Testament sources, sorting fact from myth, legend and fiction, their hermeneutic aim was to isolate an original, authentic tradition behind the distorting accretions of orthodoxy—an original core which had a firm basis in historical fact. This "pure," uninterpolated tradition was to be the "real" figure of Jesus and his original teachings. Their methodological model was, of course, the natural sciences. As Harnack, a classic example of the liberal hermeneutic, wrote:

> If the *person* of Jesus stands at the center of the Gospel, how can the foundation for a reliable and generally accepted knowledge of that person be gained except through historical-critical research? Is not such research essential to prevent the substitution of an *imagined*

Christ for the real Christ? And who can carry on this
research unless he pursues it as scientific theology?/49/

Second, as Hans Frei discusses at length in *The Eclipse of
Biblical Narrative,* the "history-likeness" of the gospel narratives
seduced modern critics, like their pre-critical predecessors, into
assuming that the intention of the Gospel stories was to give a
reliable historical report. If the biblical texts are to be treated
like other literature, the genre of this other literature was
assumed to be the historical chronicle. But implicit here is the
further assumption that the *meaning* of the stories was located
in their ostensive reference to historical events./50/

Their positivist confidence in the ability of objective research
to uncover the undistorted facts behind the texts' verbal sense was
thus paralleled by a positivistic approach to language, and, corre-
latively, by their understanding of the nature of myth as well./51/
Both liberal critics and their orthodox opponents in the early nineteenth century shared a kind of literalism with regard to the texts:
language can have only one meaning, and that meaning lies in its
reference to historical truth. Luther's doctrine of the clarity of
Scripture, as we have seen, established the basis for this kind of
approach—the form and the content of the texts, he maintained,
are strictly congruent. But for these nineteenth-century critics, the
content or meaning of Scripture was reduced to the question of its
historical veracity, so that if a particular narrative is demonstrably
without historical reference, it has no meaning at all. Thus, when
liberal and orthodox exegetes turned to narratives such as the feed-
ing of the five thousand, both assumed that the writer literally
meant what he said—"literally," that is, meaning with reference to
historical fact. Orthodox resistance to historical criticism rested on
their conviction that Christians were required to believe that all
events narrated in the texts were historically true. Liberal critics,
on the other hand, used science to test out the texts' apparent
claims to historical veracity, and dispensed with those portions of
the Gospel accounts without verifiable reference as myth, fiction,
or legend, symptoms of an outmoded, primitive system of belief
irrelevant for faith. Their enterprise was thus reductive in a double
sense: the text which could be of abiding significance for faith was
reduced to those portions of the Bible deemed most free from
myth, and language's potentiality for meaning was reduced to historical reference./52/

The liberals' avid interest in historical reconstruction curiously enough prevented them from recognizing the full extent of the hermeneutical problem historical inquiry could engender. For these critics, maintaining the dual perspectives of outsider and insider seemed easily accomplished. Science and hermeneutic recovery appeared to be compatible, criticism and exegesis identical, since what was deemed relevant for faith were the historically reconstructed teachings of Jesus and his religious personality. By arguing that the true canon within the canon was the life and teachings of the historical Jesus recoverable through historical investigation, they could maintain that theological and scientific perspectives were compatible.

Furthermore, by dispensing with those elements of the texts which were most alien to contemporary readers, and by assuming, often with the assistance of the Hegelian distinction between external ideas and temporary forms, that, as Bultmann wrote of them, "the great truths of religion and ethics are timeless and eternal," the nineteenth century critical movement did not yet face the possibility that the "essence of Christianity" could not be readily disentangled from the supernatural, messianic world presented in the texts. They could assume, in Bultmann's words, that

> the apprehension and acceptance of these principles does not depend on the knowledge and acceptance of the age in which they first took shape, or the historical persons who first discovered them. We are all capable of verifying them in our own experience at whatever period we happen to live. History may be of academic interest, but never of paramount importance for religion./53/

While applauding their insistence that the perspectives of scientific criticism and theological interpretation must both be maintained, Bultmann viewed the liberal enterprise as misconceived./54/ From a hermeneutical perspective, Bultmann accused them of misreading the New Testament and of violating the text's intentions, both consequences of an inadequate hermeneutic method. Bultmann saw their easy conflation of criticism and interpretation as a failure to meet the crucial problem: the recovery of anything of permanent validity for Christian faith cannot be legitimately won unless all of the writings are subjected to a thoroughgoing criticism of content, and the alienness of the entire New Testament is acknowledged. Bultmann's critique, of course, was offered in retrospect. Many of the presuppositions on which the liberal hermeneutic had rested had already been exposed as inadequate by the simple progress of historical research itself. Bultmann's own accomplishments as an historical critic contributed significantly to the eclipse of the liberal enterprise.

First to be questioned was their ideal of critical objectivity. Where Harnack could insist on the need for an historical Jesus purged of subjective fancy, Schweitzer in his 1906 classic, *The Quest of the Historical Jesus*, had already pointed out that there were as many pictures of the "real" Jesus as there were historians' visions of the ideal personality./55/ Secondly, attempts at historical reconstruction were also undermined when their assumptions concerning the genre of the New Testament writings were challenged. With the contributions of Wrede and Wellhausen and then of the form criticism pioneered by Bultmann and Dibelius, scholars were forced to recognize that the Gospels afforded no simple possibility for reconstructing the events of Jesus' life and inner development, because they were not biographical but highly theological documents, records of the early church's faith. It was demonstrated that the New Testament writings were not in intention solely chronicles of historical events but instead essentially religious writings, and, as form criticism attempted to show, compilations of small, isolated units of pre-literary tradition, shaped into longer narratives according to the needs of the early worshiping community. The majority of scholars consequently pronounced a negative verdict on the possibility of recovering very much, if anything, of an uninterpolated, authentic tradition with enough cohesiveness to obtain legitimate biographical information—Bultmann and others argued that all we essentially have is the "Christ of faith."/56/

Finally, the research of the History of Religions school forced scholars to acknowledge the extent to which the New Testament was pervaded by myth, and to recognize the eschatological elements in the texts as genuine. The mythological language of Gnosticism and Jewish apocalyptic had to be accepted as indispensible—and therefore, as a problem for interpretation. And so, as Bultmann wrote, the "utter strangeness of primitive Christianity" presented itself; nothing in the texts is "immediately comprehensible."/57/

The Program

Bultmann's hermeneutic turns the liberal enterprise upside down, so so to speak, transforming each of its inadequacies into a virtue. Their lack of scientific objectivity becomes, in Bultmann's program, the "pre-understanding" which is the condition for understanding history at all. Loss of the possibility of recovering the historical Jesus, and the emergence of skepticism as an inevitable consequence of historical criticism, become necessary asceses in the dialectic of faith. Acknowledgement that the New Testament writings are not historical chronicles but expressions of faith becomes the real foundation for their recovery through existential interpretation. Recognition of the radical strangeness of the texts becomes the main crux of the hermeneutical problem, for Bultmann, and the starting point for his exegetical proposal. The most central shift, however, lies in Bultmann's choice of a canon within the canon: in place of the liberal canon of the historical Jesus, Bultmann reestablishes Luther's doctrine of justification by faith through grace, the Gospel articulated most clearly, in Bultmann's view, in the theologies of Paul and John.

Bultmann's theological and hermeneutical programs seek to be faithful to this understanding of the New Testament proclamation, while at the same time fully embracing the liberals' insight that the biblical world view has been rendered untenable by modern knowledge of the world and of human existence. Where the liberals sought to declare scientific historical criticism to be the means for the recovery of the central core of Christianity, Jesus' life and teachings, Bultmann will argue, in contrast, that the central Christian proclamation itself demands a criticism of not only the biblical picture of the world, but of all world views as well. Bultmann's primary theological and hermeneutical assertion is that the New Testament, properly understood, calls for its own demythologization. Demythologizing, in his view, is both an "epistemological radicalization" of the Pauline and Lutheran doctrines of justification by faith, and the exercise of the kind of *Sachkritik* begun by Luther./58/

Bultmann's programmatic essay of 1941 begins with the acknowledgment that the New Testament writings are thoroughly shaped by a mythological view of the world untenable for modern thought. Mythology, in Bultmann's definition, is "the use of imagery to express the other-worldly in terms of this world, and the divine in terms of human life, the other side in terms of this side."/59/ In the categories of the neo-Kantian and existentialist traditions which form the philosophical foundation of Bultmann's enterprise, myth is an "objectifying" mode of thought. It represents the transcendent as an entity located spatially and temporally within the world, knowable in the subject-object form with which we cognitively grasp other objects in the world.

While myth and modern science are both objectifying, in the sense that any human attempt to construct an objective picture of reality is an instance of objectifying vision, scientific thought necessarily views nature, history, and the human self as closed, self-subsistent entities, "immune from the interference of supernatural powers."/60/ To objective observation, in Bultmann's view, modern reality is necessarily godless. Accepting the critical radicalism of his nineteenth-century predecessors, Bultmann insists that Christian faith cannot demand a blind acceptance of New Testament mythology, for this would entail a sacrifice of the intellect, the "acceptance of a view of the world in our faith and religion that we should deny in ordinary life."/61/ Modern thought, then, necessarily demythologizes, because it excludes the working of supernatural powers about which myth speaks./62/ The only meaning that modern thought can ascribe to a notion of divine action is one which refers to existential self-understanding. In Bultmann's view, one

> can understand himself in his relation to God only as a person who is addressed by God precisely in his being as a person. This means that the only divine speaking and acting he can understand as important and of concern to him are such as encounter him in his personal existence—and in fact, adhere precisely to it./63/

If the meaning of the New Testament is not in some way independent of the mythological framework in which it is represented, Bultmann argues, then the New Testament can have no meaning or religious significance for a reader who does not share its first-century world view. The crucial question, then, as Bultmann poses it, is whether the New Testament writings embody a truth independent of its mythological framework./64/ As he asks: "Can the kerygma be interpreted apart from mythology? Can we recover the truth of the kerygma for men who do not think in mythological terms without forfeiting its character as kerygma?"/65/ Bultmann's proposal is that the kerygma is recoverable through a hermeneutic of demythologizing, or, put positively, through existential interpretation.

Before examining Bultmann's hermeneutical program in detail, it is important to note that there are at least four distinct, though interrelated, dimensions to what Bultmann is attempting to achieve. First, Bultmann addresses the general hermeneutical question of how any text, particularly a text originating in a culture not our own, can be understood as significant for the present. This issue concerns the nature of historical understanding, and to explicate this aspect of his program Bultmann turns to the hermeneutical tradition of Schleiermacher and Dilthey. In addition, Bultmann's program is concerned with the nature of language, particularly of mythological language as he defines it, and with the relation between linguistic form and meaning or content. Here Bultmann introduces a subtle form of allegory, turning to the kind of existentialist "translation" of myth he observed in the writings of Hans Jonas.

The central impetus and aim of Bultmann's program is theological, however, and the above general hermeneutical concerns are governed by Bultmann's theological argument. Bultmann will argue that the kind of demythologizing or existential interpretation he recommends is actually demanded by the New Testament itself on inner theological grounds. In Bultmann's view, the New Testament, properly understood, calls for its own demythologization, a process which has already begun in the writings of Paul and John. This is a theological, as well as a hermeneutical argument, because Bultmann maintains, with Luther, that the central intention of the New Testament texts is to proclaim Christ, interpreted in terms of the tension between Law and Gospel. Like Luther, Bultmann thus argues that this kerygmatic norm makes possible a kind of *Sachkritik* whereby it can be argued that Paul and John, and even particular aspects of the theologies of Paul and John, are most faithful to the true intention of the New Testament proclamation. As we shall see, here demythologizing becomes not only a critique and interpretation of the *forms* of the New Testament writings, but of their *content* as well.

Finally, Bultmann will also argue, like Luther, that the religious significance of the New Testament is actualized in the present as a proclamation that is appropriated by faith through grace. Bultmann thus upholds Luther's distinction between the proclaimed Word and the words of Scripture: while the latter may be *understood* in the present through existential interpretation, Bultmann argues, the New Testament becomes Word of God only in the present event in which it is appropriated in faith.

Bultmann presents his theology as an interpretation of the content of the New Testament writings. In his view, the natures of faith and of the God-world relation make it possible to remain obedient to both the intention of the New Testament and to the presuppositions of modern thought./66/ Bultmann argues that God does act in the world, but in such a way that "to every eye other than the eye of faith the action of God is hidden."/67/ To objective observation the framework of nature and history is profane—there are no places or events which can be marked off as having special sacred status. The only way to preserve the unworldly, transcendent character of divine activity, then, Bultmann suggests, is to

> regard it not as an interference in worldly happenings, but as something accomplished *in* them in such a way that the closed weft of history as it presents itself to objective observation is left undisturbed. . . . Only the natural happening is generally visible and ascertainable. In it is accomplished the hidden act of God./68/

Bultmann can thus permit the "critical fires" of historical investigation to consume what they will, for there is nothing available to objective observation that could constitute proof for faith:

> The man who wishes to believe in God as his God must realize that he has nothing in his hand on which to base his faith. He is suspended in mid-air, and cannot demand proof of the Word which addresses him. . . . Security can be found only by abandoning all security, by being ready, as Luther put it, to plunge into the inner darkness./69/

Faith, then, is not an affair of objective knowledge, but of existential self-understanding, for God, both the Wholly Other beyond the grasp of propositional thought and the reality undergirding all else, is known only under the qualification of the subject's religious relation to him./70/ Faith entails, in Bultmann's appropriation of Schleiermacher's phrase, an "experience of absolute dependence," where one's being is unfolded *freely* to a power, in self-surrender./71/

Faith is therefore dialectically related to the acknowledgment of one's human limitations, and to the surrender of all claims to know, master, and secure one's existence in the world. Revelation and faith are "eschatological events," in Bultmann's interpretation, for it is only in and through the "crisis" which brings human "world" to an end, only through the surrender of all objectifying means by which we order our lives and attempt to secure our fate, that the event of revelation—God's self-disclosure as the power unifying all that is—can occur./72/

Bultmann argues that the salvation event was an actual historical occurrence and continues to be an actual historical occurrence whenever an individual decides to accept the kerygma, because the salvation event always occurs as response to a concrete personal address. The historical event of the crucifixion was merely the origin of the salvation event the kerygma proclaims. The disciples, personally bound to Jesus of Nazareth, had been confronted with a question for decision by Jesus' assertion that he was God's messenger announcing God's coming reign. For them, the crucifixion was a personal experience which raised once again the need to decide the legitimacy of Jesus' assertion. The crucifixion presented the disciples with a question and immediately disclosed to them its meaning./73/ But constitutive of both New Testament faith and our faith is the distance between those disciples and all who hear their witness without the experiential bond with Jesus of Nazareth. That bond cannot be reproduced: as an event of the past, the crucifixion can only be known by historical report. Historical reconstruction of Jesus' life and death may now be partially possible, but it is not necessary. What is necessary is the faith expressed in the proclamation that God brought salvation through the crucified and risen Christ. The resurrection was not a historical event but part of the Easter faith: "Indeed, faith in the resurrection is really the same thing as faith in the saving efficacy of the cross, faith in the cross as the cross of Christ." For the first communities of faith as for us, "Christ meets us in the preaching as one crucified and risen. He meets us in the word of preaching and nowhere else. The faith of Easter is just this—faith in the word of preaching."/74/

Bultmann therefore opposes all attempts to make Jesus of

Nazareth the source of faith in God. His words are like the words of any other historic (*geschichtliche*) figure; they can challenge our self-understanding, but they cannot mediate faith in God. Jesus' work and destiny happened within history and can be understood by the historian as part of the nexus of history. But detached inquiry "cannot become aware of what God has wrought in Christ, that is, the eschatological event."/75/ Christian faith is not a response to the words of Jesus but a response to the proclamation of the Church. The kerygma presupposes Jesus and the Cross, but it proclaims Jesus Christ.

In this way Bultmann attempts to adhere to the categories of modern historical and scientific understanding, while preserving the transcendent character of God's activity. The salvation event is continually actualized within history without miraculous interference in the closed unity of events, because salvation is wrought in one's self-understanding. Whenever the kerygma is heard as personal address is judgment day.

Since revelation is not the communication of knowledge, but an event which puts one in a new situation as a self, one can speak of God only by speaking at the same time of one's own transformed existence./76/ This double-speaking is theology. Theology is not the kerygma, but the explication of the new understanding of God, the world, and the self that is conferred in and by faith./77/ Theology is thus "a movement of faith itself"; the New Testament writings are therefore theological interpretations of the kerygma.

Since theology must speak about human beings, philosophy can assist theology by clarifying the ontological structure of human existence. Bultmann argues that Heidegger's existentialist philosophy offers the most adequate categories for understanding human existence because it is, in Bultmann's view, simply a "clear and methodical explication of the understanding of existence given with existence itself."/78/ Heidegger's philosophy is appropriate not only because human existence is the direct object of its attention, but also because it points to the *existentiell* self as the place where self-understanding is realized./79/ Philosophy enables one to understand conceptually what such things as "life in faith" or "out of faith" or "revelation" mean on a formal level, as existential possibilities. Philosophy is limited to this task because it cannot speak of the ontic (or *existentiell*) level where faith and unfaith actually occur. "Philosophy sees *that* man is only a particular concrete man who is determined by some specific 'how'; it speaks of the 'that' of this 'how,' but not of the 'how' itself."/80/ Both philosophy and theology speak of human being, but philosophy inquires into the formal structures of human existence, while theology speaks of the concrete person insofar as he or she is faithful or unfaithful, i.e., "insofar as his 'how' is characterized by the fact that he has been or is to be encountered by a specific proclamation."/81/

By using philosophy in this way, Bultmann wants to demonstrate that salvation does not produce a mysterious ontological change in human nature, which would be untenable for modern thought, but effects instead an ontic change; one's concrete, *existentiell* self-understanding is transformed./82/ At the same time, Bultmann wishes to show that while the decision for faith *is* a "leap" away from the security of all objective proof, faith is not a "blind, arbitrary resolve," but an understanding Yes or No. For Bultmann the kerygma presents us with a possible way to understand ourselves, and existentialist philosophy can clarify the meaning of this possibility. Bultmann's illustrative analogies are usually taken from the sphere of interpersonal relationships. To demonstrate his point here he employs the analogy of a friendless person longing for friendship./83/ Even without a friend, says Bultmann, I still know what friendship is. When I do enter into friendship, do I know anything more than I knew before? I cannot define the concept of friendship in a new or better way; I know nothing new *about* friendship at all. What I do know now are both my friend and myself anew, in the sense that in understanding my friend, my concrete life in all its dimensions is qualified in a new way. "In knowing my friend in the *event* of friendship," Bultmann explains, "the events of my life become new—new in a sense that is valid only for me and visible only to me, that indeed only *becomes* visible in the now and thus must always become visible anew."/84/ The analogy is transparent. What "revelation" or "life in faith" means conceptually can be known by the *lumen naturale*, and known equally well by persons in or out of faith. The proclamation gives the same objective knowledge to all. What "more" the person of faith knows is that revelation has occurred, and that through this event the events of one's life have been newly qualified.

Although the New Testament texts are pervaded by a mythological view of the world—they represent the transcendent in terms of a three-story cosmology, they picture the world and the self as open to the incursion of transcendent powers, and they contain reports of other-worldly occurrences—Bultmann nevertheless argues that the theological program outlined above *is* a valid interpretation of these texts. While New Testament myth objectifies the transcendent in a way that is incomprehensible for modern consciousness, myth's real intention, in Bultmann's view, is to speak of what is fundamentally beyond objectifying thought: it wishes to express the self's awareness of a ground and limit to human existence, of a power lying beyond everything to be found in the realm of what human beings can know in subject-object form and thus have as an object of calculation and control./85/ This awareness of the transcendent is an experience which all persons can share, although the forms in which it is expressed and experienced will be historically conditioned./86/ Myth does not intend to present an objective picture of the world as it is, in Bultmann's view, but to "express man's understanding of himself in the world in which he lives." Myth intends to express "a certain understanding of existence"—existence as it is grounded and limited by the transcendent./87/

In Bultmann's view, then, the experience and self-understanding which myth intends to speak is not bound to the forms in which it is expressed—and for Bultmann, the conceptual categories of existentialist philosophy provide a means to express the intention of New Testament myth in a form intelligible to modern readers. At this level, demythologizing, or existential interpretation, is a critique and translation of the language of the New Testament into other linguistic forms. Bultmann's presupposition here is that the forms in which the New Testament writings are represented are not constitutive of their content. As he writes of certain apocalyptic and gnostic elements in Paul and John, for example, "we can dispense with the objective form in which they are cast."/88/

Thus Bultmann translates New Testament notions concerning life in faith and out of faith into the Heideggerian framework of authentic and inauthentic existence. He interprets Paul's notion of life "in the flesh," for example, as equivalent to Heidegger's notion of inauthentic existence: "For just this is the essence of 'flesh': the essence of the man who understands himself in terms of himself, who wants to secure his own existence."/89/ Bultmann interprets John's concept of "world" in like fashion:

> By 'world' he understands humanity as it constitutes
> itself and takes pride in what it has and does; it is the
> world of sound common sense with its ideals and norms,
> its traditions and its knowledge; it is the world of possi-
> bilities that can be disposed of, which does not reckon
> with any other possibilities and looks upon what it does
> not understand as absurd and ridiculous. The 'world'
> does not know that it is limited by God, and therefore it
> does not know him even if it imagines that it does. This
> is its sin./90/

Bultmann's existentialist interpretation of justification by
faith, Law and Gospel, is clear in the above passages. As long as
we try to find our life in the "world," we are in bondage to the
past, and our notions of freedom and the future are illusions, for
"in every actual choice in which man chooses a possibility of
existing authentically he in fact always chooses what he already
is— . . . He never gets rid of the past and is therefore never
free."/91/ Conversely, life in faith can be understood in terms
of authentic existence. Life in faith is life in which bondage, to
the past is broken:

> Faith as openness to the future is freedom from the past,
> because it is faith in the forgiveness of sins; it is freedom
> from the enslaving chains of the past. It is freedom *from*
> ourselves as the old selves, and freedom *for* ourselves as
> the new selves. It is freedom from the illusion, grounded
> in sin, that we can establish our personal existence
> through our own decision. It is the free openness to the
> future which Paul acclaims in saying that 'death is swal-
> lowed up in victory.' (I Cor. 15:54)/92/

While as theologian Bultmann self-consciously stands within
the Lutheran tradition, this kind of "translation" of the New Testament forms is a clear departure from Luther's insistence on
scriptural "clarity"—on the unity between form and content. In
some respects this aspect of Bultmann's program is a form of
allegorical interpretation. Like the pre-critical interpreters, Bultmann moves beyond the surface or literal level of the writings to
expose a deeper, hidden meaning there. He can do this because
he assumes with these earlier interpreters that the content or
intention of the text (or, for the pre-critical allegorists, of the
Divine Author) is independent of the forms in which it is
expressed. Like the allegorists, Bultmann's "divination" of the
intention of the whole becomes the normative principle whereby

the forms are judged as to their appropriateness. Bultmann, unlike Luther, then, presupposes that language is polysemous: language does not always mean what it says.

Bultmann's hermeneutic is clearly not a pure example of pre-critical allegory, however. For a pre-critical interpreter, the Divine Author guaranteed not only the final cohesiveness of Scripture's various "senses," but included the exegete within its circle of meaning as well. Since Scripture contains the true meaning of existence, it was thought, then it naturally embraces the past and present of any individual reader. To understand the meaning of Scripture is to fit oneself into the biblical world, and simultaneously to learn the meaning of one's individual existence.

With the collapse of the *hermeneutica sacra*, and particularly with the rise of historical consciousness, the interpretive relation between text and reader essentially reversed its direction. As Hans Frei points out, the application of rational and then historical criticism to the biblical texts implied a logical and reflective distance between the biblical narratives and the "real" world, so that rather than fitting oneself into the biblical world, one determines the text's meaning with reference to an autonomous framework of meaning./93/ While Bultmann's hermeneutic is allegorical in the sense that he criticizes the New Testament's linguistic forms in light of what he discerns to be its central content, then, it is a distinctly modern hermeneutic in that the abiding significance of that content can no longer be immediately assumed.

Bultmann's program thus has a dual task. On the one hand, he turns to general hermeneutic theory and to an explication of the nature of historical understanding to show how the biblical texts, as texts among other texts, can have meaning for the present despite their mythological world view. But on the other hand, Bultmann will argue that the special nature of the content of the biblical writings makes demythologizing necessary in a further sense. Theologically, he will argue, demythologizing "is performing for faith the supreme service of recalling it to a radical reconsideration of its own nature."/94/ Before looking at Bultmann's theological use of interpretation theory, it will be helpful to see how he finds in the hermeneutical tradition of Schleiermacher and Dilthey a methodological foundation for his existential interpretation.

General Hermeneutics and the Problem of Meaning

Bultmann's dialectical reversal of the liberal program reflects Dilthey's distinction between historical *explanation*, conceived on the model of the natural sciences, and historical *understanding*, which shares the distinctive methodology of the human sciences. In contrast to natural science, writes Dilthey, the object of the "human studies" is "not sensory appearance as such . . . but is rather first and foremost an inner reality, a coherence experienced from within."/95/ Historical understanding aims at "the understanding of individual historical being," or "the life the soul"; it entails "our re-experiencing of alien states of mind." Genuine historical understanding, the "recomprehension" of alien individuality, seeks to overcome the temporal gap between past and present, to enable "modern man," as Dilthey writes, "to hold the entire past of humanity present within himself."/96/

For Bultmann, the nineteenth-century critical-historical paradigm, patterned after the natural sciences, is to be distinguished from the understanding of human existence, from "an interest in history as the sphere of life in which human existence moves, in which it attains its possibilities and develops them, and in reflection upon which it attains understanding of itself and its own particular possibilities."/97/ Following Heidegger as well, Bultmann argues that human being is never simply given, but is rather always in question; an individual not only has possibilities, but is a possibility. One's being must be responsibly laid hold of by continual decision. One lives by moving beyond oneself and projecting oneself into one's own freely chosen possibility of existence./98/ Consciously or unconsciously, one is always moved by the practical (*existentiell*) question of the meaning of one's existence, of who one ought to be, so that one's self-understanding at any moment always consciously or unconsciously represents an answer to this question. Human existence is thus fundamentally historical existence; one's being is unfinished, and "authentic" human existence is one in which an individual continually chooses his future in responsible decision./99/

Similarly, for Dilthey, human beings continually strive to bring their thought, feeling, and desire into a unified *Weltanschauung*. At the foundation of every world view is an endeavor to solve the "riddle of life," to deal with the problems of birth and death, human power and weakness, and one's ambiguous

position in nature./100/ Human nature is a reservoir of infinite
possibilities from which an individual chooses which to realize.
The historian explores the record of choices made, a project that
reveals to us possibilities in our own nature of which our situation had not made us aware. "Thus," Dilthey writes,

> the inner directed man can experience many other exis-
> tences in his imagination. Limited by circumstances, he
> can yet glimpse alien beauty in the world and areas of
> life beyond his reach. Put generally: man, tied and limi-
> ted by the reality of life is liberated not only by
> art . . . but also by historical understanding./101/

To study history, for both Dilthey and Bultmann, is thus not simply to chronicle facts, but to see history as a sphere of possibilities.
It is to overcome cultural and temporal distance, for history is the
"enquiry into 'human being' as one's own being."/102/

To recover the possibilities history presents is, for this tradition, primarily to interpret texts, which are, in Dilthey's terms,
"expressions of life," "residues of human reality preserved in written form."/103/ They turn to written materials because, according to Dilthey, "only in speech does the inner life of man find its
fullest and most exhaustive, most objectively comprehensible
expression."/104/ Because texts offer a possible way to understand
existence, they present to the interpreter, in Bultmann's words, a
"claim," a "summons to decide" whether or not one will make that
possibility one's own. A text thus discloses its meaning only to one
who is willing to hear its claim:

> To understand history is possible only for one who does
> not stand over against it as a neutral, non-participating
> spectator, but himself stands in history and shares respon-
> sibility for it. We speak of this encounter with history that
> grows out of one's own historicity as the *existentiell*
> encounter. The historian participates in it with his whole
> existence./105/

The meaning of a text, like the meaning of historical events, therefore belongs, in a sense, to the future. Phenomena have meaning in
the present only when one reflects on the past with one's responsi-
bility for one's future being in mind. Since the end of history is
unknown, its meaning cannot be definitively fixed, but rather continues to unfold itself to interpreters who are themselves partici-
pants in its actualization. Bultmann writes: "And therefore one can

say that the future of an historical event belongs to that event. . . .
It can definitively disclose itself only when history has come to an
end."/106/

Language is viewed here as the "objectification" of an individual life-moment. The interpreter's aim is to move back
through these fixed expressions to the life of the soul expressing
itself therein. This understanding of language is also developed
in the context of Cassirer's *Philosophy of Symbolic Forms*, by
Heidegger, and by Heidegger and Bultmann's pupil, Hans Jonas,
to whose own demythologizing project Bultmann is explicitly
indebted./107/ For Jonas as for Bultmann, demythologizing is
not solely a problem concerning myth, but one concerning the
relation between words and meaning. Language expresses an
author's intention, but it also distorts; it is a tendency of the
human spirit to represent itself in objective expressions which
lead away from the meaning it intends to express. In contrast to
the literal congruence between word and intended meaning
asserted by nineteenth-century critics, language here is viewed
as ambiguous; it can be a "distorting objectification of meaning."
To interpret, to demythologize, is to attempt to discover the
possibility of existence the author intends to express through
language's objective formulas and symbols. As Jonas writes:

> All this derives from an unavoidable fundamental struc-
> ture of the spirit as such. That it interprets itself in
> objective formulae and symbols, that it is 'symbolistic,' is
> the innermost nature of the spirit—and at the same time
> the most dangerous! In order to come to itself, it neces-
> sarily takes this detour via the symbol, in whose enticing
> jungle of problems it tends to lose itself, far from the
> origin preserved symbolically in it, taking the substitute
> as ultimate. Only in a long procedure of working back,
> after an exhausting completion of that detour, is a
> demythologized consciousness able terminologically to
> approach directly the original phenomenon hidden in
> this camouflage. . . ./108/

This hermeneutical gap between letter and spirit, language and
meaning, is what permits Bultmann to distinguish the intention
of myth, which is to express "a certain understanding of human
existence," from the language leading away from it; myth's purpose is "impeded and obscured by the terms in which it is
expressed." Existentialist interpretation seeks the understanding
of existence hidden within the camouflage of language.

To grasp the inner particularity of the "life" behind language is, for Schleiermacher and Dilthey, a process of "reproduction" (*Nachbildung*). The interpreter in effect reproduces the text in reverse fashion, working back from the fixed expressions to comprehend the original "life-moment" seeking expression. For Dilthey, understanding (*Verstehen*) is the "process by which an inside is conferred on a complex of external sensory signs."/109/ In Schleiermacher's terms, "the task of hermeneutics is to reproduce the whole internal process of an author's way of combining thoughts."/110/ This interpretive reproduction requires, according to Schleiermacher, both the analysis of "external form" through "grammatical" interpretation, and that of "internal form," through "technical," or "psychological," interpretation. Because an individual expression arises from the established vocabulary and grammatical rules and conventions of its cultural origin, grammatical investigation attempts to reproduce the language shared by author and original audience. But this philological, historical investigation is not enough, for an individual expression also reflects the particular organization of the author's thoughts. Technical interpretation, therefore, seeks to comprehend "the unity of the work . . . viewed as the dynamic principle impelling the author, and the basic features of the composition are viewed as his distinctive nature, revealing himself in that moment."/111/ Interpretation requires both "comparative" and "divinatory" methods, for "Only a divinatory method," Schleiermacher writes, "enables us to rightly reconstruct [*nachzubilden*] the creative act that begins with the generation of thoughts which captivate the author and to understand how the requirement of the moment could draw upon the living treasure of words in the author's mind in order to produce just this way of putting it and no other."/112/

The meaning of the text for both Schleiermacher and Dilthey is finally located in the interpreter's consciousness, for through the interpretive process historical distance is overcome, and interpreter and author become immediately present to each other. As Schleiermacher writes, "By leading the interpreter to transform himself, so to speak, into the author, the divinatory method seeks to gain an immediate comprehension of the author as an individual."/113/ Hermeneutics is an "art," for it requires a constant oscillation between comparative and divinatory, grammatical and technical analyses, a process which is always open to revision and thus never complete:

> In order to complete the grammatical side of interpreta-
> tion it would be necessary to have a complete knowledge
> of the language. In order to complete the psychological
> side it would be necessary to have a complete knowledge
> of the person. Since in both cases such complete knowl-
> edge is impossible, it is necessary to move back and forth
> between the grammatical and psychological sides, and no
> rules can stipulate exactly how to do this./114/

While never final, such interpretation seeks, in Schleiermacher's
noted phrase, "to understand the text at first as well as and then
even better than its author."/115/ This is possible because the process of reproduction reveals more to an interpreter than an author
could have been consciously aware. The exegete sees not only the
spontaneous, original idea and its development in the work, but
also those points at which an author "initiates something new in
the language," or "merely repeats and transmits the language he
has received."/116/ The success of the art of interpretation thus
depends, in Schleiermacher's words, "on one's ability for knowing
people."/117/ It depends as well on the mutual participation of
author and exegete in a common human nature. One can transcend one's own subjectivity without losing oneself because, as
Dilthey writes:

> In understanding, the individuality of the exegete and
> that of the author are not opposed to each other like two
> incomparable facts. Rather, both have been formed upon
> the substratum of a general human nature, and this is
> what makes possible a communion of people with each
> other in speech./118/

For Bultmann, both philological-historical criticism (explanation) and existentialist interpretation (understanding) of the biblical texts are part of the general hermeneutical task. Just as Dilthey
maintains that interpretation depends on the condition that author
and exegete "have been formed upon the substratum of a general
human nature," so Bultmann wishes to argue that any properly
trained exegete, Christian or non-Christian, can understand the
possibility for existence the New Testament texts present. The
demythologized biblical documents, as disclosures of human possibility, can be of significance to all persons, insofar as they are
aware of those fundamental questions arising out of human existence as such to which the texts provide a possible answer. This
kind of pre-understanding, Bultmann astutely perceives, is always

operative when the text to be understood is a literary work. When reading a novel, for example, one implicitly assumes that the text emerges from, speaks about, and is addressed to, human experience./119/ By placing the New Testament writings in the company of literary texts, Bultmann is thus arguing two significant points: first, that the New Testament texts, properly understood, do speak about and to one's existential situation, and second, that one of the central tasks for modern New Testament exegetes is that of *creating* the appropriate context, or pre-understanding, within which the texts can be understood./120/ For Bultmann, this proper understanding is the question of the meaning of one's existence. Every individual, that is, is moved by the *existentiell* question concerning God, regardless of the particular form that this question may take in one's own consciousness. Since to understand a text at all requires an *existentiell* encounter with the possibility it offers, Bultmann argues, each interpreter is faced with the demand to decide whether one will accept or reject its claim. "Even in the case of a no, however," writes Bultmann, "the understanding is a legitimate one, i.e., is a genuine answer to the question of the text. . . ."/121/ The nature of the hermeneutic process itself thus ensures the text's significance for the present. Historicity is overcome whenever genuine understanding occurs, because to understand is to recognize that in the text which speaks out of and to the concerns of human existence as such.

Bultmann's chief modification of the Schleiermachian tradition is his shift of the locus of meaning in a text, the object of interpretation, from the author to the "subject matter." In his most important essay on interpretation theory, "The Problem of Hermeneutics," Bultmann outlines his own program in relation to those of Schleiermacher and Dilthey./122/ In this essay he points out that their "psychological" emphasis on the "individuality" of the author is simply one kind of hermeneutic investigation among others, and one which ignores the contents directly mediated by certain texts in favor of "the inner creative process in which they arose." While a mathematical or medical text can, to be sure, be viewed as the expression of an individual life, Bultmann points out, it can also be read for its informational content. Bultmann therefore argues that interpretation is "constantly oriented to a particular formulation of a question, a particular 'objective'," and is thus "governed always by a prior understanding of the subject in accordance with which it investigates the text."/123/ One reads a text with different questions in mind, and one's inquiry is directed toward the subject matter spoken of either directly or indirectly in the text. Schleiermacher and Dilthey are correct in characterizing the relationship between author and interpreter as the foundation for comprehension of a text, Bultmann argues, but this relationship is not to be determined by "psychical processes" or one's "spiritual make-up or intellectual consanguinity"; it is determined, rather, on the basis of the author's and interpreter's relationships to the subject matter directly or indirectly expressed in the text./124/ For an interpreter to understand a text whose subject matter is music, for example, the condition for understanding is that both author and exegete "have the same relation in life to the subject matter which is under discussion"; they must both stand in the same "context of living experience."/125/ It is the interpreter's interest in and living relationship to the subject matter which motivates the interpretation and establishes its "direction of enquiry."

Bultmann's argument in this essay is not entirely clear. Simply grounding interpretation on the "author's intention," Bultmann seems to argue, does not recognize the complexity of the herme- neutical circle:

> The formula, that the comprehension of the author and his work is the real aim of exegesis . . . is right insofar as it rejects the view that the exegesis is or may be governed by dogmatic or practical interests. Otherwise it tells us abso- lutely nothing about the problem of hermeneutics. For this is where the problem really begins! What comprehen- sion of the author is intended—a psychological one, or a biographical one perhaps?—and so on. And how is the work to be understood—as a problem in an historical light, or aesthetically, and so on?/126/

Here Bultmann seems to suggest that a kind of hermeneutic pluralism is possible and valuable. One can view a text as a source for the reconstruction of its cultural context, or for the information it provides about a particular subject, for example. One can view a novel in terms of its aesthetic form, read it to be entertained by its story, or seek to obtain psychological or bio- graphical information about its author./127/ This would imply that Bultmann regards his own interest in the "understanding of existence" expressed in the New Testament texts as simply one line of inquiry among others, to be placed beside other interests such as historical reconstruction.

Bultmann also wishes to claim, however, that only an existentialist interpretation of certain texts produces genuine understanding. When he pursues this argument Bultmann seems to suggest that some directions of inquiry are "alien," or "extrinsic," to a text, while others are in accordance with the text's "intrinsic" intention. Reading a text which intends to impart information—a scientific text, for example—as a source for understanding the history of science is problematical, because it "subordinates its interpretation to an alien interest." Bultmann argues that "the orientation of the interpretation is not problematical, however, when guided by enquiry into that particular subject, the imparting of which is the intention of the text itself."/128/

What is clear, in any case, is why Bultmann wishes to shift the object of interpretation from the author's consciousness to the subject matter. What is "reproduced" through interpretation, for Bultmann, is not the individual life-moment of an author, but rather the author's relationship to the subject matter expressed in the text. The interpreter is not, so to speak, transformed into the author, but instead seeks to grasp the subject matter the author also sought to grasp. What is sought is an "immediate comprehension" of the subject matter, not of the author as an individual personality.

From General to Theological Hermeneutics

Bultmann's shift from author to subject matter is necessary if he is to place this general hermeneutical framework in service of the specifically theological task demanded by the New Testament texts. For Bultmann, recognition of the original authors' intentions cannot be the final interpretive goal, because the focus of the biblical authors is not finally on themselves, but on that of which they are attempting to speak—the transcendent. The understanding of existence in the New Testament texts is an understanding of existence as it has been transformed by faith in God. The "subject matter" that biblical interpreters strive to grasp is, in keeping with the kind of "double-speaking" characteristic of theological statements, both the transcendent and the possibilities for new self-understanding made possible in Christ. What awakens faith, however, is the kerygma, which, for Bultmann as it was for Luther, is genuinely understood only as it is heard as a word addressed to one's concrete existence. Truly to understand the kerygma is to experience it as God's Word addressing one as a questioning and promising word, a condemning and forgiving word.

While the kerygma is the object of faith and in one sense the true subject matter of the New Testament, what we find in the texts are theological responses to and interpretations of the kerygma. As Bultmann writes, "it is not possible simply and sharply to distinguish kerygmatic statements in the New Testament from theological ones," since because it can never be spoken except in human language and as formed by human thought, the kerygma never appears without already having been given some theological interpretation./129/ Thus, just as we can learn *about* friendship without entering into that relationship itself, the New Testament writings can tell us what life in or out of faith means as possibilities for existence. The theological interpreter cannot presuppose his or her faith as a methodological instrument, but must come to the texts with the proper pre-understanding—with openness, with an awareness that existence can be lost or gained, and with a sense of the questionability of existence. Whether or not the kerygma will become a vehicle of grace for the interpreter is therefore outside the task and possibility of interpretation.

In this theological context, demythologizing takes on new dimensions. To "translate" the texts into existential categories is the means for their recovery for contemporary readers. In theological terms, demythologizing is necessary to remove the false "stumbling block" that mythological statement presents for modern thought, so that the true and permanent *skandalon*, the kerygma, can come into view. Translating the New Testament forms of expression is in the "service of faith" in this first sense.

In addition, however, Bultmann's existential interpretation of the central New Testament message—of justification by faith, Law and Gospel—becomes a further argument for demythologization. As we have seen, in Bultmann's interpretation faith can rest on no objective proof, and it requires that one abandon one's attachments to any form of objectifying thought. As "eschatological event," faith calls all objectifying forms into question, with myth and science both examples of objectifying thought. While the new self-understanding awakened by faith will continually be re-articulated in varying forms under different historical conditions, the event of faith will again and again call all particular forms into question. "For the Revelation," Bultmann writes, "is represented as the shattering and negating of all human norms and evaluations. And precisely by virtue of being such a negation, the Revelation is the fulfillment and affirmation of human longing for life, for true reality."/130/

Demythologizing is thus in this further sense demanded by the character of the New Testament itself. Because Bultmann's interpreters have often obscured this point, his statement merits quoting at length:

> If the challenge of demythologizing was first raised by the conflict between the mythological world view of the Bible and the modern scientific world view, it at once became evident that the restatement of mythology is a requirement of faith itself. For faith needs to be emancipated from its association with every world view expressed in objective terms, whether it be a mythical or a scientific one . . . . Starting as it does from the modern world view, and challenging the biblical mythology and the traditional proclamation of the church, this new kind of criticism is performing for faith the supreme service of recalling it to a radical reconsideration of its own nature. It is just this call that our demythologizing seeks to follow./131/

In Bultmann's view we see that this process has already begun in Paul's and John's rejection of certain gnostic views. According to Bultmann, Paul means by "life according to the Spirit" not a new supernatural state but the possibility of a new life which must be appropriated by a "deliberate resolve."/132/ And while Paul employs the gnostic myth of redemption to convey that all persons participate in Christ's life and death, the Pauline imperative demythologizes the gnostic indicative, stressing that one must continually decide whether to accept the possibility presented by the Cross. In John, we see an elimination of the cosmological presuppositions and the rational and speculative insights of gnostic myth, and of the preaching by the historical Jesus. For John, Jesus "reveals nothing but that he is the Revealer. . . . John, that is, in the Gospel presents only the fact (*das Dass*) of the Revelation without describing its content (*ihr Was*)."/133/

Demythologizing thus becomes a contemporary form of Luther's "Christ against Scripture." With the kerygma as hermeneutical norm—an internal norm in that the highest intention of the New Testament is to preach Christ; an external norm in that Christ is an event witnessed to, but distinct from, Scripture— Bultmann can argue that the interpreter is required to make theological judgments as to the adequacy of the content of any particular theological statement in the New Testament. It is possible, Bultmann notes, that

> these statements may be only relatively appropriate, some more so, some less so. The possibility exists that in some of them the believing comprehension itself may not be clearly developed, that it may be hindered— bound perhaps by a pre-faith understanding of God, the world, and man and by a corresponding terminology. . . . From this possibility arises the task—even in the case of the New Testament writings—of content criticism (*Sachkritik*) such as Luther, for example, exercised toward the Epistle of James and the Revelation of John./134/

Bultmann, then, attempts to recover the meaningfulness of the biblical writings by criticizing the adequacy of their mythological forms for both modern thought and the content of the New Testament itself. Beyond this, he argues that a theological critique of the content of these texts is demanded as well. Like Luther, Bultmann measures the "believing comprehension" of the various writers against an interpretation of the heart of the Christian message—the canon within the canon of justification by faith.

In the years following the publication of "New Testament and Mythology," Bultmann's proposals were subject to extensive debate. As Schubert Ogden notes, critics on both the right and left of Bultmann focused on the same difficulty—the question of just how far demythologization of the New Testament was to extend./135/ While in Bultmann's view what the New Testament says about human existence prior to faith and about the existence of the believer may both be demythologized, the question remains whether the affirmation that the transition from the former to the latter is conceivable only through faith in God's act in Christ is also a mythological affirmation./136/ As we have seen, Bultmann argues that the true intention of the New Testament writings, despite their objectifying forms, is not to view the Christ occurrence as a mythological event. Bultmann insists that the cross of Christ, as "eschatological event," is a "genuinely historical event" that takes place as salvation or judgment *within* the individual's decision for faith or unfaith./137/ While the biblical texts can tell us about what existence in faith means, the power to awaken the transition from unfaith to faith lies solely in the proclaimed word of the Cross.

One of the most undeveloped aspects of Bultmann's thought— and one of the points at which the recent explorations of religious language can make a significant contribution—is Bultmann's insistence that one can speak directly of God's act in Christ in a non-mythological way. For the most part, Bultmann's hermeneutic seems to acknowledge only two types of New Testament language. On the one hand, there are statements concerning human existence in or out of faith. While often expressed in mythological terms, these statements concern one's existential self-understanding, and can be interpreted in existentialist categories. On the other hand, there is the kerygma—the proclaimed word which demands decision. The kerygma's status as language is not entirely clear, since, as we have seen, in Bultmann's view the biblical texts themselves are for the most part not the kerygma but responses to the kerygma. For Bultmann as for Luther, the kerygma is fundamentally a preached word, a word of address, rather than an inscribed word. And in general Bultmann seems to conceive of the meaning of the kerygmatic proclamation wholly in terms of the event of salvation effected in the believer's self-understanding. The demythologized texts can tell us about Christian self-understanding, but the transition to existence in faith occurs only within the event of individual decision, as the "eschatological event" which the kerygma proclaims is "reactualized" in the concrete existence of the believer. The proclaimed word is thus in a sense a statement of pure faith which seems to have no objective content, for its meaning or content *becomes* meaningful only in the event of its actualization. Because Bultmann seems to place myth and kerygma in opposition, and because he "translates" myth into philosophical statement, his program seems to have no place for a language of faith that is neither the "objectifying" language Bultmann assigns to myth, nor the conceptual discourse of philosophy.

What is at stake here is the question of whether there is a language for revelation. Christian theologians have often spoken of revelation as "event," indicating that revelation is a manifestation from beyond, and an act of God's personal self-disclosure.

Can the event of revelation be mediated by language? While Bultmann is undoubtedly correct in acknowledging that the objectifications of the transcendent which we find in the New Testament pose a problem for modern thought, the question remains whether Bultmann would have us abandon all direct speaking of God altogether. In addition to the anthropological language of existentialism and to the proclamation of the kerygma, is there any language in which one can appropriately speak of the transcendent?

The issue here is in many respects an ancient one—the capacity of human thought and language to refer to the transcendent. Plato, of course, first raised the question as a philosophical issue, and he provided the arguments for both sides. On the one hand, myth and poetry are subjected to radical criticism: they tell stories which give a false picture of the gods. Furthermore, they are to be excluded from *paideia* because they appeal to the passions rather than to reason./138/ On the other hand, the "likely story," the *Timaeus* suggests, is the closest we can come to true insight; the limits of thought and language make it impossible for us to have unmediated knowledge of truth itself./139/ Pre-critical biblical interpreters tended to uphold both sides of the question by arguing that in the biblical writings the Divine Author reveals and conceals truth in figures to "accommodate" the limitations of the human intellect.

Bultmann seems to maintain both positions as well. His critique of the adequacy of objectifying language is clear. There is some indication that Bultmann also saw a place for a language of faith, an "analogical language" distinguishable from myth on the one hand and from what he describes as a purely "symbolic description of subjective experience" on the other./140/ Bultmann argues that if speaking about God is to be meaningful,

> it must denote an act in a real, objective sense, and not just a symbolical or pictorial expression. . . . Such language is therefore neither symbolical nor pictorial, though it is certainly *analogical*, for it assumes an analogy between the activity of God and that of man and between the fellowship of God and man and that of man with man./141/

In *Jesus Christ and Mythology* he pursues a similar argument, again suggesting that to speak analogically of God as acting does not mean to speak in symbols or images, but "must be able to convey its full, direct meaning . . . . God's love and care, etc., are not images or symbols; these conceptions mean real experiences of God as acting here and now."/142/

It is not clear precisely what Bultmann means by his notion of analogy, or how it is distinct from myth and conceptual statement. In his insistence that God's action can be spoken of in terms of analogies drawn from human existence, Bultmann is perhaps suggesting that, just as our human words and deeds provide the occasion and outward expression for, but are never simply identical with, our acts of communion with others, so also is the act of God only "paradoxically" present in the event of Jesus Christ and the proclamation of the Church./143/

While Bultmann has left this significant aspect of his program undeveloped, it is precisely at this point that a number of his students, under the rubric of the "New Hermeneutic," and, most recently, those New Testament scholars who have turned to literary criticism, have begun their reflection./144/ As the following chapters will examine in detail, this recent "literary turn" stands in complex relation to Bultmann—a relation sometimes self-consciously addressed; in other cases implicit. In some respects, the use of literary criticism to investigate the variety of linguistic forms in the New Testament writings can be seen as an attempt to carry further Bultmann's own preliminary efforts to describe a language of faith, a language that can in some way mediate revelation. One of the central issues to be explored in what follows, however, is to what extent such literary investigations are, in fact, compatible with the larger framework of Bultmann's theological and hermeneutical proposals. For this literary turn is also a turn to the imagination: a dimension of human existence for which Bultmann's existentialist theology, centered as it is in the act of human decision in faith, has little room. One question to be kept in view is how an affirmation of the mediating capacities of the imagination can be integrated with a theology like Bultmann's which focuses on revelation as an event of encounter and response to proclamation.

Even more central is the question of the relation between language and meaning, form and content. As the next chapter will explore in detail, a central axiom of modern formalist literary criticism is that linguistic form and content are inseparable—an axiom which clearly calls into question the foundation of Bultmann's demythologizing program. Another question to be considered, then, is how one may affirm, with literary criticism, that form and content belong together, while also being responsible, with Bultmann, to the problem of historicity and of the scandalous foreignness of the biblical texts. An evaluation of these issues must be postponed until the final chapter of this project. The central principles and presuppositions of modern formalist literary criticism are the subject of the chapter which follows.

NOTES

/1/   Günther Bornkamm, for example, points out that: "In fact, in Rudolf Bultmann's own view the issue and concept of demythologizing is relatively speaking confined to the surface of the matter. It is not new, and calling attention to it is really a *testimonium pauperitatis*. For it has necessarily always been taking place in various ways, although usually without adequate hermeneutical reflection." "Die Theologie Rudolf Bultmanns in der neuren Diskussion," *Theologische Rundschau* n.F., 29 (1963):125, cited by James Robinson, "Hermeneutic since Barth," in *The New Hermeneutic*, ed. James Robinson and John B. Cobb, Jr., New Frontiers in Theology, no. 2 (New York: Harper & Row, 1964), p. 38, n. 98.

/2/   Bultmann's definition of the modern perspective as one primarily shaped by scientific thought provoked intense discussion in the earlier demythologizing controversies. While Bultmann does often equate modern consciousness with scientific consciousness, to focus exclusively on the validity of this assertion is to ignore Bultmann's chief hermeneutical concern, the problem of historicity.

/3/   As Carl Braaten observes, the early demythologizing debate tended to focus on the question of the mythological elements in primitive Christian preaching. Subsequent discussion shifted to the question of "kerygma and history," and thus to the relation between kerygma, myth and history. See *Kerygma and History*, ed. Carl Braaten and Roy A. Harrisville (New York: Abingdon Press, 1962), p. 10. I would add that even with this shift of focus, criticial interest in historical understanding as a hermeneutical issue seems often to have been eclipsed by concern with the narrower problem of the "historical Jesus."

/4/   For perspectives on the interpretation of all normative texts, see Jerome Mazzeo, *Varieties of Interpretation*, and Robert M. Grant, *The Letter and the Spirit* (London: Oxford University Press, 1957).

54   Literary Criticism and Biblical Hermeneutics

/5/   For the history of New Testament study, see Robert M. Grant, *The Bible in the Church* (New York: Macmillan Co., 1948); *The Cambridge History of the Bible*, vol. 1: *From the Beginnings to Jerome*, ed. P. R. Ackroyd and C. F. Evans; vol. 2: *The West from the Fathers to the Reformation*, ed. G. W. H. Lampe; vol. 3: *The West from the Reformation to the Present Day*, ed. S. I. Greenslade; 3 vols. (Cambridge: Cambridge University Press, 1963–70); and Werner Georg Kümmel, *The New Testament: A History of the Investigation of Its Problems*, trans. S. Maclean Gilmour and Howard C. Kee (Nashville: Abingdon Press, 1972). For a theory concerning Christian classics, see David Tracy, *The Analogical Imagination* (New York: Crossroad, 1981).

/6/   Among contemporary literary theorists, discussions of the relation between form and content and language and meaning take various directions. For the positions of "stylistic" criticism see the essays in Seymour Chatman, ed., *Literary Style: A Symposium* (New York: Oxford University Press, 1971). See also E. D. Hirsch, *Validity in Interpretation* (New Haven: Yale University Press, 1967), and *The Aims of Interpretation* (Chicago: University of Chicago Press, 1976), esp. his critique of stylistics in Chapter IV. For the position of the "New Critics" and of Paul Ricoeur, see Chapters II and IV below. For a quasi-deconstructionist position applied to the New Testament, see Frank Kermode's provocative study, *The Genesis of Secrecy: On the Interpretation of Narrative* (Cambridge: Harvard University Press, 1979).

/7/   For Heraclitus, see Grant, *Letter and Spirit*, pp. 9–11. For Augustine, see *On Christian Doctrine* (trans. D. W. Robertson) 3.27.38.

/8/   Augustine *On Christian Doctrine* 2.6.7–8.

/9/   Origen *On First Principles* (Harper Torchbooks) 4.2.7.

/10/   Philo *Leg. All.* 11, 19; *De Plant.* 32, cited by C. K. Barrett in *The Cambridge History of the Bible*, 1:381.

/11/   Augustine *On Christian Doctrine* 2.18.28.

/12/   "Thus the Wisdom of God, setting out to cure men, applied Himself to cure them, being at once the Physician and the Medicine." Ibid. 1.14.13.

/13/   For studies on Paul, see Rudolf Bultmann, *Theology of the New Testament*, trans. Kendrick Grobel; 2 vols. (New York: Charles Scribner's Sons, 1951–55), 1:190–325. See also Günther Bornkamm, *Paul*, trans. D. M. G. Stalker (New York: Harper & Row, 1971), and *The Cambridge History*, 1:412–26.

/14/ See Paul Ricoeur's interpretation of Christ as both "exegete" and "exegesis" in "Preface to Bultmann," published in *The Conflict of Interpretations*, ed. Don Ihde (Evanston: Northwestern University Press, 1974), pp. 381–401.

/15/ T. S. Eliot, "Tradition and the Individual Talent," in *The Sacred Wood* (London: Methuen and Co., University Paperbacks, 1960), p. 49.

/16/ See Hans von Campenhausen, *The Formation of the Christian Bible*, trans. J. A. Baker (Philadelphia: Fortress Press, 1972), and David H. Kelsey, *The Uses of Scripture in Recent Theology* (Philadelphia: Fortress Press, 1975), Chapter 5.

/17/ M. F. Wiles, "Origen as Biblical Scholar," in *The Cambridge History*, 1:463–65.

/18/ Cited by Grant, *The Bible in the Church*, p. 113. See also James Samuel Preus's excellent study of Luther's hermeneutics, *From Shadow to Promise* (Cambridge: Harvard University Press, The Belknap Press, 1969), esp. pp. 184–99.

/19/ Augustine *On Christian Doctrine* 1.36.40.

/20/ See, for example, Irenaeus *Adversus Haereses* 4.33.8; and 3.2.3: "Every Church, that is, the faithful everywhere, must needs agree with the Church at Rome, for in her the Apostolic tradition has ever been preserved by the faithful from all parts of the world." See also Tertullian *De Praescriptione Haereticorum* 13.

/21/ See especially Origen *On First Principles* Book 4.

/22/ See Roland Bainton, "The Bible and the Reformation," in *The Cambridge History*, 3:1–37.

/23/ Martin Luther, *D. Martin Luthers Werke: Kritische Gesamtausgabe*, 58 vols. (Weimar: 1883–1963), 7:97.

/24/ Martin Luther, *Luther's Works*, ed. Jaroslav Pelikan, American ed., 55 vols. (St. Louis: Concordia Publishing House, 1958–76), 39:178.

/25/ See, for example, Gerhard Ebeling, "The Significance of the Critical Historical Method for Church and Theology in Protestantism," in *Word and Faith* (Philadelphia: Fortress Press, 1960), pp. 17–61.

/26/ For Luther's notion of the internal and external clarity of Scripture, see "The Bondage of the Will," in *Martin Luther: Selections from His Writings*, ed. John Dillenberger (Garden City: Doubleday Co., Anchor Books, 1961), pp. 166–206.

/27/   Luther, Weimar 56:169, cited by Bainton, "The Bible in the Reformation," p. 20.

/28/   Martin Luther, "Preface to the Epistles of St. James and St. Jude," in Dillenberger, *Martin Luther*, pp. 35–36.

/29/   Luther, Weimar 12:259.

/30/   K. Fullerton, "Luther's Doctrine and Criticism of Scripture." *Bibliotheca Sacra* 3 (1906): 16, cited by Grant, *The Bible in the Church*, p. 113.

/31/   Luther, Weimar 50:245–46.

/32/   Bainton, "The Bible in the Reformation," p. 24.

/33/   It can be argued, for example, that the roots of modern scientific criticism lie in scholasticism's view of reason as an autonomous agent, as does Grant in *The Bible in the Church*, pp. 98–108. That the Reformation and Renaissance gave impetus to modern historical criticism has by now been amply demonstrated. See in this regard Ebeling, "The Significance of the Critical Historical Method," pp. 17–61.

/34/   Rudolf Bultmann, *Essays Philosophical and Theological*, trans. James C. G. Greig (London: SCM Press, 1955), p. 256; and Hans Werner Bartsch, ed. and trans., *Kerygma and Myth* (New York: Harper & Row, Harper Torchbooks, 1961), p. 4 (hereafter cited as KM).

/35/   Schleiermacher's manuscripts on hermeneutics, edited by Heinz Kimmerle, are translated by James Duke and Jack Forstman as *Hermeneutics: The Handwritten Manuscripts*, AAR Texts and Translations Series, vol. 1 (Missoula, Mont.: Scholars Press, 1977).

/36/   Ibid., pp. 216, 255.

/37/   Ibid., p. 216: "Inspiration, as an infusion into the mind (*Gesinnung*), should not influence the work of interpretation. If in the case of the Bible, as in every other case, the goal of hermeneutics is to understand the texts as their original readers understood them, the fact that they are inspired does not affect the interpretation at all."

/38/   See Hirsch's rehearsal of the principal argument in favor general hermeneutics in *Aims*, pp. 17–19.

/39/   On this point see Ebeling, *Word and Faith*, pp. 17–61, and Ted Peters, "Sola Scriptura and the Second Naivete," *Dialog* 16 (1977): 268–80.

/40/   Ernst Troeltsch, *Gesammelte Schriften* (Tubingen: J. C. B. Mohr, 1913), 2:730, cited by Van Harvey, *The Historian and the Believer* (New York: Macmillan Co., 1966), p. 5.

/41/   See Ted Peters, "Sola Scriptura," pp. 272–73.

/42/   Cf. Hans W. Frei's comment that: "Biblical interpretation since the eighteenth century has always proceeded in two directions which sometimes have appeared to be on collision course. On the one hand there has been the question of the origin and, in some respects, the reliability of biblical writings. On the other there has been inquiry into the proper ways of learning what abiding meaning or value these writings might have. Collision threatened whenever the answer to the second question seemed to be partially or wholly dependent on the answer to the first. The task of interpretation has frequently been taken to be that of plotting a chart for the narrows between these two shoals." *The Eclipse of Biblical Narrative* (New Haven: Yale University Press, 1974), p. 17.

/43/   Frei uses the term "history-likeness" throughout *Eclipse*, but see especially his introductory chapter, pp. 1–16.

/44/   Kermode, *Genesis*, p. 106.

/45/   Harvey, *Historian*, pp. 6–8.

/46/   Ibid., p. 7.

/47/   Ibid., esp. pp. 38–101.

/48/   Cf. Hans-Georg Gadamer's perception that: "The kerygmatic meaning of the New Testament, which gives the form of application of the *pro me* to the Gospel, cannot ultimately contradict the legitimate investigation of meaning by historical science. This is, I contend, an unalterable requirement of the scientific consciousness. It is impossible to assume a relation of mutual exclusion between the meaning and salvation-meaning of a scriptural text." *Philosophical Hermeneutics*, trans. David E. Linge (Berkeley: University of California Press, 1976), pp. 209–10.

/49/   Adolf von Harnack, "Fifteen Questions to Those among the Theologians Who are Contemptuous of the Scientific Theology," in *The Beginnings of Dialectical Theology*, ed. James Robinson (Richmond: John Knox Press, 1968), p. 166.

/50/   I am indebted to Frei's discussion of ostensive reference in *Eclipse*.

/51/   Cf. Hirsch's discussion of "positivism" in *Aims*, pp. 22–25.

/52/   The development of biblical criticism through the eighteenth and nineteenth centuries is, of course, much more complex than is indicated by the outline sketched here. See Frei's excellent review of "Hermeneutical Options at the Turn of the Century" in *Eclipse*, pp. 245–66.

/53/   KM, p. 13.

/54/   See, for example, "Liberal Theology and the Latest Theological Movement," in *Faith and Understanding*, ed. Robert W. Funk (New York: Harper & Row, 1969), pp. 28–52 (hereafter cited as FU).

/55/   Albert Schweitzer, *The Quest of the Historical Jesus*, trans. W. Montgomery (New York: Macmillan Company, 1964).

/56/   See, for example, "On the Question of Christology," in FU, p. 132: "I have never yet felt uncomfortable with my critical radicalism; on the contrary, I have been entirely comfortable. . . . I calmly let the fire burn, for I see that what is consumed is only the fanciful portraits of the Life-of-Jesus theology, and that means nothing other than 'Christ after the flesh'."

/57/   See Bultmann's introduction to Adolf von Harnack, *What is Christianity?*, trans. Thomas Bailey Saunders (New York: Harper and Bros., Harper Torchbooks, 1957), pp. vii–xviii.

/58/   See KM, p. 211: "Our radical attempt to demythologize the New Testament is in fact a perfect parallel to St. Paul's and Luther's doctrine of justification by faith alone apart from the works of the Law. Or, rather, it carries this doctrine to its logical conclusion in the field of epistemology." Cf. KM, p. 11.

/59/   KM, p. 10.

/60/   KM, p. 7. See also Bultmann's discussion of "objectification" in "On the Problem of Demythologizing," *Journal of Religion* 42 (April 1962): 96–97.

/61/   KM, p. 4.

/62/   Bultmann, "On the Problem of Demythologizing," p. 96.

/63/   "Zum Problem Der Entmythologisierung," in *Kerygma und Mythos, d* ed. Hans Werner Bartsch, 5 vols. (Hamburg-Volksdorf: Herbert Reich, 1948–1955), 2:182. This section is omitted from the translation in KM, pp. 191–211.

/64/ KM, p. 3.

/65/ KM, p. 15.

/66/ The relation between God and world is primary in John B. Cobb, Jr.'s interpretation of Bultmann. See his *Living Options in Protestant Theology* (Philadelphia: Westminster Press, 1961), pp. 227–58.

/67/ KM, p. 197.

/68/ Ibid.

/69/ KM, p. 211.

/70/ "Religion and Culture," in *The Beginnings of Dialectical Theology*, p. 216. Bultmann's reflections on the second edition of Barth's commentary on Romans, for example, describes his own endeavor as well:

> The book attempts to prove the independence and the absolute nature of religion. It thus takes its place . . . with such works as Schleiermacher's *On Religion* and Otto's *The Idea of the Holy*, with modern attempts to demonstrate a religious a priori, and finally with the letter to the Romans itself, which, with its radical contrast between works and faith, basically has no other intention than this. However different all these attempts may be in detail, they seek to give verbal expression to the consciousness of the uniqueness and absoluteness of religion. (Ibid., p. 100)

/71/ FU, p. 53.

/72/ KM, p. 211.

/73/ Bultmann argues for some continuity between Jesus and the Church in *The Theology of the New Testament*, 1:44.

/74/ KM, p. 41.

/75/ Rudolf Bultmann, *Jesus Christ and Mythology* (New York: Charles Scribner's Sons, 1958), p. 80 (hereafter cited as JCM).

/76/ Bultmann presents this view in numerous essays. See, for example, *The Beginnings of Dialectical Theology*, pp. 205–20, and FU, pp. 92–110.

/77/ See, for example, *Theology of the New Testament*, 2:39, and *Existence and Faith*, ed. Schubert Ogden (New York: Meridian Books, 1960), pp. 88, 93–95, 120. (The latter is cited hereafter as EF).

/78/   KM, p. 193.

/79/   JCM, p. 56.

/80/   EF, p. 94.

/81/   Ibid. While Bultmann usually argues that philosophy has a strictly formal function, many of his statements presuppose that philosophy has material significance as well. See Ogden's discussion of this issue in *Christ Without Myth* (New York: Harper and Bros., 1961), pp. 68–70.

/82/   Thus Bultmann can write:

> The only way to preserve the unworldly, transcendental character of the divine activity is to regard it not as an interference in worldly happenings, but as something accomplished *in* them in such a way that the closed weft of history as it presents itself to objective observation is left undisturbed. To every eye other than the eye of faith the action of God is hidden. Only the 'natural' happening is generally visible and ascertainable. In it is accomplished the hidden act of God. (KM, p. 197)

/83/   Bultmann introduces his notion of analogy in KM, p. 196, where he attempts to argue that analogy is non-objectifying and non-mythological. The above analogy appears in EF, pp. 99–100.

/84/   EF, pp. 99–100.

/85/   Bultmann, "On the Problem of Demythologizing," p. 100. Bultmann can thus distinguish even primitive proto-science, a "work-thinking" that seeks ordered explanations for events in natural causes, from "myth," which refers the world to its ground in supernatural powers. See, for example, FU, pp. 247–61.

/86/   Ibid.

/87/   JCM, p. 19; KM, p. 10.

/88/   KM, p. 35.

/89/   EF, p. 81.

/90/   Ibid.

/91/   EF, p. 107.

/92/   JCM, pp. 77–78.

/93/ See Frei, *Eclipse*, pp. 4–5. See also Theodore Ziolkowski, "Religion and Literature in a Secular Age: The Critic's Dilemma," *Journal of Religion* 59 (January 1979): 18–34.

/94/ KM, p. 210.

/95/ Wilhelm Dilthey, "The Rise of Hermeneutics," in *Wilhelm Dilthey: Selected Writings*, ed. and trans. H. P. Rickman (Cambridge: Cambridge University Press, 1976), p. 247.

/96/ Ibid., p. 246.

/97/ Bultmann, *Essays*, p. 253.

/98/ Bultmann, "On the Problem of Demythologizing," p. 96.

/99/ Ibid., p. 97.

/100/ Dilthey, "The Rise of Hermeneutics," p. 136.

/101/ Ibid., p. 228.

/102/ Bultmann, *Essays*, p. 253.

/103/ Dilthey, "The Rise of Hermeneutics," p. 220.

/104/ Ibid., p. 228.

/105/ EF, p. 294. See also Rudolf Bultmann, *History and Eschatology: The Presence of Eternity* (New York: Harper & Row, Harper Torchbooks, 1957), p. 120.

/106/ EF, p. 294; *History and Eschatology*, pp. 120–122. Cf. Dilthey, "The Rise of Hermeneutics," pp. 235–36.

/107/ I am indebted here to Robinson's discussion of Jonas in "Hermeneutic since Barth," pp. 34–39.

/108/ Hans Jonas, *Augustine und das paulinische Freiheitsproblem*, Forschungen zur Religion und Literatur des Alten und Neuen Testaments, Heft 44, ed. Bousset and Gunkel, cited by Robinson, "Hermeneutic since Barth," p. 36.

/109/ Dilthey, "The Rise of Hermeneutics," p. 232.

/110/ Schleiermacher, *Hermeneutics*, p. 188.

/111/ Ibid., p. 147.

/112/ Ibid., p. 192. It should be noted that Schleiermacher's understanding of the language-thought relation is debated among his interpreters. See, for example, Kimmerle's argument that Schleiermacher shifts from an early hermeneutic position oriented toward language to one oriented toward the author's subjective consciousness in his "Editor's Introduction," ibid., pp. 21–40. Cf. James Duke's response, pp. 9–12, and Frei's comments in *Eclipse*, p. 345, n. 30.

/113/ Schleiermacher, "Hermeneutics," p. 150.

/114/ Ibid., p. 100.

/115/ Ibid., p. 112.

/116/ Ibid., p. 148.

/117/ Ibid., p. 101.

/118/ Dilthey, "The Rise of Hermeneutics," p. 135.

/119/ That formalist literary theory tends to exclude this dimension from the literary situation is argued in Chapter II.

/120/ Modern New Testament exegetes, then, have not only the negative task of criticizing the texts' outmoded world view, but also the positive one of establishing a hearing ground into which the texts may speak. Cf. Ricoeur's remarks in this regard in *Philosophy*, pp. 223–38.

/121/ EF, p. 296.

/122/ Bultmann, "The Problem of Hermeneutics," in *Essays*, pp. 234–61.

/123/ Ibid., p. 239.

/124/ Ibid., p. 241.

/125/ Ibid.

/126/ Ibid., p. 239, n. 2.

/127/ These examples and others are found ibid., pp. 243–48. See also *History and Eschatology*, pp. 114–15.

/128/ *Essays*, pp. 244–45.

/129/ *Theology of the New Testament*, 2:240.

/130/ Ibid., p. 67.

/131/ KM, p. 210.

/132/ KM, p. 22.

/133/ *Theology of the New Testament*, 2:66.

/134/ Ibid., 2:238.

/135/ Ogden, *Christ Without Myth*, pp. 95–126.

/136/ KM, p. 33.

/137/ KM, p. 37.

/138/ Plato *Republic* 2.9.380b–89; 10.37.606.

/139/ Plato *Timaeus* 30c.

/140/ KM, p. 134.

/141/ KM, pp. 196–97.

/142/ JCM, pp. 68–69. See also FU, pp. 53–65. Ogden discusses this problem in *Christ Without Myth*, pp. 90–93; 146.

/143/ Ibid., pp. 91–94. Hans Frei takes up this issue in his (implicit) critique of Bultmann. See Chapter III.

/144/ For essays representative of the New Hermeneutic, see Robinson and Cobb, eds., *The New Hermeneutic*.

CHAPTER II
THE LIMITS OF FORMALISM

New Testament critics advocating the importance of literary criticism for biblical study have charged Bultmann with a failure to understand the specifically literary properties of the New Testament writings. Our retrospective study of Bultmann indicates that these charges must be qualified—Bultmann addresses in a significant way many of the issues involved in interpreting all texts, including works of literary art. As theologian, Bultmann argues that the true subject matter of the New Testament is the Christ kerygma, which is always a scandal to human understanding. If the meaning of the New Testament writings is limited to the conceptual statements of existentialist philosophy, however, then the texts themselves cannot speak of the otherness, the scandal, of the kerygma; for if the disclosive possibilities of language are confined to philosophical statement, then Bultmann must say that the kerygma is "unutterable." Furthermore, since Bultmann argues that philosophy explicates *all* that human beings can know about existence, he also tends to assert that the "new" introduced by faith in the kerygma has no revealed, knowable content of its own—it is wholly an *event*, by which one's existence is qualified in a new way. Bultmann's gropings toward a theory of "analogy" indicate his awareness of these problems, and my study concluded with the suggestion that Bultmann's hermeneutic needs to be supplemented by an understanding of the language of faith—a language that can indeed speak of both the self and of God, of human experience and what is always a scandal for human experience, as Bultmann prescribed.

It is at this point, with the question of religious language, that this chapter takes up another aspect of the hermeneutical problem. In moving to this question, the logic of this discussion parallels the developments within theology and New Testament studies, where the problem of demythologizing has given way to the question of

"God-talk."/1/ Theologians and certain New Testament scholars have turned to twentieth century language philosophy, and to a re-investigation of the nature of symbol, metaphor, and analogy, as new ways to come to terms with the problem of religious language. The application of certain literary-critical techniques to New Testament study belongs in this context.

Before looking directly at several New Testament scholars who have employed literary criticism in their work, however, this chapter will provide a brief background in critical history. The New Testament critics to be examined have turned to a particular orientation in literary criticism, the orientation I will call "formalism," which itself has an historical context and makes certain assumptions about the nature of a literary work and its relation to the larger human situation. An understanding of both the positive tenets and the underlying presuppositions of formalist criticism is therefore a necessary prerequisite for understanding and evaluating the contributions of these New Testament scholars.

This chapter takes that phase of twentieth-century Anglo-American literary criticism often referred to as the New Criticism as its chief representative of the formalist orientation. The writings of the New Critics are those to which the New Testament critics most often refer, explicitly and implicitly. While putting forward this body of critical writings as paradigmatic, however, it is understood that their general principles are shared, at least in part, by a variety of other "schools" of criticism within the formalist orientation—including the Russian Formalists, the Prague School, certain dimensions of the neo-Aristotelian Chicago School, and structuralism./2/ It is also recognized that even within the New Criticism individual scholars set out programs which are by no means identical, and are sometimes in conflict on particular issues. The purpose of this chapter, then, is not to illuminate the theory or practice of any particular critic or critical movement, but to outline certain general tendencies and attitudes characterizing the formalist orientation. This limited intention is appropriate to the larger purposes of my study, for it is the general direction of formalist theory, rather than the writings of any individual critic, that will be most pertinent to my analysis of New Testament scholarship.

This chapter will argue that the central weakness of formalist literary theory is its failure to develop adequately the *interpretive* dimension of literary study. It will further suggest that

Bultmann's hermeneutical program and formalist theory stand, in a sense, in inverse relation: each provides a dimension which the other inadequately develops. In its capacity to explicate how poetic language can disclose the "new" in a way that other discourse cannot, formalism can assist in constructing a theory of the language of faith. Insofar as formalism ignores the problems of interpretation, Bultmann's reflections on hermeneutical issues are formalism's complement.

Formalism in Context

In 1953, Meyer Abrams presented a schema for classifying the predominant types of literary theory in the Western critical tradition./3/ Setting out the four elements that comprise the total situation of a literary work of art—the work itself, the artist, the world the work creates or reveals, and the audience to whose attention the work is directed—Abrams outlines four correlative critical orientations, each deriving its principle categories from one of these four elements. While any literary theory must take the total situation of the work into account, in Abrams' view each of the elements will vary in meaning and function depending on the central orientation of the theory in which it appears. Abrams' four typical orientations are the objective, expressive, mimetic, and pragmatic.

Whatever their primary focus, most literary theories share one noteworthy feature—their defensive stance. As Abrams writes elsewhere,

> Alone among the major disciplines the theory of literature has been mainly a branch of apologetics, and we shall mistake the emphases of many critical documents, whether or not they are labelled a Defense of Poetry, if we fail to recognize the degree to which they have constituted the rebuttal in a persistent debate./4/

In every age, the seemingly positive programs of literary theory have been designed for poetry's defense, and the terms of the debate have more often than not been set by the opposition./5/ The debate to which Abrams refers began at least as early as Plato, who, it was observed in the preceding chapter, forced poetry into competiton with other human attempts to arrive at knowledge of the True, the Good, and the Beautiful. Poetry's chief contender, for Plato, was philosphy. At various times literary theory has done battle on other fronts as well, competing for the status of privileged access to certain kinds of truth with history, theology, the New Philosophy in the seventeenth century, and, since the eighteenth century, with modern science./6/

The defense of poetry's cognitive status has been most prominent in those types of theory concerned with the relation between the literary work and that which it "imitates." The mimetic orientation, inheriting from Plato the traditional analogies for describing the relation between literary art and the world—mirror, copy, image, counterfeit, representation—has been preoccupied with the the oldest of the critical orientations, it is also perhaps the most persistent. A glance at the history of mimetic theories shows, for example, that the "nature" a literary work is to reflect has been variously conceived: as a transcendental realm of eternal ideas or essences, as it was by Plato (and in different ways by neo-Platonic, Idealist, Jungian, and modern "myth" critics); as the statistical average; as the typical and universal; or as the particular and unique (for the advocate of realism, Stendahl, "a novel is a mirror riding along a highway")./7/ Scriptural interpretion shares the central issues raised by mimetic literary theory: the need to distinguish biblical "truth" from "mere" poetry and myth, and later, from scientific truth, has been a major concern of biblical interpretation since its inception.

In what Abrams calls the pragmatic orientation, a literary work's effect on its audience is the primary focus. What the work imitates and the manner in which it does so become in this orientation instrumental properties of an artifact deliberately designed to achieve a foreknown end. What this *telos* was traditionally assumed to be is expressed in typical fashion by Sidney:

> Poesy therefore is an art of imitation . . . a representing,
> counterfeiting, or figuring forth . . . a speaking picture;
> with this end, *to teach and delight.*/8/

Since the essence of a literary work here lies in its moral implications, critics of this orientation have had to defend poetry vis-a-vis other forms of moral discourse. Its chief weapon in this battle has been poetry's capacity to instruct *through* delight, to seduce its readers into learning by pleasing, diverting, or, in the twentieth-century Auden's phrase, by "the luck of verbal playing."/9/ This capacity has been noted by scriptural interpreters as well: theories of accommodation, for example, provided that biblical truth was hidden in figures not only because the human intellect was

incapable of understanding unmediated truth, but also because, as
Augustine writes

> this situation was provided by God to conquer pride by
> work and to combat disdain in our minds, to which those
> things which are easily discovered seem frequently to
> become worthless. . . . That which is sought with diffi-
> culty is discovered with more pleasure./10/

The expressive orientation, while it has roots in Plato's
notion of poetic inspiration and in Longinus' concern with the
special powers of the poet to evoke the "sublime," finds its chief
representatives in eighteenth and nineteenth-century romantic
theories of literature./11/ Their point of departure is the literary
artist's capacity for expression, together with an unprecedented
exaltation of the role of the imagination. Since romantic expressive theories were influenced by the development of historical
consciousness and its consequent interest in other, more primitive cultures, the common expressive origins of poetry, myth,
and religion became a favored topic for exploration. This alli-
ance between poetry and religion represents an interesting irony
in the history of literary theory, since until the eighteenth century, post-classical Western literature was virtually coterminus
with Christian literature, and literary and biblical hermeneutic
theories and interpretive techniques were closely related./12/
On the one hand, the rapid process of secularization following
the Renaissance and Enlightenment meant that the cohesiveness
of Western Christian culture was increasingly diminshed. On the
other hand, just as literature and religion began to come apart,
they found themselves co-defendents before the growing claims
of science to be arbiter of what constitutes true knowledge. The
developing tendency toward scientism in the modern period,
with its inevitable divorce of values and facts, subjective "feeling" and objective "reason," has provided such diverse twentieth-
century phenomena as various literary theories, existentialist
philosophy, and certain kinds of Protestant theology, with a
common enemy.

Within romantic literary theory we actually find two ways
of defending poetry, each with twentieth-century representatives. They are often divided for convenience into theories
emerging from, or at least related to, those of Wordsworth and
Coleridge./13/ Accepting science's positivistic criteria for truth,

that orientation following Wordsworth argued that poetry (and sometimes religion as well) is an emotional, in contrast to a rational, use of language. In expressive theories of this type, plot, character, and other considerations of form are subordinated to an interest in language as expressive of the poet's "feeling." For Wordsworth, "all good poetry is the spontaneous overflow of powerful feelings," which "takes its origin from emotion recollected in tranquility."/14/ The mirror of art here does not so much reflect "nature" as it does the poet's "soul," and the writer's "sincerity" becomes the primary standard for judging poetry's excellence./15/ The split between "feeling" and "reason" is, of course, not wholly new with the eighteenth and nineteenth centuries. In biblical interpretation, for example, as early as the seventeenth century the rationalist Spinoza recommended that in interpreting Scripture "we are at work not on the truth of passages, but solely on their meaning," and that Scripture's object "is not to convince the reason, but to attract and lay hold of the *imagination*."/16/

Nor was the defense of poetry as emotion limited to expressive theories. From the pragmatic perspective, for example, John Stuart Mill, reacting against the strict rationalism of Bentham's utilitarianism, became the defender of a poetry whose aim "is confessedly to act upon the emotions," in contrast to "what Wordsworth affirms to be its opposite, namely, not prose, but matter of fact or science. The one addresses itself to the belief, the other to the feelings."/17/ Not long after, Matthew Arnold was to state programmatically that "the future of poetry is immense," because with the increasing loss of religious belief, it is in poetry that "our race, as time goes on, will find an ever surer and surer stay."/18/ Religion's difficulty, according to Arnold, is that "it has materialized failing it." Because its effectiveness has to do with the emotions, poetry maintains its consolatory and sustaining capacity independent of its "truth" or its readers' beliefs. "Most of what now passes with us for religion and philosophy," Arnold proclaims, "will be replaced by poetry."/19/ Arnold's position is taken up in the twentieth century by the early I. A. Richards, who argued in *Science and Poetry* that poetry is composed of "pseudo-statements." Poetry is "capable of saving us" precisely because, unlike non-poetic statements which refer to empirical evidence, it satisfies our need to "cut our pseudo-statements free from belief and yet retain them, in this released state, as the main instruments by which we order our attitudes as to one another and to the world."/20/

The second line of defense, while represented in its romantic phase by Coleridge's expressive theory, is typical of what Abrams refers to as the objective orientation, and what, in this essay, is spoken of as formalism./21/ While formalism has made numerous appearances in the history of literary theory, it is the characteristic orientation of many twentieth-century theorists, and the one to which contemporary New Testament critics have most often turned./22/

For Coleridge, the poem is not primarily an expression of the poet's feelings, but a product of "that synthetic and magical power, to which we have exclusively appropriated the name of imagination."/23/ In Coleridge's view, the poetic imagination shares in the dynamic principle underlying the universe itself: the "primary imagination" is "a repetition in the finite mind of the eternal act of creation in the infinite I AM."/24/ Unlike the mechanical operations of the "fancy," according to Coleridge, the creative imagination, emulating the creativity of God, possesses its own inner source of motion. Governed by its own internal laws, and propelled by the tension of contraries seeking resolution in a new whole, the synthetic imagination assimilates disparate materials into an "organic" unity. The resulting literary work is an "organism" which, in Coleridge's famous words, exhibits its unity "in the balance or reconciliation of opposite or discordant qualities: of sameness with difference; of the general, with the concrete; the idea, with the image; the individual with the representative. . . ."/25/

The emphases in Coleridge's theory, and in other representatives of this critical orientation, are somewhat contradictory. On the one hand, poetry is defined as a special mode of knowing—it provides a special access to what is beyond the grasp of logic or reason, or it represents a special fusion or reconciliation of logically incompatible elements. On the other hand, Coleridge and other formalist theorists conceive of the poem as a kind of heterocosm, or second creation, which is complete in itself, has its own reason for being, and is free from the burden of having to "reflect" the world, the poet's soul, or to work some emotive or moral effect in the reader.

The poem as an autonomous end in itself has roots in the Renaissance notion of the poet as "maker" who, like the Divine

Creator, creates *ex nihilo.*/26/ Sidney, for example, chief defender of the moral value of poetry against the Puritan opposition, also argued that in contrast to the "natural and moral philosophers," historians, logicians, and a host of others, "only the poet, disdaining to be tied to any such subjection, lifted up with the vigor of his own invention, doth grow in effect another nature, . . . freely ranging only within the zodiac of his own wit."/27/ In the seventeenth and eighteenth centuries, this became the primary line of defense against the empirical philosophy of Hobbes and others, who demanded that the mythical and the marvelous, "monsters and beastly giants," had no place in poetry. Since for Hobbes poetry is "an imitation of human life," and "the description of great men and great actions is the constant design of the poet," poetry must not go "beyond the conceived possibility of nature."/28/ This view continued to develop through the eighteenth century, from Addison's reflections on "the pleasures of the imagination,"/29/ through the aesthetics of Baumgarten, Coleridge, and Kant, to nineteenth-century varieties of *l'art pour l'art*, influenced by Poe's insistence that poetry exists only "for the poem's sake."/30/

While René Wellek is undoubtedly correct to remark that Kantian aesthetics survives in twentieth-century literary theory only as a "most general attitude," many of the ideas most fundamental to twentieth-century versions of the objective orientation can be traced back to Kant as well as to Coleridge./31/ In a general sense, of course, Kant's epistemological "Copernican revolution" has indirectly affected literary theory as it has all critical thinking, and much of the American New Criticism as well as the principle of "symbolic forms" in Cassirer and his followers relies on a neo-Kantian theory of knowledge. In the more specialized arena of aesthetics, two elements in Kant's third *Critique* illustrate central attitudes in twentieth-century formalist theory.

In the *Critique of Practical Reason*, Kant distinguishes aesthetic from teleological judgments./32/ Aesthetic judgments are singular: they do not refer the object under consideration to any external criteria concerning how it should be used or what it ought to be./33/ An aesthetic object exhibits, in Kant's paradoxical terms, a kind of purposiveness without purpose: "*Beauty* is the form of the *purposiveness* of an object, so far as this is perceived in it without any representation of a purpose."/34/ The standard for aesthetic judgment is therefore generated by the singular internal purpose of the individual object, so that questions concerning a work's truth to nature, implied by the notion of imitation, become irrelevant. Second, while aesthetic judgment is ultimately grounded in subjective experience, it must be "disinterested," indifferent to the object's reality or utility, since the work is not to be related to any exterior purpose or ideal./35/ A literary theorist following Kantian principles is thus concerned with a work's internal unity and form. The text's truth is judged in terms of coherence, rather than by its correspondence to some external state of affairs. Criticism is disinterested, in keeping with the inutility of art, and the work of art's formal structure governs its meaning./36/

While the first strategy of defense entails the surrender of poetry's turth claims and the fortification of its emotive capacities, the second, formalist, orientation claims that poetry can grasp and represent certain kinds of truth to which science is barred access. How its emphasis on art's autonomy, inutility, and internal coherence can be reconciled with these assertions of poetry's special cognitive status, however, remains a perpetual difficulty in formalist literary theories.

Modern Formalism

The romantic legacy of twentieth-century formalism—the desire to set poetry against the various evils of science—needs to be kept in view, since from the outset its proponents were stridently anti-romantic. T. E. Hulme defined the mood and perspective of modern formalism when he called for a "classical" poetry of restraint, wit, and irony, and for a "religious attitude" that postulates absolute values by which humankind is judged as limited and imperfect./37/ As R. W. Stallmann observes, "there is one basic theme in modern criticism: it is the dissociation of modern sensibility."/38/ Hulme and Eliot, and then the company of New Critics—Ransom, Tate, Blackmur, Brooks, and others—take this theme as a major premise. From their perspective, the romantic cult of originality and self-expression was symptomatic of the erosion of a spiritual order and the loss of integrity in the modern consciousness. With the absence of a unified religious and cultural tradition, and of a rational structure of absolutes, the poet is deprived of moral and intellectual standards for evaluating personal experience and the social order. As a consequence, in the formalists' view, the romantics substituted their own personalities as the center of experience and meaning, creating their own set of values and a world order out of themselves. As Eliot wrote of Blake, he lacked "a framework of traditional ideas which would have prevented him from indulging in a philosophy of his own."/39/ For Hulme, the romantic attitude, with its trust in the natural goodness of humanity, entails a confusion between the divine and the human, a "blurring of the clear outlines of human experience . . . like pouring a pot of treacle over the dinner table."/40/ The romantic poet is "always flying over abysses, flying up into the eternal gases," replacing belief in God with belief in the divinity of the human imagination./41/ Romanticism, in short, lacks an understanding of original sin./42/

The central doctrines of formalist theory—the autonomy and inutility of art, the impersonality of the artist, and the disinterestedness of criticism—must be understood in this context, a context obviously shared by certain kinds of Protestant theology, including that of Bultmann, and by existentialist philosophy after World War I./43/ This is especially important in light of the criticisms brought against formalist theory in the past several years. As Gerald Graff summarizes these challenges, "all of them agree that the New-Critical style objective interpretation is an extension of the Western technological mentality with its aggressive need to transform its world into objects."/44/ The term *New Criticism* has come to mean simply a quasi-scientific technique for close reading, one which views the text as an object whose ambiguities and complexities are surgically exposed under the critic's scalpel./45/ To accuse these critics of scientism, however, is to forget that their program was mounted to defend literature as a mode of knowledge precisely against its disvaluation by science, and, with the romantics, to look to the humanities as the agency of cultural redemption./46/

The formalist critics' animosity toward romanticism was, in fact, related to their quarrels with science: they saw romantic humanism continued in science's optimistic faith in human progress, in its will to power, and in its restriction of value to the pragmatic. Their advocacy of the non-utility of art, of the disinterestedness of criticism, and of the special properties of poetic language, is thus aimed at combating science's purposive reduction of the world to abstracted types and forms. As Tate

writes, "poetry finds its true usefulness in its perfect inutility."/47/ For Ransom, poetry, through its "sense of the real
density and contingency of the world," restores the "world's
body" stripped away by scientific abstraction./48/ Eliot's notion
of the "impersonality" of the poet, in like manner, is put forward
not only in opposition to the Romantic doctrines of poetic
expression, but also to combat the absolutist claims of science by
asserting poetry's own absolute independence. Thus, for Eliot,
"poetry is not the turning loose of emotion, but an escape from
emotion; it is not the expression of personality, but an escape
from personality."/49/ It is the poem itself that contains "the
work to be done"; poetry involves "a continual surrender of [the
poet] as he is at the moment to something which is more
valuable."/50/

Once the motivating forces of formalist theory are duly considered, however, we still encounter the difficulty mentioned
above—these high claims and hopes for literature are invested in a
theory of literary autonomy that seems to undermine precisely
these claims. Eliot's understanding of "Tradition and the Individual Talent" will serve as a final example. Eliot argues against the
romantic celebration of poetic originality that "if we approach a
poet without this perspective we shall often find that not only the
best, but the most individual parts of his work may be those in
which the dead poets, his ancestors, assert their immortality most
vigorously."/51/ Poetry, Eliot affirms, is not made from personalities, but from words, which is to say, from tradition, for "language
embodies in some real sense the funded experience of the
race."/52/ Thus, the poet must feel that that "the whole of the
literature of Europe from Homer . . . has a simultaneous existence
and composes a simultaneous order," and

> what happens when a new work of art is created is
> something that happens simultaneously to all the works
> of art which preceded it. . . . The past [is] altered by the
> present as much as the present is directed by the
> past./53/

While Eliot's call for an historical sense demonstrates the formalists' concern to "redeem the time," the force of his argument is
undercut when we note that the simultaneous order to which he
refers is the specifically *literary* tradition. The poet's struggle is
not so much with the particularities of human experience as it is

and has been, but with *language*, and with the literature of the poet's ancestors. Literary tradition, like a single poem, is itself an autonomous structure, the meaning of which is derived from the internal ordering of its various elements, rather than from its relationship to the ordinary universe, past and present./54/

If literature is to have the culturally transformative power that the formalists, together with theorists of most critical orientations, wish to affirm, then their emphasis on literary autonomy presents certain difficulties. A way must be found to speak about how the experience of a literary work is related to extra-literary human experience, and to those larger social, moral and spiritual values present in what Bultmann speaks of as our self-understanding. The problem is, in short, to speak adequately of each of the elements in the total situation of the literary work: of the work's relation to its author and genetic context, as do expressive theories; of the "nature" the work may disclose or illumine, as the mimetic orientation considers; and, with theorists of the pragmatic orientation, of the work's special design upon its readers. How these difficulties are addressed by that modern American phase of formalism, the New Criticism, is explored in more detail in the following sections.

Poetry Is Poetry and Not Another Thing

That formalist theories seem to pursue two somewhat antithetical aims is in part a consequence of the polemical situation to which they are responding: science and the excesses of romanticism are not their only opponents. In the nineteenth century, the historical method, with its own kinds of emphases and excesses, had established itself in literary study as it had in biblical scholarship. Romantic preoccupation with literature as "expression" took various forms, ranging from interest in the individual poet's personality, to Taine's view of literature as expressive of "race, milieu, and moment."/55/ Like the liberals' quest after the historical Jesus, these sometimes passionate and often nationalistic concerns could go hand in hand with the most rigorous, skeptical, and fact-finding procedures of historical criticism. The results were often reductive. The assumption that literature can be explained by external determining forces—whether by the artistic personality, or by causal antecedents in the political, social, or economic spheres—meant that the "meaning" of the literary text was transferred to its genetic context./56/ Victorian philology and literary history often became a kind of "petty antiquarianism," in Wellek's phrase, with vigorous research devoted to the accumulation of unrelated facts and to investigations of minute details in the lives and quarrels of authors./57/ In America in particular, early twentieth-century literary scholars were fascinated with literature's relation to the whole range of influences that fall within Taine's three categories, under the doctrine that, as Wimsatt writes, "literary criticism should be neutral and tolerant and devote itself to discovering the natural forces by which literature is caused."/58/

In light of this situation, Eliot's dictum that "poetry is poetry and not another thing" served to recall critical attention to the literary text as a work of art./59/ Despite the numerous challenges to the New Criticism in recent years, the new directions initiated by Eliot and those influenced by him has had an enormous and positive impact on the study of literature, especially in America./60/ To this orientation is owed the development of a specifically *literary* criticism which studies both the complex ways in which a single work of literature can be said to "mean," and that text's relation to the "simultaneous order" of the Western literary tradition. In place of the prevailing modes of historical scholarship—often "merely a tour through a refined kind of Madame Tussaud's," in Brooks' description—there developed a vocabulary and technique of close textual analysis, including important investigations of the nature of metaphor, paradox, and irony, which has significantly altered the way we read a literary work.

One of the clearest and most influential statements of a formalist program for critical study, and one self-consciously proposed in opposition to the "genetic fallacy" endemic to historical literary scholarship, is that outline for an "intrinsic" criticism presented by Wellek and Warren in their *Theory of Literature.*/61/ Since a literary scholarship chiefly concerned with "extratextual circumstances" has resulted in "the astonishing helplessness of most scholars when confronted with the task of actually analyzing and evaluating a work of art," they propose instead that "the natural and sensible starting point for work in literary scholarship is the interpretation and analysis of the works of literature themselves."/62/ After designating textual criticism, or the "ordering and establishing of evidence," as a "pre-critical activity," Wellek and Warren briefly outline various "extrinsic" approaches to literature. In their view, an extrinsic approach is one which relates literature to, or brings to the analysis and evaluation of a literary work, the insights and methods of non-literary areas of study, such as biography, psychology, society, ideas, or the other arts./63/

Their proposal for an intrinsic study of literature rests on their conviction that the proper context for viewing a literary text is other works of literature—and the text in itself. With Kant and Coleridge present in the background, they argue that a literary text is a "structure of norms,"/64/ a "highly complex organization of a stratified character with multiple meanings and relationship."/65/ In keeping with this "mode of existence of a literary work of art," an intrinsic study of literature will view the work as an autonomous structure, each constituent element deriving its meaning from its place within the whole. In place of the inevitable dualism which results from the traditional distinction between "form" and "content," they propose to call all aesthetically indifferent elements "materials," and to speak of the manner in which these elements acquire aesthetic efficacy as "structure."/66/ Recalling Coleridge's view of the literary work as an organism with its own internal law, and Kant's emphasis on the purposelessness of art, they define the intrinsic approach: "The work of art is, then, considered as a whole system of signs, or structure of signs, serving a specific aesthetic purpose."/67/

These positive principles constitute the basic doctrines of formalist literary theory. While the specific programs set out by critics of this orientation are by no means identical, restatements of these basic tenets can be found in most of their writings. A few examples must suffice: For A. C. Bradley, writing in 1901, the nature of poetry

> is to be not a part, nor yet a copy, of the real world . . .
> but to be a world by itself, independent, complete,
> autonomous./68/

According to Ransom,

> The intent of the good critic becomes therefore to exam-
> ine and define the poem with respect to its structure and
> texture/69/

and to consider "the autonomy of the work itself as existing for its own sake."/70/ R. P. Blackmur recommends his "technical approach" to criticism, as distinguished from one which has "ulterior purposes"; the former will never violate "the thing in itself from its own point of view."/71/

The Heresies

The principles of formalist theory have also been spelled out through analyses of numerous heresies and fallacies in literary criticism. (As Blackmur writes, "the approaches to—or escapes from—the central work of criticism are as various as the heresies of the Christian Church. . . ."/72/) Two of the best known are those set out by Wimsatt and Beardsley in their essays "The Intentional Fallacy" and "The Affective Fallacy."/73/ The intentional fallacy, a subspecies of the genetic fallacy, is epitomized by romantic expressive theories. This fallacy is the confusion of the designing intellect of the author as *cause* of the poem with the use of the poet's design or intention as a *standard* by which a critic judges a poem's worth./74/ They argue that even if we could determine the author's intentions for a poem, the object of critical evaluation is the poem itself. If the poet did not succeed in what he or she set out to do, the poem is not adequate evidence for determining the author's intentions; if the poet did succeed, the poem itself, which "belongs to the public," shows what the author was attempting. There is criticism of poetry and there is author psychology, and the latter, while interesting in itself, is extrinsic to the "true and objective way of criticism."/75/ In sum, the intentional fallacy "begins by trying to derive the standard of criticism from the psychological cause of the poem, and ends in biography and relativism."/76/

The affective fallacy is a problem typical of the pragmatic orientation. It is a "confusion between the poem and its *results* (what it *is* and what it *does*), a special case of epistemological skepticism."/77/ The affective fallacy "begins by trying to derive the standard of criticism from the psychological effects of the poem, and ends in impressionism and relativism." /78/ In this essay, I. A. Richards' identification of poetic meaning with reader response is their primary example. It is also aimed at the residues of another kind of critical tendency that flourished in late nineteenth and early twentieth-century France and England: impressionist criticism. The doctrine of "Art for Art's Sake" was accompanied by an equally autotelic "criticism for its own sake."

The impressionist critic explores the most vivid of the sensations and attitudes the poem evokes; the resulting criticism is, in effect, a second work of art. Criticism becomes Anatole France's "adventures of the soul" among literary masterpieces./79/ Their credo is summed up by Pater:

> in aesthetic criticism the first step toward seeing one's object as it really is, is to know one's own impression as it really is, to discriminate, to realize it distinctly. /80/

Against these emphases on the reader's response, Wimsatt and Beardsley argue that "emotion" in poetry is not separable from the complex organism which is the poem itself, for "poetry is characteristically a discourse about both emotions and objects, or about the emotive quality of objects."/81/ Here they set out another tenet of formalist theory, originating in Eliot's notion of the "objective correlative":

> The emotions correlative to the objects of poetry become a part of the matter dealt with—not communicated to the reader like an infection or disease, not inflicted mechanically like a bullet or a knife wound . . . but presented in their objects and contemplated as a pattern of knowledge./82/

While the concept of an objective correlative is rather mystifying, the intention of all arguments to this effect is simply to underscore a view of the poem as an entity complete in itself, with its elements fused by the "pressure of the total context" into a unique artifact. Wimsatt and Beardsley's obvious concern is that the outcome of either fallacy "is that the poem itself, as an object of specifically critical judgment, tends to disappear."/83/ It is also apparent that by insisting on poetry as a structured system made of *language*, they wish to rescue critical evaluation from relativism.

Just as emotive elements are to be subservient to the poem's presiding executive principle, so are "ideas." While a poem may contain ideas and emotions as "materials," it is the poetic structure or context that gives them a unique aesthetic being peculiar to the poem. The role of ideas in poetry is the subject of Cleanth Brooks' essay, "The Heresy of Paraphrase," a phrase that has become a catchword in the formalist movement in America. The polemical situation prompting Brooks' caveats was, again, the proliferation of "extrinsic" criticisms already outlined. In particular, Brooks was taking a stand against those critics too eager to confuse poetry with propaganda, politics, or morals, in the form of message hunting, genteel moralism, or "vulgar Marxism."/84/

The question of paraphrase is one point at which the differences between formalist literary criticism and the Bultmannian hermeneutic are sharply focused. Bultmann's proposal for the "translation" of the mythological forms of the New Testament writings into the conceptual statements of existential philosophy is a kind of paraphrase: for Bultmann, the meaning or content of the texts is identical with, and reducible to, the philosophical "paraphrase" he provides./85/ For the literary formalists this kind of paraphrase violates the principle of the unity of form and content. Their own treatment of this subject, however, is also not without difficulties. Since Brooks' writings are some of the most typical and widely read of the American New Critics, his treatment of the heresy of paraphrase deserves close scrutiny./86/

"The Heresy of Paraphrase" is the final essay in Brooks' collection, *The Well Wrought Urn*. Brooks has examined ten poems varying widely in historical period, thematic content, and style, from Shakespeare through Donne, Wordsworth, and Yeats./87/ His purpose is to discover what these pieces have in common, and in particular, to see what each of the poems shares with the "metaphysicals" and the "moderns." In striking contrast to Bultmann's stress on evaluation of the content of the biblical texts, Brooks contends that the excellence these poems share must be stated as a quality belonging to their *structure*, rather than to their content or subject matter. The "beauty" of a poem is an effect of the poem's "total pattern," which can incorporate within itself materials that are themselves intrinsically unattractive.

What Brooks means by "structure" is continuous with the tenets of formalism already discussed. Poetic structure, he says, is not "form," in the usual sense of an "envelope" that contains content, but rather "a structure of meanings, evaluations, and interpretations; and the principle of unity which informs it seems to be one of balancing and harmonizing connotations, attitudes, and meanings."/88/ Like Coleridge's reconciliation of discordant qualities, this unity is an "achieved harmony." As it is for Wellek, poetic unity is the solution to a problem set by the nature of the materials.

The form-content distinction creates a false dilemma, according to Brooks. It suggests that a poem constitutes some sort of "statement" that can be a true or false proposition about the world, and that "form" has to do with how that statement is expressed.

The chief difficulty with this view, for Brooks, is that it suggests that a poem's meaning can be summed up in a paraphrase of its content. "Most of our difficulties are rooted in the heresy of paraphrase," Brooks proclaims; this heresy results from

> yielding to the temptation to make certain remarks which we make *about* the poem—statements about what it says or about what truth it gives or about what formulations it illustrates—for the essential core of the poem itself./89/

Brooks does not mean to say that we cannot paraphrase in general terms what a poem is "about." The point is that all of the elements in a poem, including its ideas, imagery, rhythm, and feelings, set up tensions with any single statement the poem may seem to assert, "warping and twisting it" in such a way that all good poems *resist* attempts to paraphrase their meaning./90/ To refer the structure of a poem to a paraphrase is, in Brooks' view, to refer it to something outside the poem itself, and to bring the poem into "unreal competition with theology or philosophy."/91/ If the poet wished to state ideas, Brooks notes, he critic discovers, then, that the more adequate one's propositions concerning the meaning of a poem become, the longer and more full of qualifications, reservations, and metaphors they become: "In sum, his proposition, as it approaches adequacy, ceases to be a proposition."/92/

Against the "distempers" resulting from the paraphrastic heresy, Brooks offers his positive "principle of dramatic propriety." The structure of a poem, as a pattern of resolved stresses, resembles the structure of a drama, which arrives at its conclusion through conflict. Like drama, poetry makes use of ideas, emotions, and attitudes, but its coherence comes from the "dramatic process" (not a logical process, says Brooks) that subordinates the "attitudes in tension" to a "total and governing attitude." A poem's conclusion is proved as a dramatic conclusion is proved—by its ability to resolve conflicts which have been accepted as the *données* of the drama./93/

Irony is the term Brooks uses to describe the way in which the various elements of a poem are qualified by its total context./94/ Irony, Brooks explains, is what makes a poem most unlike scientific propositions, whose terms aspire to be pure denotations, unchanging in meaning regardless of the context in which they appear. As he writes in another essay:

> The tendency of science is necessarily to stabilize
> terms, to freeze them into strict denotations; the poet's
> tendency is by contrast disruptive. The terms are
> continually modifying each other, and thus violating
> their dictionary meanings./95/

Poetry, in other words, has an advantage over science—through
the use of irony, paradox, and metaphor, poetry can bridge
"unlikes" in a way that scientific propositions cannot. Brooks does
not deny that words naturally refer ostensively to something,
actual or ideal. He is insisting, however, that in contrast to the
discursive use of language, when words enter the structure of the
poem their meaning is altered by the context. In contrast to both
scientific and ordinary discourse, the real meaning of a poem lies
in the action of the words upon each other, and the "partial" or
"unit" meanings in a poem may take two opposing stands at once.
The prose meaning of various elements in a poem are, in a sense,
negated, so that they can mean in a poetic sense./96/ Through
such procedures as metaphor and irony, it is claimed, poetry has
the unique capacity to transcend the subject-object schema, fusing
emotion and idea and fact, concrete and universal, into a special
kind of experiential poetic meaning.

Brooks' view here is widely held, and versions of his account of
irony reappear in the writings of numerous other formalist critics.
Tate will serve as an example. For Tate, science

> demands an exact one-to-one relevance of language to the
> objects and the events to which it refers. In this relevance
> lies the 'meaning' of all terms and propositions insofar as
> they are used for the purpose of giving us valid
> knowledge./97/

In contrast,

> in poetry the disparate elements are not combined in
> logic, which can join things only under certain categories
> and under the law of contradiction; they are combined in
> poetry rather as experience, and experience has decided to
> ignore logic. . . . Experience means conflict, . . . and con-
> flict means drama. . . . Serious poetry deals with the fun-
> damental conflicts that cannot be logically resolved: we
> can state the conflicts rationally, but reason does not
> relieve us of them. Their only final coherence is the formal
> re-creation of art. . . ./98/

"Experience means conflict": this is a fundamental assumption

of twentieth-century formalist criticism. Brooks concludes his
essay, echoing Tate, with his reflections on why the poet chooses
ambiguity and paradox, and why "dramatic propriety" is an
appropriate critical principle. Because their evocative use of the
term "experience" represents a central difficulty in formalist theories, the passages are quoted at length.

> It is not enough for the poet to analyze his experience as
> the scientist does, breaking it up into parts. . . . His
> task is finally to unify experience. He must return to us the
> unity of the experience itself as man knows it in his own
> experience. The poem, if it be a true poem, is a simil-
> acrum of reality—in this sense, at least, it is an 'imita-
> tion'—by *being* an experience rather than any mere
> statement about experience or any mere abstraction from
> experience./99/

Paradox and ambiguity are necessary in order to "dramatize the
oneness experience," for the poet

> is giving us an insight which preserves the unity of expe-
> rience and which, at its higher and more serious levels,
> triumphs over the apparently contradictory and conflic-
> ting elements of experience by unifying them into a new
> pattern./100/

Finally, Brooks quotes Robert Penn Warren's resonant statement
that

> the poet, somewhat less spectacularly [than the saint],
> proves his vision by submitting it to the fires of
> irony—to the drama of the structure—in the hope that
> the the fires will refine it. In other words, the poet
> wishes to indicate that his own vision has been earned,
> that it can survive reference to the complexities and
> contradictions of experience./101/

That human experience is disordered, atomized, contradictory; that with science's corruption of the authority of tradition
and the power of religious symbols human experience has lost
touch with its sense of unity with nature, the social order, and
with other humans, are perceptions of the human situation characteristic of the modern period. But even if we grant this
assumption validity, Brooks still seems to work a kind of
mystification. What has been throughout his essay an argument
about poetic structure stressing that the poem does not refer to
anything "outside" itself now becomes an assertion that poetry

The Limits of Formalism 85

unifies "experience." Does Brooks mean the poet's experience?
The reader's experience? Human experience as it is in the
ordinary world? Since the several fallacies, taken together, have
pared away poetry's relation to the other elements in Abrams'
schema, Brooks cannot spell this out. The poem does not "refer,"
and yet it is in some respect a "simulacrum," an analogy of
human experience. It is not "about" experience, but *is* an
experience, Brooks says, and yet he leaves us unsure for whom.

The notion of the poem as an analogy, rather than an imitation, of the universe is employed by many formalist critics. In
Auden's view, for example, the poem is a "verbal society" that, like
any society, has its own laws; the laws of prosody and syntax are
analogous to those of physics and chemistry. In its capacity to reconcile contradictions, for Auden, "every poem . . . is an attempt to
present an analogy to that paradisal state in which Freedom and
Law, System and Order are united in harmony."/102/ Brooks and
Auden both use the term "parable" as well: the ten poems he has
discussed, Brooks contends, are not only poems, but also "parables
about poetry."/103/ The achieved harmony in a poem is analogous to the coherence of a vision which has been tested in the fires
of experience—the analogy moves in both directions.

The brief summary of the development of the notion of poem
as "heterocosm" above mentioned its transformation from a
defense of the "fairy way of writing" against the empirical philosophers, to Coleridge's notion of the poetic process as a recapitula-
tion of the continuous creation of the universe. For Coleridge, the
reconciliation in a poem is analogous to the dynamic principle of
the universe itself, so that poet, reader, poem and universe are
joined by a principle of transcendental unity. But for Brooks and
other formalist critics, lacking some such metaphysical basis, the
appearance of a unified theory seems to be achieved by the swift-
ness with which they shift the referent of the term *experience*
from one thing to another./104/ The relation between the internal
workings of a poem (*as* experience) and human experience as it is
lived and reflected on is simply asserted to be a relation of analogy,
without clarification.

This sleight-of-hand returns us again to the conflicting emphases of formalist theory, and to the variety of fronts on which its
defense of poetry has been conducted. Against the numerous fallacies robbing literature of its integrity as art, their insistence on
poetic autonomy is a valuable strategy. But in their stance against

science, it is the special "experiential knowledge" they claim for poetry that is important. Now that the tenets of the formalist orientation have been examined more thoroughly, we can better investigate this latter claim.

Poetry and Knowledge

Brooks' argument against the heresy of paraphrase, if taken to its logical conclusion, makes of the hermeneutical circle a procedure which mysteriously occurs entirely within the poem itself. This circle relates parts to whole, to be sure, but when the poem is viewed as an "ownerless, unasserted, non-referential, uncredited, and thoroughly insulated something," in Abrams' catalogue, the reader seems to have no role in the interpretive process. The "meaning" to be understood seems to lie not in the author's intention, in the reader's consciousness, nor even in the poem's relation to the universe, ideal or actual, but to rest, in some manner, in the "being" of the poem itself. The suspicion that the term *meaning* may even be inappropriate to this view of poetry is confirmed by Macleish's often cited pronouncement that

> A poem should be equal to:
> Not true . . .
>
> A poem should not mean
> But be./105/

The justifiable impulse to discuss poetry as poetry seems to lead to critical silence.

Yet in the Preface to Brooks and Warren's *Understanding Poetry* we read:

> Poetry gives knowledge. It is knowledge of ourselves in relation to the world of experience, and to that world considered, not statistically, but in terms of human purposes and values. . . . It involves [a] kind of experiential knowledge. . . . We have access to this special kind of knowledge only by participating in the drama of the poem, apprehending the form of the poem./106/

This passage makes it clear that the formalists do wish to endow poetry with a unique cognitive status—unique, because it provides us with a kind of knowledge other discourse cannot. It is also clear that when these critics present their case on this front, they move outside the poem itself to speak of the poet, the reader, and the world. Poetry gives knowledge, they are here not afraid to say, because it is created by a thinking, feeling and imagining human being, whose insight recovers a more "original world" than the one most of us commonly inhabit. When pursuing this line of argument, our critics are not adverse to the ancient notion of the Muse: poetry is "no mere action of the conscious will," writes Brooks; it involves "a submission of one's consciousness to the darker subliminal forces of one's own mind."/107/ For Ransom, the poetic process entails an "ontological insight." According to Blackmur, the "mixture of a word, an image, a notion," is made in the preconscious, where the artist adventures through intuition./108/ In Tate's view, the poem gives us "complete knowledge" because the poet has an "inner field of experience" denied to the scientist./109/

Now the poem does seem to give knowledge "about" something as well; for Tate it is knowledge "not of the experimental order, but of the experienced order: it is, in short, of the mythical order."/110/ Nor do they exclude the reader's response. The reader "participates in" and "apprehends" what the poem represents, in Brooks' view. The poem, in Ransom's account, "leaves us looking, marvelling, and and revelling in the thick *dinglich* substance that has just received its strange representation."/111/ Finally, however profoundly the meanings of words are altered by their placement within the poem, language itself carries us outside the the poem. "The funded experience of the race [is] contained in, and refracted through, language," Brooks writes: language reflects "the world of sense and contingency, which is the difficult and tangled world that we know in our mundane experience."/112/

In statements like these, formalist critics resist the centripetal force of their own theory of autonomy, moving toward the positive contributions of other critical orientations. Their view that poetry presents a special order of knowledge is, of course, at least as ancient as Plato. While for these critics, poetic knowledge does not consist in the apprehension of a transcendental realm of Ideas, they do seem to say that poetry is concerned with the human condition at those deep levels where it wrestles with what Dilthey speaks of as the "riddle of life." They also wish to say that through one's participation in the drama of the poem, one may arrive at a new knowledge of human possibility.

One of the formalists' most significant contributions to literary study, in this context, is precisely their insistence that because the poem is an artifact made of words, it is as complex as human existence itself. The force of their notion of the poem as "analogy" lies just here, in their demonstration that there are no shortcuts to proper understanding—of poetry, or of human existence. Because a poem resists any easy translation into conceptual statement, and because it does not work on our emotions in any immediate way that would release us from the labors of understanding, poetry can give us a kind of experiential knowledge that is not different from, but rather inclusive of, all of our faculties of cognition, imagination, and affection.

Given these intentions, the content of the particular experiential knowledge a poem provides becomes important—the questions of the "truth" of the poem, and of the reader's critical appropriation of that truth through an interpretive process which includes reflection, must be addressed. These issues are familiar to us from from the preceding chapter, which indicates that they are concerns which go beyond the problem of the "mode of existence of a literary work of art," in Wellek's phrase, to the question of the nature of *interpretation*. The tension between the formalists' concern with the autonomy of poetry on the one hand, and with poetry's status as a vehicle of knowledge on the other, however, prevents them from developing, and perhaps even from perceiving the need for, a theory of interpretation as sophisticated as their poetics. It is this particular failure, it seems to me, that marks the limits of formalist criticism. These limits are apparent in Brooks' treatment of the problems of "belief" and evaluation in literary criticism./113/

The problem of belief, as it has been posed in modern literary criticism, arises out of the confluence of elements that characterize the modern cultural situation: the development of historical consciousness, the loss of traditional religious faith, cultural pluralism, and the rise to power of modern science. In its modern form, the problem chiefly concerns the relation between the reader and the literary work./114/ I. A. Richards formulated the problem in this way: "Must we believe what an utterance says if we are to understand it fully? Does the *Divine Comedy* or the Bible tell us something we must accept as true if we are to read it aright?"/115/ In addition to Richards' concern with the relation between belief and understanding, the problem includes the question of how one ought to deal with the commensurate excellency of poems whose

truths or world views conflict—and with poems whose truths
conflict with their readers' beliefs. Part of the problem obviously
turns on the way truth or belief is defined. For the early Richards,
as noted above, the problem was solved by defining poetry as emotive "pseudo-statement." Here, poetic truth never conflicts with
the truths of science or the beliefs of its readers, because poetic
truth has only to do with its effects on our feelings and attitudes./116/ Eliot developed no formal position on the problem of
belief, and his comments are scattered among various essays. His
most often quoted statement concerning the issue places him close
to Richards: the poet does not advocate or assert certain beliefs, he
writes, but rather "enacts what it feels like to hold certain
beliefs."/117/ It is only when certain beliefs are strikingly puerile,
for Eliot, that they call attention to themselves and stand in the
way of our sympathetic enjoyment of the poem. The truth or falsity of a poem's beliefs are therefore not an issue for Eliot either,
although these beliefs must be fairly "mature," "coherent," and
"founded on the facts of experience."/118/

Because Brooks claims that poetry does present truth concerning human experience, he cannot follow Richards and Eliot.
Brooks shifts from Eliot's attention to the *content* of particular
beliefs to a consideration of their *function* within the structure of
the poem. For Brooks, if ideas or beliefs in a poem stand out, they
have not been properly assimilated into the total context of the
poem. They then "wrench themselves free from the context and
demand to be judged on ethical or religious grounds."/119/ This
may be the fault of the poet, who has not adequately dramatized
the statement, or of the reader, who has failed to consider the
statement in its context. Brooks therefore insists on the "total
meaning" of the poem as the proper place to address the problem
of belief. In so doing, he distinguishes between the "total meaning"
of a work and the "partial" or "unit meanings" of which it is composed. While the poet employs the language of a particular time
(and with the language, the ideology and the valuations of a particular time), Brooks suggests, we do not need to agree with the
ideology and the valuations in order to accept the poem. Any "unit
meaning" in a poem—the nature and importance of Greek burial
rites in *Antigone* is his example—is to be judged only in terms of
its relation to the poem's total effect./120/ While we must suspend
our own beliefs about burial practices in order to understand what
is at stake for the characters, it is only in terms of the total meaning

that the problem of evaluation properly arises.

When Brooks attempts to address the problem in terms of the "total meaning," however, he simply turns back to his principle of dramatic propriety and asserts a view of truth as "coherence." Transposing Eliot's three criteria into structural properties, Brooks argues that the critic

> will regard as acceptable any poem whose unifying atti-
> tude is one which really achieves unity ('coherence'), but
> which unifies, not by ignoring but by taking into
> account the complexities and the contradictions of the
> situation concerned ('mature,' and 'founded on the facts
> of experience'). . . . A poem, then, to sum up, is to be
> judged, not by the truth or falsity as such, of the idea
> which it incorporates, but rather by its character as
> drama—by its coherence, sensitivity, depth, richness,
> and tough-mindedness./121/

The same difficulties we noted in Brooks' notion of "experience" are apparent here. If the poem is to be "founded on the facts of experience," must we not ask about its relative adequacy to experience as we know it? Will any experience that achieves coherence in spite of contradiction make an equally "sensitive," "deep," "rich," "tough-minded," or true poem? Granting the formalists their insight that the meaning of a poem is an affair of its total structure, is it not possible to evaluate the substance of that total meaning? And to evaluate this meaning, must we not test it against what we recognize to be true, however unarticulated that recognition may be? Is there not some interpretive process between the experience which "is" the poem and the reader's own experience of what it is to be human? Does not experience include reflection as well as feeling and imagining?

In his concern to preserve the literary work against the heresy of paraphrase, Brooks insulates the poem from interpretation itself, at least in theory. In practice, of course, Brooks and other formalists have given us a body of practical criticism that not only analyzes poetic structure with sophistication, but also unfolds the full density of human experience disclosed in works of literary art with sensitivity and insight. That Brooks fails to recognize the importance of these questions is evident in the concluding pages of his essay on the problem of belief, where he engages the philosopher Wilbur Marshall Urban in dialogue. While the passages from Urban's *Language and Reality* selected

by Brooks seem to point precisely to the importance of interpretation, Brooks consistently resists these suggestions, and perhaps
misunderstands Urban's argument./122/

As Brooks presents him, Urban rejects the dualism between
emotive and referential uses of language imposed by nominal-
istic positivism, arguing that language also has a "representa-
tional" (intuitive or symbolic) function. Poetry is cognitive, and
presents its truth in symbols "by means of which we embody any
ideal content not otherwise expressible."/123/ Brooks finds here
support for his own view that metaphor is not "mere decora-
tion," but the vehicle of a kind of knowledge unstateable in any
other way. A more interesting point arises when Brooks examines Urban's solution to the problem of paraphrase. Urban contends that theory of knowledge faces a dilemma: if we are to
interpret the "sense" of a symbol, we must expand it, and this
must be in terms of "literal sentences." But if we so expand it,
we lose the "sense" or value of the symbol *as symbol*. The solution, Urban writes,

> seems to me to lie in a theory of interpretation of the
> symbol. It does not consist in substituting literal for sym-
> bolic sentences, in other words substituting 'blunt' truth
> for symbolic truth, but rather in deepening and enrich-
> ing the meaning of the symbol./124/

Ignoring Urban's reference to a theory of interpretation,
Brooks instead immediately expresses doubts about Urban's further statement that "only [by expansion of the symbol] . . . can
its truth or falsity be determined," suspecting that Urban may
here be viewing poetry as "distorted philosophy." Urban writes:
"Poetry says what it means but it does not say *all* that it means;
in attempting to say this 'all' it often ceases to be poetry." Poetry
is "covert metaphysics," and the

> transition to metaphysics is inevitable, but the poet, as
> poet, is not the one to make it. He does well . . . to keep
> to his own symbolic form. For precisely in that symbolic
> form an aspect of reality is given which cannot be ade-
> quately expressed otherwise./125/

It seems to me that Urban is suggesting that symbolic language
is polysemous—that "symbol gives rise to thought," in Paul
Ricoeur's evocative phrase. While poetry always "says" more than
any single literal statement can propose, the poem (or the symbol)

can and should be "expanded" through interpretation, relating its possible meanings to the insights of other modes of reflection on human experience and the universe. Further, by "covert metaphysics" Urban may simply mean that the "total meaning" of a poem, in Brooks' terms, inevitably, if implicitly, touches that more "original world" Ransom refers to as the "mythical order." Rather than taking up these suggestions, Brooks instead remarks that Urban must mean that "expansion" is necessary only if we "wish to relate the 'truths' given by poetry to the truths given in other realms of discourse."/126/ This, says Brooks, is something for the philosopher, not the poet. He does not consider that it might be part of the critic's task. Brooks correctly observes that Urban shares his own view that poetry is "revelatory." He then argues, however, that in insisting that the poet keep to his own symbolic form, "Urban refuses to set the poet the task of revealing some extra-poetic truth: poetry is not merely the vehicle of a content which it is to express."/127/

Brooks misses the point, it seems to me. He does not recognize that expansion is something any reader or critic does as he or she "participates" in the "experience" of a poem. He does not consider that this experiential process is one which engages one's whole self, including one's reflection on the "truths given in other realms of discourse." Brooks instead immediately assumes that expansion must result in the heretical form-content dualism. Brooks thus simply refuses to address the question of testing the truth or falsity of the total meaning of a poem. Instead, he claims Urban, who seems to be suggesting precisely such a testing, in support of his own contention that (and here he cites the early Richards with approval) "it is never what the poem *says* that matters, but what it is."/128/ Poetry, Brooks finally seems to maintain, yields no extra-poetic truth. In short, if the coherence of a poem's structure is the main criterion for good poetry, and not what the poem "says," then the critic has nothing to say. In his fear that any reference to the content of poetry will introduce a dualism between form and content and provoke the heresy of paraphrase, Brooks cannot adequately explain how it is that poetry gives us "complete knowledge."

Literary Formalism and the Bultmannian Hermeneutic

It should be noted that Bultmann and the formalists share a common cultural context. For both, the dominating influence of

science and positivism on the modern consciousness is to be
abhorred; both oppose science, with its attendant categories—
objectification, abstraction, generalization—to the concrete and
personal arena of human "experience" or "existential awareness."
Both contrast two general attitudes toward existence: the "romantic" or "liberal" optimism, which trusts in the ultimate
goodness of human nature, is set against a "classical" or "religious," or "dialectical" attitude which acknowledges the limits of
human knowledge, the depth of its sinfulness, and the dangers of
human willfulness. The dissociation and corruption of the modern situation is a shared theme—history seems to be a "pano-
rama of futility," nature and culture both profoundly godless.
Both look toward some absolute which is independent of the
present cultural situation as the source of both judgment and
redemption.

The New Critics were quite uneasy with attempts to identify
the functions of religion and literature./129/ The Arnoldian-
Ricardian program, which viewed poetry as providing the emotive
satisfactions of belief without ascribing any cognitive content to
those beliefs, was, of course, their chief example here. Nevertheless, the formalists' interest in the autonomous and absolute status
of poetry at least parallels their view of religion as a set of absolutes
which contrasts with the dissociation of the modern sensibility.
Those literary critics who did finally opt for Christianity in their
personal lives (Eliot, Auden, and Tate are three examples), turned
to orthodoxy (and neo-orthodoxy), to Kierkegaard, Reinhold Niebuhr, and Karl Barth, even when the confessions they chose were
Roman Catholicism or the Anglican Church. And many of the
metaphors these critics employ to set out their literary theories are
borrowed from Christianity. Wimsatt and Brooks, for example,
thus conclude their history of literary criticism:

> The kind of literary theory which seems to us to emerge
> the most plausibly from the long history of the debates is
> far more difficult to orient within any of the Platonic or
> Gnostic ideal world-views, or within the Manichaen full
> dualism and strife of principles, than precisely within the
> vision of suffering, the optimism, the mystery which are
> embraced in the religious dogma of the Incarnation./130/

Certainly it is the mystery and the dissimilarity of poetry to all
other forms of discourse and cognitive processes that the formalists
stress./131/ The kind of new knowledge poetry provides through

its paradoxical, non-logical, (Incarnational) reconciliation of discordant qualities is viewed as radically discontinuous with the
ordinary and scientific ways in which we "objectify" the world.
Poetic meaning is unique because it negates or suspends the usual
referents of words, the words "crack and strain under the burden,"
in Eliot's phrase, so that a new poetic meaning can come into
being. The new word the poem presents is not put forward as a
means for escaping from the disorders of history into some static
purity of art, but rather as a means for restoring human culture
precisely through its absolute autonomy and otherness.

The objectivity and otherness of the poem is also preserved
Without giving undue weight to the analogy, the parallels
between this view of poetry and Bultmann's understanding of
the kerygma deserve consideration. The poem, for the formalists, is in some respects both a *skandalon* and a saving word. For
Bultmann, the ordinary ways in which we make sense of the
world—assembling a cohesive world view, objectifying nature
and other persons in order to place them at our "disposal,"
attempting to secure our existence by adhering to the past—are
negated or overturned by the scandal of the Cross. And just as
the internal ordering of the poem is an "experience" which
transforms the ordinary value-laden meanings of its materials, so
the false cohesiveness of human experience is broken and transformed by "participation" in the paradox of the Cross. Both
Bultmann and the formalists reject the dominance of the historical method because its investigations are finally irrelevant to
what is at issue. For Bultmann, it is not the historical Jesus but
the Christ kerygma, the preaching, which is central; the details
of Jesus' life and death are taken up into the Word of the Cross.
For the formalists, similarly, it is not the historical persons and
events that constitute a text's genetic context which are significant, but the unique word which is the poem itself, and this
word "belongs to the public." The author surrenders himself to
something more valuable, according to Eliot.

The objectivity and otherness of the poem is also preserved
by the formalists' advocacy of a "disinterested" criticism. As
noted earlier, part of the formalists' motive here is to protect
poetry from violation by the utilitarian, and thus "interested"
grasp of science, of message hunters, of those who would turn
art into propaganda; these "uses" of poetry, in their view,
manipulate art into serving some end pre-determined by the
critic. The formalists' caveats concerning paraphrase also intend

to preserve the integrity of poetry from its critics' claims to "possess" the poem by abstracting from it a set of ideas. In like manner, Bultmann aims to preserve the scandal of the kerygma against the all too interested intentions of those who would make of it a series of propositions to which faith assents. For Bultmann, faith entails the surrender, not the confirmation, of what one already securely knows.

Both Bultmann and the formalists seem to suggest that, while neither poetry nor the kerygma can be completely alien to our common human experience if either is to be in some sense a redeeming word, it will always appear as a wonder and a threat. This is so because as finite human beings we cannot clearly perceive, and as sinful beings we willfully refuse to see, the truth concerning human existence which we at some deep level do already know. Finally, the problems in both Bultmann's program and formalist theory are in some ways parallel: insofar as each emphasizes the absoluteness and the discontinuity of the poetic or kerygmatic "word," they find it difficult to speak of the meaningful content of that word and to specify how it is that we "experience" it.

This analogy obviously cannot be pushed too far. It does, nevertheless, point to a significant way in which formalist theory might assist in remedying certain difficulties in the Bultmannian program. Bultmann's discontent with the adequacy of philosophical statement as a vehicle for expressing the scandal of the kerygma led him, on the one hand, to sever the kerygma from all direct expression in language, and, on the other, to make gestures toward a theory of religious language with his remarks on "analogy." By showing us how language can disclose the "new" through the warping and twisting of meaning worked by metaphor and other poetic forms, the formalists provide a significant basis for reconsidering the problem of the language of faith.

The analogy also suggests that we can consider the limits of formalism in relation to Bultmann's proposals. Given our analysis of formalism's difficulties with the interpretive dimension of literary study, it seems to me that, to the extent that it is possible to distinguish the general from the theological perspectives in Bultmann's hermeneutic, Bultmann's reflections on general hermeneutical issues offer a corrective, or complement, to the formalist orientation. Formalist theory, it was argued, cannot specify how poetry provides experiential knowledge, because it fails to relate the "meaning" of a poem to other arenas of meaning outside the poem. Formalism cannot, then, speak adequately about how poetic "truth" might be evaluated and appropriated so that it can indeed offer transformative knowledge. While one may not wish to subscribe to Bultman's treatment of these problems in every detail, his general hermeneutic does address these issues in a significant manner.

Bultmann's hermeneutical model, as it was outlined in the preceding chapter, is one which insists that the truths disclosed by literary, religious, and philosophical texts are only properly understood by one who is existentially engaged with the text's subject matter in an "interested" way. Bultmann emphasizes that this process of "participation" involves one's "life-relation" to the subject matter expressed there: one brings to the text questions arising from one's pre-understanding, so that the interpretive process resembles a dialogue. /132/ And while a reader whose pre-understanding is in question does not simply read into the text what he or she already knows, the context for understanding a text is outside the text itself. The context for understanding is not the work itself, nor only other literary works, but human experience, for without such a "hearing ground," Bultmann saw, the texts have no one to address, and are thus without anything to say.

Evaluating the truth of a text is of central importance for Bultmann, since as theologian he wishes to ascertain which of the New Testament's "mythological statements" present true "believing comprehension"—Christ. But in his reflections on general hermeneutical issues as well, Bultmann also contends that the interpretive process entails a testing of what the text sets forth against our own deepest sense of the truth concerning human existence. Philosophy, in this regard, is not Brooks' feared "abstract philosophical yardstick," but a critical tool for expanding the "covert metaphysics" of a text, since philosophy, according to Bultmann, simply explicates what we in some sense already know—an understanding of existence is given with existence itself. Unlike the formalists, Bultmann thus assumes that "experience" and reflection on experience are continuous; experience includes understanding.

Finally, while neither Bultmann nor the formalists equate the meaning of a text with its author's intention, Bultmann does not share the formalists' tendency to sever the text from its origins in human experience. /133/ This is partly a consequence of the understanding of language Bultmann appropriates from Dilthey and others. Language, in this tradition, is not the expression of feelings in a Wordsworthian sense, but it *is* the "objectification" of human life. In this view, it is only by deciphering the linguistic signs into which the human spirit projects itself that we can come to understand ourselves at all. While the New Critics would wish to affirm, with Bultmann, that through literature, however intricate the process of mediation may be, persons do, finally, speak to persons, the strictly formalist elements of their program tend to represent the poem as an artifact without content, communicating only with itself. The emphasis of Bultmann's hermeneutic, in contrast, is that through the New Testament writings, however "mythological," faith speaks to faith.

The strengths and limitations of these two perspectives are thus in several ways inversely related. The task now is to examine how they interact in the projects of three contemporary New Testament critics.

NOTES

/1/   See, for example, Langdon Gilkey, *Naming the Whirlwind* (Indianapolis: Bobbs-Merrill Co., 1969).

/2/   The term *formalism* has been used in the same inclusive way by numerous literary critics. For example, see Hoy, *The Critical Circle*, pp. 8–9.

/3/   M. H. Abrams, *The Mirror and the Lamp* (New York: Oxford University Press, 1953), pp. 3–29.

/4/   M. H. Abrams, "Belief and the Suspension of Disbelief," in *Literature and Belief: English Institute Essays 1957*, ed. M. H. Abrams (New York: Columbia University Press, 1958), pp. 2–3.

/5/   As is customary in literary criticism, the term *poetry* represents all works of literary art in this discussion.

/6/   My discussion of the defensive strategies of literary theory is especially indebted to Abrams' essay, "Belief and the Suspension of Disbelief."

/7/   Cited by Abrams in "Poetry, Theories of," in *Princeton Encyclopedia of Poetry and Poetics*, ed. Alex Preminger, enlarged ed. (Princeton: Princeton University Press, 1974), p. 641.

/8/   My emphasis. Sir Philip Sidney, "An Apology for Poetry," in *Critical Theory since Plato*, ed. Hazard Adams (New York: Harcourt, Brace, Jovanovitch, 1971), p. 158. Sidney, of course, is using Horace's noted discussion in "The Art of Poetry," also in *Critical Theory*, p. 73.

/9/   W. H. Auden, "The Truest Poetry is the Most Feigning," in his *Collected Shorter Poems 1927–1957* (New York: Random House, 1966), pp. 315–16.

/10/   Augustine *On Christian Doctrine* 2.6.7–8.

/11/   See Longinus, "On the Sublime," in Adams, ed., *Critical Theory*, pp. 77–102.

/12/   See the excellent discussion of this relation by Ziolkowski, "Religion and Literature in a Secular Age."

/13/   Abrams so divides them in "Belief and the Suspension of Disbelief." See also Giles B. Gunn's introduction to *Literature and Religion*, ed. Giles B. Gunn (New York: Harper & Row, Harper Forum, 1971), pp. 1–33.

/14/   William Wordsworth, "Preface to the Second Edition of the Lyrical Ballads" (1849–50), in Adams, ed., *Critical Theory*, pp. 435–41.

/15/   See Lionel Trilling, *Sincerity and Authenticity* (Cambridge: Harvard University Press, 1972), for a modern perspective on this problem.

/16/   Emphasis mine. *The Chief Works of Benedict de Spinoza*, trans. R. H. M. Elwes (New York: Dover, 1951), 1:91, cited by Frei, *Eclipse*, pp. 42–43.

/17/   John Stuart Mill, "What Is Poetry?" (1833), in Adams, ed., *Critical Theory*, p. 537.

/18/   Matthew Arnold, "The Study of Poetry" (1833), in *Selected Poetry and Prose*, ed. Frederick L. Mulhauser (New York: Holt, Rinehart and Winston, Rinehart Editions, 1953), p. 299.

/19/   Ibid. For a twentieth–century representative of this view, see Wallace Stevens' comment that "In an age of disbelief, it is for the poet to supply the satisfactions of belief, in his measure and in his style." "Two or Three Ideas," in *Opus Posthumous*, ed. Samuel French Morse (New York: Alfred A. Knopf, 1957), p. 206.

/20/ I. A. Richards, *Science and Poetry* (New York: W. W. Norton, 1926), pp. 57–58.

/21/ Samuel Taylor Coleridge, *Biographia Literaria* (1817). Chapters 12–14 appear in Adams, ed., *Critical Theory*, pp. 468–71.

/22/ Examples of the formalist orientation are prominent in Italian thinkers of the Renaissance, including Christoforo, Landino, Tasso, and Scalinger. For a brief but excellent summary of the development of this orientation, consult Abrams, *Mirror*, pp. 26–29, and his "Poetry, Theories of," pp. 645–47.

/23/ Coleridge, *Biographia*, p. 471.

/24/ Ibid., pp. 470–71.

/25/ Ibid., p. 471.

/26/ See Abrams' essays cited in n. 22, above.

/27/ Sidney, "Apology," p. 157. Cf. Julius Caesar Scalinger, "Poetics" (1561), in Adams, ed., *Critical Theory*, p. 139, where he suggests that poetry, in contrast to history, is "conjectural." While Sidney's remarks have often been taken by modern critics to anticipate the romantic notion of the creative imagination, the latter is based on an epistemology foreign to Sidney and his contemporaies.

/28/ Thomas Hobbes, "Answer to Davenant's Preface to *Gondibert*" (1650), in Adams, ed., *Critical Theory*, p. 215.

/29/ Joseph Addison, "On the Pleasures on the Imagination" (1712), in ibid., pp. 288–92.

/30/ See, for example, Edgar Allan Poe, "The Poetic Principle" (1850), in ibid., pp. 564–74. For a discussion of Baumgarten's aesthetics, see Abrams, "Belief and the Suspension of Disbelief."

/31/ René Wellek, "Philosophy and Postwar American Criticism," in *Concepts of Criticism*, ed. Stephen G. Nichols, Jr. (New Haven: Yale University Press, (1963), p. 327.

/32/ Immanuel Kant, *Critique of Judgment*, trans. J. H. Bernard, 2d ed. (New York: Hafner Publishing Co., 1931).

/33/ Ibid., 1:8 (Analytic of the Beautiful).

/34/ Ibid., 1.17.

/35/ Ibid., 1.11–12. See Hirsch's discussion of the Analytic of the Beautiful in *Aims*, pp. 95–109. It should be noted that Kant distinguishes between aesthetic judgments and judgments of the "sublime": the latter are purely subjective; the aesthetic are not.

/36/   Truth as coherence and truth as correspondence are discussed in the context of the history of literary theory by Adams in his introduction to *Critical Theory*, pp. 5–7.

/37/   T. E. Hulme, "Romanticism and Classicism" (1913-1914), ibid., pp. 766–74.

/38/   Robert Wooster Stallman, "The New Criticism," in *Critiques and Essays in Criticism: 1920–1948*, ed. R. W. Stallman (New York: Ronald Press, 1949), p. 488.

/39/   T. S. Eliot, "Blake," in *The Sacred Wood*, pp. 157–58.

/40/   Hulme, "Romanticism and Classicism," p. 769.

/41/   Ibid.

/42/   See Gerald Graff's excellent discussion of the New Criticism in *Literature Against Itself*, pp. 129–49.

/43/   It would be interesting to explore further the relationship between post-World War I literary criticism, with its emphasis on language, and the concurrent developments of theologies of the Word by Barth, Bultmann, Tillich, and others. Tillich, for example, certainly acknowledged the affinity between his theological program and the theories and practices of German Expressionistic art.

/44/   Graff, *Literature Against Itself*, p. 130.

/45/   Cf. ibid., p. 133.

/46/   For a discussion of the New Criticism's ties to romanticism see Richard Foster, *The New Romantics* (Bloomington: Indiana University Press, 1962). See also Gerald Graff, *Poetic Statement and Critical Dogma, d* pp. 3–86.

/47/   Allen Tate, *On the Limits of Poetry: Selected Essays 1928–1948* (New York: Swallow Press, 1948), p. 113.

/48/   John Crowe Ransom, "Poetry: A Note on Ontology," in *The World's Body* (New York: Charles Scribner's Sons, 1938), pp. 111–42.

/49/   Eliot, "Tradition and the Individual Talent," p. 58.

/50/   Ibid., pp. 52–53.

/51/   Ibid., p. 48.

/52/   See Stallman's discussion of tradition and language in the New Criticism in "The New Criticism," pp. 488–91.

/53/   Eliot, "Tradition and the Individual Talent," p. 49.

/54/   Cf. Nathan A. Scott, Jr.'s discussion of Malraux's *"le musée imaginaire"* in his "Criticism and the Religious Horizon," in *Humanities, Religion and the Arts Tomorrow*, ed. Howard Hunter (New York: Holt, Rinehart and Winston, 1970), pp. 39–60.

/55/   See William K. Wimsatt, Jr. and Cleanth Brooks, *Literary Criticism: A Short History* (New York: Random House and Alfred Knopf, Vintage Books, 1957), pp. 454–74; 522–49.

/56/   Cf. the discussion of meaning as "ostensive reference" in Chapter I, above.

/57/   René Wellek, "The Revolt Against Positivism in Recent European Literary Scholarship," in *Concepts*, p. 256.

/58/   Wimsatt and Brooks, *Literary Criticism*, pp. 543–44.

/59/   Eliot, *The Sacred Wood*, p. viii.

/60/   For a perceptive discussion of the positive and negative impact of the New Criticism on American academia, see Frederick Crews, "Anaesthetic Criticism," in *Out of My System: Psychoanalysis, Ideology, and Critical Method* (New York: Oxford University Press, 1975), pp. 63–88.

/61/   René Wellek and Austin Warren, *Theory of Literature* (New York: Harcourt, Brace and World, Harvest Books, 1942).

/62/   Ibid., pp. 127–28.

/63/   These are chapter titles in Part Three: "The Extrinsic Approach to the Study of Literature," ibid., pp. 61–127.

/64/   Ibid., p. 138.

/65/   Ibid., p. 16.

/66/   Ibid., p. 129.

/67/   Ibid.

/68/   A. C. Bradley, "Poetry for Poetry's Sake" (1910), in Adams, ed., *Critical Theory*, p. 737.

/69/   John Crowe Ransom, "Criticism as Pure Speculation" (1941), in

The Intent of the Critic, ed. D. A. Stauffer (Princeton: Princeton University Press, 1969), pp. 92–124.

/70/   Ransom, *The World's Body*, esp. pp. 327–28.

/71/   R. P. Blackmur, "A Critic's Job of Work," in *Language as Gesture* (New York: Harcourt, Brace, Jovanovitch, 1952), pp. 381–83 and passim.

/72/   Ibid., p. 373.

/73/   Both essays appear in William K. Wimsatt and Monroe C. Beardsley, *The Verbal Icon* (Lexington: University of Kentucky Press, 1954), pp. 3–18; 21–39.

/74/   Ibid., p. 21.

/75/   Ibid.

/76/   Ibid.

/77/   Ibid.

/78/   Ibid.

/79/   This is the title of an essay by France. First published in *La Vie Littéraire (1888–1893), it appears in* Adams, ed., *Critical Theory*, p. 671.

/80/   Walter Pater, "Preface to *Studies in the History of the Renaissance*," (1873), ibid., p. 643. See also Wimsatt and Brooks, *Literary Criticism*, pp. 475–98. The varieties of reader response criticism which have emerged in recent years, together with deconstructionist modes of criticism, are clearly related to this critical orientation. For the former, see *The Reader in the Text*, Susan R. Suleiman and Inge Crossman, eds. (Princeton: Princeton University Press, 1980), and David Bleich, *Subjective Criticism* (Baltimore: Johns Hopkins University Press, 1978). For the latter, see *Deconstruction and Criticism*, ed. Harold Bloom (New York: Seabury Press, 1979).

/81/   Wimsatt and Beardsley, *The Verbal Icon*, p. 38.

/82/   Ibid.

/83/   Ibid., p. 21

/84/   See Gerald Graff, *Literature Against Itself*, pp. 140–41. See also Wellek, "The Revolt Against Positivism," pp. 256ff.

/85/   It should be noted that for both Bultmann and the New Critics theory and practice are not necessarily identical. In practice, Bultmann often does explicate a text by attending to the movement of its formal structure. See, for example, his discussion of John 9, in his *The Gospel of John*, trans. G. R. Beasley-Murray (Philadelphia: Westminster Press, 1971).

/86/   Brooks often speaks of the similarities between his views and those of other New Critics. Gerald Graff also treats Brooks as representative of the New Critical view in *Poetic Statement*, pp. 87–111. See his defense of this treatment of Brooks in note 1, p. 87.

/87/   Cleanth Brooks, *The Well Wrought Urn* (New York: Reynal and Hitchcock, 1947), pp. 176–96 (cited hereafter as WWU).

/88/   WWU, p. 178.

/89/   WWU, pp. 184, 182.

/90/   WWU, p. 180.

/91/   WWU, p. 184.

/92/   WWU, p. 181.

/93/   WWU, p. 189.

/94/   WWU, p. 191. See also Brooks' essays "The Language of Paradox," in WWU, pp. 3–20, and "Irony as a Principle of Structure," in *Literary Opinion in America*, ed. Morton D. Zabel, 3d rev. ed. (New York: Harper & Row, 1962), pp. 729–41.

/95/   WWU, p. 8.

/96/   On this point see Robert Langbaum, *The Modern Spirit* (New York: Oxford University Press, 1970), pp. 10–11.

/97/   Allen Tate, "Literature as Knowledge," in *The Man of Letters in the Modern World* (New York: Meridian Books, 1955), pp. 38–39.

/98/   Ibid., p. 335.

/99/   WWU, p. 194.

/100/   Ibid., p. 195.

/101/   Robert Penn Warren, "Pure and Impure Poetry," in *Selected Essays* (New York: Random House, 1958), p. 29.

/102/   W. H. Auden, *The Dyer's Hand* (New York: Random House, Vintage Books, 1968), pp. 69–71.

/103/ WWU, p. 195. Cf. ibid., pp. 456–61.

/104/ It should be noted with regard to this point that Wimsatt and Brooks appeal to the Christian dogma of the Incarnation in their history of literary criticism.

/105/ Archibald Macleish, "Ars Poetica," in *Chief Modern Poets of England and America*, ed. G. D. Sanders, 4th ed., 2 vols. (New York: Macmillan Co., 1962), vol. 2: *The American Poets*, p. 333.

/106/ Cleanth Brooks and Robert Penn Warren, *Understanding Poetry (New York: Holt, Rinehart and Winston*, 1960), p. xiii.

/107/ Brooks, "Implications of an Organic Theory of Poetry," in Abrams, ed., *Literature and Belief*, pp. 65–66.

/108/ Blackmur, *Language as Gesture*, p. 398.

/109/ Tate, *Letters*, p. 35.

/110/ Ibid., p. 63.

/111/ Ransom, *The World's Body*, p. 142.

/112/ Brooks, "Implications of an Organic Theory," pp. 66–67.

/113/ The essay discussed here is "The Problem of Belief and the Problem of Cognition," in WWU, pp. 226–38. Brooks advances a similar argument in ibid.

/114/ For a brief overview of this problem, see Murray Krieger, "Belief, Problem of," in *Princeton Encyclopedia of Poetry and Poetics*, pp. 74–76.

/115/ I. A. Richards, *The Philosophy of Rhetoric* (New York: Oxford University Press, 1936), pp. 134–35.

/116/ Richards, *Science and Poetry*, pp. 58–59. See also Stallman's discussion of the problem in *Critiques*, pp. 494–95.

/117/ T. S. Eliot, "The Social Function of Poetry," in Stallman, ed., *Critiques*, p. 107.

/118/ Ibid.

/119/ WWU, p. 227.

/120/ Ibid.

/121/ WWU., pp. 228–29.

/122/ It should be made clear that in what follows I am relying on Brooks' citations of Urban. My point is not to explicate Urban's own views, but to show how Brooks understands, or misunderstands, the passages which he cites.

/123/ WWU, p. 232.

/124/ WWU, p. 233.

/125/ Ibid.

/126/ WWU, p. 234.

/127/ Ibid.

/128/ WWU., p. 236.

/129/ See, for example, Brooks, "The Implications of an Organic Theory," pp. 77–79.

/130/ Wimsatt and Brooks, *Literary Criticism*, p. 746.

/131/ See R. S. Crane's discussion of this "dialectical" procedure in *The Languages of Criticism and the Structure of Poetry* (Toronto: University of Toronto Press, 1953), pp. 85-88.

/132/ Hans-Georg Gadamer, *Truth and Method*, trans. Garrett Barden and John Cumming (New York: Seabury Press, 1975).

/133/ An excellent discussion of the personal dimensions of literary understanding is that of Walter J. Ong, Jr., "Voice as Summons for Belief," in Gunn, ed., *Literature and Religion*, pp. 68–86.

CHAPTER III
LITERARY CRITICISM
AND BIBLICAL NARRATIVE

The three case studies that follow examine the relation between literary critical and theological presuppositions in the writings of John Dominic Crossan, Dan Otto Via, Jr., and Hans W. Frei. Each scholar in his own way accepts the normative status of the biblical texts and understands the task of interpretation to include that of rendering the biblical writings meaningful for the present. Each, furthermore, maintains that the proper starting point for this task is a consideration of the texts (for Crossan and Via, the parables, for Frei, the Gospel narratives) as cohesive literary works.

Crossan and Via each employ different dimensions of the Bultmannian and post-Bultmannian (New Hermeneutical) programs, and join these presuppositions to aspects of the New Critics' understanding of the literary text. Crossan's several studies introduce various theological and literary critical perspectives, although his overarching aim remains the same: Crossan wishes to use literary analysis as a means to recover the historical Jesus' "experience of transcendence," and to show how the parables, as literary structures, can mediate that experience as "language event" to contemporary readers or auditors. I will argue that Crossan's Bultmannian or post-Bultmannian focus on an eschatological event reactualized in the present prevents him from fully exploring the resources of poetic language, particularly its capacity to disclose new meaning.

Via retains a different aspect of the Bultmannian program: he aims to demythologize, or translate, the parables into existentialist terms, so that they can convey their original "understanding of existence" to contemporary audiences. In this way the parables can again become "language events" that bring us to the "place of decision." Via attempts to integrate this project with a New Critical understanding of the parables as "aesthetic objects." While Via's intent—to combine the strengths of the Bultmannian and New Critical frameworks—is in my view both perceptive and sound, I will argue that Via's assumption that the parables require "translation" prevents him from successfully achieving this aim.

In contrast to both Via and Crossan, Frei self-consciously eschews all the presuppositions of the Bultmannian hermeneutic. Frei's work is of direct interest for this study because, I will argue, it demonstrates the dangers in adopting a New Critical position without qualification—qualifications which certain aspects of Bultmann's interpretation theory could provide.

John Dominic Crossan: The Paradoxes of Parable

Crossan borrows the pun in the title of Joyce's *Finnegan's Wake* (wake for day, wake for death) for his survey of contemporary biblical scholarship, "Waking the Bible." In this time "between Bultmanns," Crossan defines his own projects as experiments in biblical theology, speculations about "what a future theology might look like once the literary imagination has been unleashed on the Bible itself."/1/ The possibilities for developing the pun with regard to Crossan's own work are tempting, for the biblical awakening he proposes lies in the dark night of negative theology. The wake Crossan has in mind is not a time for lamenting what is lost, but the condition for an experience of transcendence.

Crossan's penchant for citation assists us in following his progress from the New Critics and the New Quest through Levi-Strauss and Popper to Derrida and Stanley Fish. In what follows I will suggest that there is a paradoxical character to this development, for in many respects Crossan's turn to language and literature is at the same time a progressive diminution of language's capacity to speak. Crossan begins, with the New Critics, with what seems to be an attempt to describe the disclosive power of metaphor. While this undertaking could help remedy some of the weaknesses in Bultmann's theology—by demonstrating how metaphor can mediate the event of God's encounter and faith's response, for example—Crossan's theological preferences prevent him from pursuing this direction of inquiry. Rather than enriching the Bultmannian program with his sensitivity to the textures of poetic language, Crossan instead extends

Bultmann's suspicion of language even further. While Bultmann cautioned against our all-too-human tendency to pronounce our world views (our "stories," in Crossan's terms) to be the *final* word about reality, Crossan offers a critique of all attempts to order and interpret the world. In his most recent studies, Crossan celebrates the "playful creativity that is the core of all language," while he simultaneously denies language the power to plot a shape for the world and the God we seek to know.

Crossan's *In Parables* is both a study of the literary form of the parables of Jesus and an interpretation of Jesus' understanding of the Kingdom of God. The project begins with an analysis of metaphor, and Crossan's debt to the New Critics here is clear. Eschewing the distinction between form and content, Crossan argues that metaphor does not simply ornament or illustrate some information that could be communicated in another form. In "true metaphor," he writes, "participation precedes information"; what a metaphor says can only be grasped through the metaphor itself./2/ Like the New Critics' poem, Crossan's metaphor yields a special kind of non-discursive, experiential knowledge: metaphor, he writes, "can articulate a referent so new or alien to consciousness that this referent can only be grasped within the metaphor itself."/3/ Metaphor is not an imitation of reality (it does not simply "repaint the same old tired [world] we know"), but is instead what the New Critics called an analogy or similacrum: metaphor establishes a new "world" with its own autonomous criteria for "greatness" and "truth."/4/ Finally, these characteristics of metaphor make it singularly appropriate to express the object of religious experience, the Wholly Other, which is always "radically new" and "permanently inexpressible." Religious experience, Crossan suggests, demands and creates its own extraordinary form of expression, fusing "the moment of disclosure or perception itself" and "the embodiment of the experience in poetic form."/5/

Crossan's application of this analysis of metaphor to Jesus' parables takes its starting point from Bornkamm's *Jesus of Nazareth*. In contrast to the rabbinic use of parables as explanatory or illustrative aids for teaching and exegesis, writes Bornkamm, for Jesus "the parables are the preaching itself and not merely serving a lesson which is quite independent of them."/6/ The parables are Jesus' "preaching," first of all, because in Crossan's view the heart of Jesus' message is his preaching of the

Kingdom of God, and the parables are the primary and paradig-matic vehicles of that proclamation. In this and each of his sub-sequent undertakings, Crossan's experiments with contemporary literary criticism are performed on his careful reconstructions of the parables' original form. Each of Crossan's studies, that is, aims to retrieve the "historical Jesus" in some way, although with each project this intention becomes increasingly puzzling, since the literary theories he appropriates and the theological interpre-tations he proposes both lead away from any historical investiga-tion of this kind.

In Parables, for example, suggests that an understanding of the parable's metaphorical "mode of experience" will illuminate "the experience that begot it," Jesus' "experience of God."/7/ Since Crossan's New Critical theory of metaphor stresses the man-ner in which it fuses "experience" and "expression," form and con-tent, however, then to attempt to separate Jesus' experience from its parabolic expression in order to learn something about the for-mer through the latter is to work at cross purposes—and, in New Critical terms, to commit the "intentional fallacy." Crossan does recognize this difficulty, and cautions that his project is "not an attempt to probe the self-consciousness of Jesus."/8/ Instead, he argues, "the term 'historical Jesus' really means the language of Jesus and most especially the parables themselves."/9/ Even leav-ing aside the problem of reductionism here (Jesus employed other forms of language and performed a variety of actions as well), however, this caveat simply brings us full circle, since the relation-ship between Jesus' language and his "experience" is what Crossan seemed to wish to uncover./10/ Crossan's difficulty here is one aspect of a more pervasive problem: that of explicating the rela-tion between what is "in parables," or in language, and what tran-scends language.

The parables are the preaching itself, secondly, because, as metaphors, their message and their form are inseparable. The surface structure of a parable, Crossan notes, is a narrative—a realistic story which captures its auditors' imaginations and shapes their expectations as to the story's outcome by the "nor-malcy" of the situation it narrates./11/ The metaphorical aspect of the parable emerges as certain elements in the parable contra-dict the apparent and expected normalcy of the narrative situa-tion. Just as the poem in New Critical theory warps and twists the ordinary referents of its words, creating a tension or discord which forces the reader to new insight on a higher level, so the contradictions that the parable effects provoke its hearers to "see" the metaphorical point—what the Kingdom of God is "like."

In the parable of The Good Samaritan, for example, what begins as a realistic story about a man who fell among thieves becomes a situation which overturns its auditors' self-understandings. Within the "world" of the parable's audience, to ascribe the adjective "good" to the figure of a Samaritan is a contradiction in terms. The hearers are compelled to "say the impossible," their world is "turned upside down," and they are forced to "radically question its presuppositions." The metaphorical point of the parable is thus disclosed:

> The metaphorical point is that *just so* does the Kingdom of God break abruptly into human consciousness and demand the overturning of prior values, closed adoptions, set judgments, and established conclusions./12/

While it would seem that Crossan intends to show us how the parables, as metaphors, have some cognitive value—how they help us imagine the inbreaking of the Kingdom—it is not clear exactly how this is accomplished. Crossan's analysis suffers from the weaknesses of the New Critical theories he appropriates. Perhaps because the New Critics had little to say about narrative, Crossan is more interested in describing how the parable becomes metaphor than he is in the parable narrative itself. And like the New Critics, Crossan focuses on the structure and function, at the expense of the content, of the meanings and beliefs embodied in the story./13/ Crossan demonstrates that a parable "works" by disrupting its hearers' expectations and in this way is dependent on a world outside the parable, but he does not seem to see that the content, as well as the function, of metaphor is also dependent on the concrete situation that the narrative depicts and its auditors recognize. While the metaphorical process is, indeed, one of disruption, the meaning of a metaphor, the content of its disclosure, emerges from the contrast or conflict it works on the ordinary meanings of its words at a specific time in a given cultural situation.

Crossan's analysis of The Good Samaritan turns on the "shock" effected by the juxtaposition Good/Samaritan, but he does not allow the specific image of the Samaritan—or of treasure, householders, or tenants—any part in the meaning of the

Kingdom disclosed. Crossan argues that the Kingdom of God is "like" what happens in the parable story, but he is not really interested in the story. Because Crossan ignores the content of the narrative, all he can say about what "happens" is that it disorients. Any story will do, it seems, because all parable narratives are functionally identical. Without the horizon of meanings already associated with the term 'Kingdom of God,' and without the specific images and events depicted in the narrative, however, the parable cannot reveal; it can simply shock or surprise. Crossan thus seems to suggest that what the Kingdom of God is "like" is, simply, reversal.

If Crossan empties the parables of disclosive power other consequences follow. The only distinguishing trait Crossan could ascribe to Jesus on this basis would also have to be purely functional: Jesus may be one who overturns established meanings, but he offers no positive vision of the Kingdom he proclaims. On this basis, furthermore, Crossan cannot explain what distinguishes Jesus' parables from one another, or indeed from any linguistic form which functions in the same way—from the parables of Kafka and Borges, for example, or from the koans of a Zen master. For the parables' auditors the same problem obtains. They may be disoriented, but they will not receive any new, or transformative, knowledge.

An analogous difficulty appears in Crossan's interpretation of the eschatology of the Kingdom. Crossan proposes to view time in a "Heideggerian," rather than a "linear" sense. In this view, "beginning" and "ending" are not chronological concepts, but terms expressing value, purpose, and destiny. Human time and human history arise from response to Being (for Crossan, the Kingdom) which comes always out of the unexpected and unforeseen, destroying one's planned projections of a future and demanding a radical reappraisal of one's past. This advent and reversal create the time, the present, of authentic humanity./14/ With this understanding of human historicity, Crossan argues that Jesus' understanding of the Kingdom's advent should be termed "permanent eschatology": "the permanent presence of God as the one who challenges world and shatters its complacency repeatedly."

> Jesus was not proclaiming that God was about to enter
> *this* world, but, seeing this as one view of world, he was

announcing God as One who shatters world, this one and
any other before or after it./15/

Crossan's choice of the term "shatters" is at least open to
misunderstanding. Metaphor does not derive from the absolute
negation of the ordinary reference of words; its shock or surprise
and its meaning depend on the preservation, as well as the
deformation, of established meanings. If a parable completely
"shatters" world, or language, there could be no parable at all.
Similarly, if the Kingdom's advent shatters world altogether, not
only is the future tension in Jesus' message ignored, but there
can be no possibility of a true metanoia—no transformation of
world or self-understanding. Eschatological advent becomes simply a negation.

The ambiguity in Crossan's interpretation is underscored in
the way he concludes his discussion of The Good Samaritan:

> But the full force of the parabolic challenge is that the
> *just so* of the metaphorical level is not ontologically dis-
> tinct from the presence of the literal point. The hearer
> struggling with the contradictory dualism of Good/
> Samaritan is actually experiencing in and through this
> the inbreaking of the Kingdom. *Not only does it happen
> like this, it happens in this.*/16/

Does Crossan mean to suggest that the Kingdom of God *actually*
arrives in the "experience" of the parable? Where? In the consciousness of its auditors? Which auditors? What does he mean
by "actually" and "ontologically" here?

Crossan's project in *In Parables* is undertaken within the
framework of the post-Bultmannian "New Quest," and as such
seems to have as its implicit purpose an investigation of the conti-
nuities between the historical Jesus and the Christ proclaimed in
the kerygma./17/ In any case, the Bultmannian character of Crossan's interpretation is evident. Like Bultmann, Crossan employs
a Heideggerian anthropology to propose that God's eschatological advent entails the dialectical reversal of one's ordinary
"world."/18/ Both speak of this process using the language of
"event" and "confrontation": While history (*Historie*) may be, as
Bultmann suggests, "profoundly godless," this is finally irrelevant,
for the sphere of "historicity" (*Geschichte*) in which God encounters us is that of our individual and inner lives. Crossan and Bultmann both speak of eschatological advent as a powerful and

unmediated encounter with the Wholly Other; apart from its immediate event character, this advent is an undefined, "unpicturable" existential possibility in the individual.

Crossan's hesitancy fully to embrace metaphor's capacity for disclosure and his tendency to ignore the narrative dimension of the parables may therefore spring as much from persistent Bultmannian presuppositions as from the weaknesses of New Critical theory. There is some irony here, for to take language seriously, as Crossan seems to intend, one would have to attend to the corporate historical situation in a way that Bultmann and his successors do not. The images in the parables, including that of the Kingdom of God, rest on deep cultural associations; language, as even the New Critics remind us, bears within it the store of human experience, the "funded experience of the race." Our historical situation provides the words and images within which even our individual inner selves must discover our identities. The narrative form, furthermore, has itself a world-ordering function. Since it is such "stories" that, in Crossan's view, must be "overturned" in God's encounter with us, there is theological warrant for Crossan's preference for metaphor. Crossan's refusal to reckon with the content of the parable narratives, then, yields more than the logical difficulty of explaining how the parables disclose a glimpse of the Kingdom. It also sustains the theological assumption that God meets us only in an unmediated encounter, and only at the margins of that public and ordinary history to which our very language testifies to our embeddedness.

Whether Crossan's final emphasis is on language's capacity to express something positive about the Kingdom through the tortures of metaphor, or rather on the Kingdom as that which undermines language altogether is not resolved in this project. Crossan's next study, *The Dark Interval*, provides an unambiguous answer to this question, and establishes the course he will pursue in each of his subsequent undertakings. The parable now does not initiate metaphorical disclosure; it has instead an exclusively negative function. By disrupting, the parable creates a space, a "dark interval," in and through which an experience of transcendence may occur. The parables do not speak about God, but "give God room."/19/

Crossan's interest in the New Critics and his Heideggerian reflections on time and history are here replaced by a "philosophical theology of story." His fundamental premises: "reality is

language," "story creates world," and "we live in language like
fish in the sea."/20/ Appropriating the insights of Kuhn, Popper,
and Hesse, Crossan argues that the reality in which we dwell is
always an interpreted reality. "Story," he suggests, does not tell
us about a "world out there objectively present before and apart
from any story concerning it," but rather "creates world," so that
"we live as human beings in, and only in, layers upon layers of
interwoven story."/21/ This "limit," as fundamental as our mor-
tality, ought not provoke despair (Crossan's characterization of
existentialism), but "exhilaration." Language, or "story," should
not be divided between the direct, objective language of science
and the indirect language of the imagination, for all language is
indirect. The real distinction, he argues, is between language
which is aware of its limits, and that which is not./22/

Crossan accordingly arranges several types of "story" on a
spectrum, with "myth" and "parable" at either pole. Adopting
Levi-Strauss' analysis of myth as a mediator of irreconcilable
opposites, Crossan argues that through its process of attempted
mediation, myth achieves an "ontological gain": it "establishes
the possibility of reconciliation itself."/23/ Crossan's earlier analysis of the parable's function is basically unchanged: parable,
myth's binary opposite, creates contradictions within a given situation of "complacent security." In so doing, parable challenges
the fundamental principle of reconciliation "by making us aware
of the fact that *we made up* the reconciliation." Parable, that is,
is that language most aware of its limits; it is "story grown self-
conscious and self-critical."/24/ In Crossan's new schema, parable (now more often "paradox" than "metaphor") is the most
appropriate language for religious experience because the transcendent "appears" as event only in and through the "cracks" in
our stories of which parables make us aware.

While this shift does clarify some of the ambiguities of *In
Parables*, how Crossan perceives the relation between "language"
and "reality" continues to be a problem. In his pronouncement
that "we live in story," Crossan sometimes seems to be claiming
that we know reality only as it is shaped by our linguistic paradigms, so that the kinds of truths we know are related to the
forms through which we come to know them. "Reality," he
writes, "is the interplay of mind and world in language"; our
paradigms are "possible ways of imagining the world."/25/ Such
a view is not only not incompatible with an understanding of

metaphor as a vehicle of insight, it is the basis for the claim that poetry, or metaphor, can provide a kind of knowledge that other forms of discourse cannot.

At other points, Crossan seems to conflate all kinds of language into one. All language now seems to be not only "indirect" but also non-referential. Instead of offering us a plurality of possible ways to imagine reality, language does not refer to anything that transcends it. Reality and human experience are not interpreted through "story," they *are* "story." Crossan is thus forced to pose the problem of transcendence in an unfortunate way:

> If there is only story, then God, or the referent of transcendental experience, is either *inside* my story, and in that case, at least in the Judeo-Christian tradition I know best, God is merely an idol I have created; or, God is *outside* my story, and I have just argued that what is "out there" is completely unknowable. So it would seem that any transcendental experience has been ruled out if we can only live in story. In all of this I admit most openly a rooted prejudice against worshipping my own imagination and genuflecting before my own mind./26/

With this either/or dilemma before him, Crossan must conclude that all attempts to speak of God are idolatrous—even such New Testament metaphors as "King," "Shepherd," or "Rock." Ironically, the only effective religious language in Crossan's view, the parable, is a language which does not say anything at all. The parables are not disclosive, but subversive, or, as Crossan will describe them in *Raid on the Articulate*, "aniconic." In this later study, Crossan argues that Jesus extends ancient Israel's prohibition against graven images to language itself:

> If the name of Moses is synonymous with the prohibitions against . . . images of God in gold and silver, it is Jesus who issues the most magisterial warning against graven words, against images of God in form and genre.

In Jesus we see the "full flowering of Israel's aniconic faith, the consummate creativity of Israel's iconoclastic imagination."/27/

In *The Dark Interval*, however, Crossan seems to move back and forth between these two understandings of "reality is story." One consequence is that we are not sure precisely what the parable "disrupts"—the complacency and self-righteousness of the everyday life-world of its auditors (as this, to be sure, is articulated in language), or simply language itself, as he later proclaims in *Raid*. If language does not refer to reality at all, as he sometimes seems to suggest, then parable is indeed simply "*story* grown self-conscious and self-critical"; it can neither transform the lives and actions of its auditors, nor elicit a new, more adequate interpretation of the real.

Crossan's functional definition of the parable now permits him to explore the similarities among the parables of Jesus, Borges, Kafka and others. Because Crossan has located the "religious" character of parable in its capacity to expose the limits of our stories, he must admit all of these parables into his genre of religious discourse, just as he had to exclude other biblical forms of expression./28/ Crossan's use of the terms "limit" and "religious" here is quite different from their use by other theologians, even those he most often cites. While religious language is characterized as a form of "limit-expression" in the analyses of Paul Ricoeur and David Tracy, for example, this term is not synonymous with Crossan's much broader use of "limit" for all parables or "paradoxes." For Tracy and Ricoeur, furthermore, these religious expressions do not simply bring us to an awareness of the limits *to* our ordinary constructions of meaning, as Crossan would have it; they disclose something of the character of the transcendent as well./29/ Crossan's religious parables may create a "dark interval," but they cannot tell us whether what appears in that space is gracious, or, like the referent of Kafka's parables, absurd.

In *Raid on the Articulate* and *Cliffs of Fall* Crossan turns to Jacques Derrida to help him explicate his thesis that "reality is language." Language does not refer to a reality external to it, in Derrida's view, but to other signs; to live "in story" is to live within the interplay of signification. There is no "outside-the-text," for there is nothing in the world which is not itself a text:

> This field is in fact that of freeplay, that is to say, a field of infinite substitutions in the closure of a finite ensemble./30/

In Derrida's critique of traditional metaphysics, there is no absolute foundation outside the play of language itself which can "center" the structure of the linguistic system and thus guarantee a determinate meaning for any utterance within that system.

The desire for such a foundation (be it Platonic essence, Kantian *Ding an sich*, or Heideggerian Being) is a nostalgic quest for "presence" destined to fail. Since there is no such ground, the specification of meaning can move from substitute sign to substitute sign without end.

Crossan still wishes to define the parable as a means to evoke the transcendent, but to do so within this new framework, Crossan must devise new strategies to explain how parable is subversive. As Crossan recognizes, "we have no words for what is outside words. . . . We have only ones which draw attention to that borderline and that limitation from the inside."/31/ Since parable, too, cannot escape the process of infinite freeplay, Crossan now locates its subversiveness in its self-reflexive nature. Parables become "metaparables," or parables about parabling: parable is "language made deliberately self-revelatory of its playful roots, language kept constantly self-manifestive of its ludic reality."/32/

Crossan finds one strategy in Stanley Fish's notion of the "self-consuming artifact."/33/ This kind of literary presentation, Fish argues, calls attention to the insufficiency of its own procedures, and thereby calls into question the sufficiency of the minds it unsettles. In *Finding Is the First Act*, Crossan argues that Jesus' parable of the Hidden Treasure (Matthew 13:44) is an "artifact" of this kind. Far from disclosing an image of the Kingdom, the parable instead shows us how language fails to refer beyond itself:

> I will tell you, it says, what the Kingdom of God is like.
> Watch carefully how and as I fail to do so and learn that
> it cannot be done. Have you seen my failure? If you
> have, then I have succeeded. And the more magnificent
> my failure, the greater my success./34/

A second strategy concentrates on the inevitable plurality of interpretations any utterance will generate. Jesus' parable of The Sower, in Crossan's view, is about this "polyvalence." Just as seed sown on bad soil (path, rocks, thorns) meets with three stages of failure, so the seed falling on good soil yields a multiple pattern of success (the harvests are 30-, 60- and 100-fold). The parable is thus a "perfect mirror of itself," like an onion "whose manifold layers constitute its totality and whose multiplicity is its message."/35/

As Crossan extends the dominion of language he shifts, or at least clarifies, his theological intention. The parables do not, even enigmatically, reveal something of the character of the transcendent, because it is a wholly unknowable divine. God's actions are not "hiddenly present" in the movements of history, as Bultmann would have it, but present only as void, as the absence of meaning and order. The narrow gate to transcendence lies in our recognition both that "the Holy has no plan at all," and that "that is what is absolutely incomprehensible to our structuring, planning, ordering minds."/36/ Crossan's "aniconic" Jesus is now less a prophetic figure, shocking us into an awareness of the falsity and complacency of our stories, than he is an "ancient Palestinian mystic" whose "serene and iconoclastic spirit" places him in the company of the Zen masters, Dionysius the Areopagite, and the anonymous author of the *Cloud of Unknowing*./37/ The understanding of eschatology Crossan designs for Jesus is neither that of the prophetic nor apocalyptic traditions, but "comic"—an "ending of the story of the end," and a laughing at our inventions of a divinity whose coherent plan is moving toward some final consummation. The religion of Jesus is "ecumenic, problematic, and unconsoling"; he is not Bultmann's "presupposition of Christianity," but a "pre-Christian."/38/

Crossan's title for *Raid on the Articulate* does well to invert Eliot's "raid on the inarticulate," then, for this program departs from the intentions of the New Critics as well as from those of Bultmann. Despite the weaknesses in their theory, the New Critics clearly sought to *restore* our sense of the real density and substance of "the world's body," under the theological symbol of the Incarnation. They aimed to combat the dissociation of the modern sensibility by revealing a more original and cohesive world, a "mythic order," beneath the conflicts and contradictions of the world we commonly inhabit.

Why Derrida is attractive to Crossan is understandable, for he is, in Meyer Abram's apt characterization, the Zen master of Western philosophy, undertaking to shock us out of our habitual linguistic categories./39/ Some of Derrida's language, furthermore, echoes the Bultmannian language which Crossan initially found most congenial—Derrida calls us, for example, to "overcome our age old nostalgia for security." But Crossan's assumption that this theory supports his own attempt to retrieve negative theology entails a misreading of Derrida. Derrida uses the term *absence* to note the lack of a center outside of language, and to refer to the "gap" at the heart of the sign which generates the play of infinite substitutions. Crossan, however, hypostatizes absence as "the foundation and horizon of all thought," the perpetually absent Wholly Other of which language continually attempts and fails to speak./40/ From Derrida's perspective, this "negative theology," or even "negative atheology," would also be "logocentric": it still pronounces the absence of a center, when it is play that should be affirmed./41/ By positing an absent transcendent as the motive for metaphor, Crossan restores the "outside-the-text" which Derrida deconstructed. While Crossan must do so if he hopes to construct a negative theology, he will have to seek a different basis for his hermeneutic of freeplay.

In so doing, Crossan might reconsider Kafka's parable of the leopards:

> Leopards break into the temple and drink to the dregs what is in the sacrificial pitchers; this is repeated over and over again; finally it can be calculated in advance, and it becomes part of the ceremony./42/

Words, like leopards, as Crossan rightly sees, belong to the profane; they contaminate the sacred and rob it of its otherness. While Crossan may choose to pursue a *via negativa*, the literature in which he so clearly delights remains a stubborn witness for the opposite path, its violations part of a different sacred ceremony.

Hans W. Frei: The Realistic Reading of the Gospels

The Eclipse of Biblical Narrative is a carefully researched and detailed examination of eighteenth and nineteenth-century biblical hermeneutics. Frei's project is not a complete history of biblical criticism at this time, but rather, as he describes it, "a historical study under a thesis."/43/ Frei's thesis is that the "realistic" or "history-like" character of many biblical narratives requires a correlative interpretive procedure, a kind of "realistic reading," appropriate to it. Before the rise of historical criticism, the precritical methods of literal and figurative reading were appropriate interpretive processes. With the breakdown of the credibility of pre-critical forms of reading, biblical critics sought alternative ways to approach the texts. While most interpreters continued to recognize the history-like quality of the narratives, the failure to develop appropriate modern forms of realistic reading meant that this characteristic of the narratives—or, better, the capacity to read the narratives *as* realistic narratives—was eclipsed.

Frei's criticism of the development of biblical hermeneutics during this period is implicit, but clear: not only is the eclipse of "realistic narrative" to be lamented, but the alternative, and to Frei mistaken, approaches to Scripture developed in the eighteenth and nineteenth centuries have continued to direct twentieth-century interpreters in a mistaken direction. Frei's attempt at an exegesis which avoids these errors is set out in his study *The Identity of Jesus Christ: The Hermeneutical Bases of Dogmatic Theology.*/44/ Nevertheless, the framework of Frei's constructive project guides his historical study as well.

Central to both projects is his notion of "realistic narrative." Despite its centrality, the concept is elusive. While Frei repeats aspects of the notion in various contexts so that we can come to appreciate why, in terms of his program, he defines it as he does, more concrete examples of what kinds of narratives would, or more importantly, would not, fit his definition, would help us understand and assess his proposal. Frei's notion has two components, one pertaining to the "realism" of the narratives, the other to the question of literary meaning. Realistic narratives are, in Frei's words, stories where

> . . . the narrative depiction is of that peculiar sort in which character or individual persons, in their internal depth or subjectivity as well as their capacity as doers and sufferers of actions or events, are firmly and significantly set in the context of the external environment, natural but more particularly social. Realistic narrative is that kind in which subject and social setting belong together, and character and external circumstances fitly render each other./45/

Following Erich Auerbach's classic study of "the representation of reality in Western literature," *Mimesis*, Frei notes that the style as well as the content of realistic narrative mingles the sublime, or at least serious, effect with what is casual, random, ordinary and everyday./46/ In contrast to the ancient Greco-Roman doctrine of the "separation of styles," whereby any serious subject is bound to be treated in elevated, epic style, in the biblical and other realistic narratives,

> Believable individuals and their credible destinies are rendered in ordinary language and through concatenations of ordinary events which cumulatively constitute the serious, sublime, and even tragic impact of powerful historical forces./47/

The weight which this aspect of the definition bears becomes more apparent in *Identity*, where Frei argues that the Gospel narratives, particularly the passion narrative and resurrection sequences, are "realistic" in this sense. Frei also develops there a notion of identity and identity description which he argues is appropriate to the way in which character and circumstance "fitly render" each other in realistic narrative. Frei suggests that realistic novels, certain biblical narratives, and historical accounts proper all fall under the rubric of realistic narrative as he defines it. While historical accounts are realistic in narrative form, however, they, unlike fictional narratives, must refer, and refer accurately, to events which have actually taken place, and the connections between those events must be rendered without recourse to supernatural agency. For Frei, the biblical stories—even those which include miracles—can be realistic, whether or not they are factually true, as long as "the depicted action is indispensible to the rendering of a particular character, divine or human, in a particular story."/48/

What Frei wishes to exclude by this definition are stories which simply illustrate something we already know independently ("an intellectually pre-subsisting or preconceived archetype or ideal essence"), allegories, and myth (stories that "function in such a way as to express or conjure up an insight or affective state that is beyond any and all depiction")./49/ This points to the second aspect of Frei's definition. Here, rather than following Auerbach, Frei comes close to the New Critics' theory of literary autonomy. For Frei, the crucial point to be stressed is that the narrative form does not "illustrate" its meaning, but "constitutes" it. The "meaning" of the story is located nowhere but in the narrative sequence itself. It is just this cohesiveness of meaning with narrative form that in Frei's view was eclipsed in modern biblical criticism. As a cautionary statement concerning the integrity of a literary work, Frei's point here is accurate and justified. It will be seen, however, that as a theory of the self-sufficiency and autonomy of literary meaning, Frei's argument becomes subject to the criticisms of the New Critical program outlined in Chapter II.

Some further clues to what Frei intends here can be garnered from what he has to say about pre-critical methods of reading. What made them appropriate ways to interpret realistic narratives, in Frei's view, was precisely that they assuumed the subject matter of the texts, what the stories were taken to be about, to be cohesive with their literal meaning: to read the stories literally was at the same time to read them as historically true. The world depicted by the biblical narrative as one temporal sequence, beginning with the creation of the world and ending with its apocalypse, was taken to be identical to the actual course of history. Furthermore, since Scripture depicts the one and only real world, the story necessarily embraces the experience of any present age and reader. To read and understand the biblical narratives was thus to appropriate their abiding religious significance by fitting oneself into the narrative depiction./50/

As Auerbach points out, it does not matter whether we take the Homeric poems as "make believe" or not, for their effectiveness lies in their capacity to ensnare us, to take us into their own world. The biblical stories, in contrast, do not aim aim to bewitch, but claim to be true, and this claim is tyrannical—it excludes all other claims.

> Far from seeking, like Homer, merely to make us forget our own reality for a few hours, it seeks to overcome our reality: we are to fit our own life into its world, feel ourselves to be elements in its structure of universal history./51/

Figural (typological) reading, a natural extension of literal interpretation, was at once a literary and historical procedure. If the literal senses of the narratives seemed to diverge, figuration was a way to fit them into one cumulative story. It was, in addition, a way of making sense of the general extra-biblical structure of human experience. Frei adopts Auerbach's description of the figural procedure:

> Figural interpretation establishes a connection between two events or persons in such a way that the first signifies not only itself but also the second, while the second involves or fulfills the first. The two poles of the figure are separated in time, but both, being real events or persons, are within temporality./52/

Figuration is obviously a delicate procedure, for it must keep together the meaning pattern perceived and the concrete events in time. Sensory occurrence and meaning are easily sundered, the reader turning his or her attention to the meaning rather than the event. This happens in allegory, where, in Frei's definition, "a temporally free-floating meaning pattern" is attached to

"any temporary occasion whatever, without any intrinsic connection between sensuous time-bound picture and the meaning
represented by it."/53/

In Frei's view, the importance of the figural procedure is that
it maintained unity of literal sense, historical sense, and the unity
and abiding religious significance of Scripture. Frei also maintains,
and this is central, that the perception of a figural pattern was not a
material contribution of the interpreter, or a unique perspective
he or she might represent, for then, in his view, figuration would
be an arbitrary forcing together of events and patterns of meaning.
The meaning pattern is not a new dimension added to the text,
stresses Frei, but a function of the narrative itself. Since (pre-
critical) interpreters are part of the same sequence of history
depicted by the story, figural reading is simply a comprehension
and a mimesis—a following of the way things really are./54/

Frei sees the seeds of the dissolution of this framework as early
as the seventeenth century. The first subtle transformations
appear, for example, when Cocceius and Bengel attempt to locate
the events of their day by means of biblical sayings, and to predict
future stages and the actual end of history in the same way. For
here, in Frei's view, the real events of history begin to be viewed as
autonomous; there begins to be a "logical distinction" and "reflective distance" between the stories themselves and the "reality" they
depict./55/ The direction of interpretation thus begins to be
reversed: rather than understanding self and world by finding
their place within the biblical narrative, the story becomes a
means of verifying or predicting the world independent of and
outside it. In time, this dissociation between the literal and the historical becomes the "category error" of historical criticism. The
"history-likeness" of the narratives is read as a putative claim of
fact to be subjected to independent investigation.

In the wake of these transformations, the chief problem for
biblical interpreters is the question of where the meaning and
abiding religious significance of the biblical texts are now to be
located. As historical criticism grew to be exclusively concerned
with ascertaining the veracity of the events depicted in the stories, explication of the literal or verbal sense became increasingly
a task for philological investigation. Subjected to the grammatical and lexical rules of language, the literal sense came to mean
the text's verbal sense for its original audience. Neither investigation assured that the biblical writings have any abiding truth

or significance, however, particularly as the sense of cultural and temporal distance between text and reader increased.

The religious significance of the texts, their subject matter or "real meaning," in Frei's analysis, while located variously (in the texts' historical reference, in some ideal referent such as a general religious or moral idea, or, later, with the mythophiles, in an authorial "folk consiousness" or genetic context) were in every case taken to be something other and external to the narrative *qua* narrative. The connection between the narrative depiction and what the stories were construed as actually about was viewed as only apparent and not real.

Frei discerns one broad approach to the problem of abiding significance in a large number of biblical interpreters whose programs are in other respects quite various. Though varying with the degree of historical truth it was thought the biblical writings contained, in general terms the logic of this argument, in Frei's view, has remained constant from the eighteenth century through the present./56/ According to these interpreters, in Frei's analysis, the religious meaningfulness of the biblical texts depends in part on their relation to independent accounts of general human experience. The meaningfulness of the claim 'Jesus is redeemer', for example, however closely or loosely it is tied to actual historical events, rests on the ability of natural insight to perceive the need for redemption. Whether this need is interpreted as one's moral imperfection, or despair and longing for grace, or the loss of true selfhood in alien social structures, Christian revelation can be understood as a meaningful possibility only if it seems to be a significant answer to, or illumination of, this condition.

It is this broad spectrum of "apologetics"—both a way of doing theology and a type of hermeneutic—toward which Frei's criticisms are directed, and which in *Identity* he attempts to outflank. One of the difficulties with both books is that Frei does not name his conversation partners. Nor does he clarify his relation to Karl Barth. Frei holds up Barth's biblical exegesis as a model of the kind of reading he proposes:

> [Barth] distinguishes historical from realistic reading of the theologically most significant biblical narratives, without falling into the trap of instantly making history the test of the *meaning* of the realistic form of the stories./57/

At the same time Frei suggests that he does not wish simply to identify his program with that of Barth ("In his hands theology becomes an imperious and allegiance-demanding discipline")./58/ Nevertheless, Frei's description of Barth's critique of apologetic theology seems to be his own as well. Barth, writes Frei, refused

> any attempt to show that Christianity is the ultimate cutting edge of the radical, autonomous quest for meaning and self-understanding of modern despisers (and non-despisers) of religion./59/

For in such an attempt, the interpretation of Christianity is "constituted by an anthropo-theology, in which understanding God and genuinely authentic human self-understanding are mutually indispensable—each being interpreted through the other."/60/ Frei argues that this has been the (misguided) preoccupation of theologians and philosophers of religion since the eighteenth century, "with few exceptions."/61/

It is of course Schleiermacher (with whom Frei's historical study concludes) who was the watershed figure for specifying the connection between "apologetic" theology and hermeneutics. Just as it became a steady preoccupation among theologians in the context of post-Kantian German romanticism to focus on faith as a distinctive, irreducible and self-conscious human stance, and to set it in the context of a general inquiry into human nature, so for Schleiermacher, to inquire about interpretation was to "step backward into the inwardness of our own consciousness to find out what is going on there and how well it is equipped to perform its proper function."/62/ From the principles and rules for the exegesis of texts, hermeneutics becomes, in Schleiermacher's hands, a coherent and systematic inquiry into the operations involved in understanding.

For Schleiermacher, interpretation is, as Frei writes, "a confrontation of one life in its inner particularity by another, a penetration through reconstruction (*Nachbildung*) of the former by the latter."/63/ Interpretation is thus a way of overcoming the walls of time, which depends on a homogeneity at the level of basic humanity; through interpretation, in Frei's words, "the original and the interpreter are directly, in unaltered shape present to each other, in a heterogeneity which is at the same time a mutual fitness, affinity, or even homogeneity."/64/

Before Schleiermacher, explication of a text's meaning was still considered logically separable from the process of "application," the question of the text's abiding significance. Once consciousness conceives itself as possessing a uniquely present location, however, the difference between original and present time becomes a problem, and application a significant issue. As Frei perceives (and laments), in Schleiermacher's hermeneutic historicity is dealt with by making the meaning of a text hover between the work's explicative sense and its significance for someone; the sense of the narrative merges into its significance for the interpreter, and explication becomes identical with application./65/ Meaning, for Schleiermacher, is finally located in neither the historical referent nor the text's genetic context, but in the interpreter's consciousness. This hermeneutics of reconstruction is clearly far from Frei's characterization of pre-critical reading as a "mimesis" in which understanding was "simply a picture of the normative subject matter."/66/

Frei's criticism of this tradition and its twentieth century heirs is resolute. In Frei's view, this kind of hermeneutic and apologetics make the meaning and significance of the biblical texts (and thus Christian concepts or fact claims) at least partially dependent on a sphere of meaning external to them. The hermeneutical circle implies that any interpretation rests on a shared structure of distinctively human being between interpreter and what is interpreted. This prevents the content of the texts from preserving the status of "neutral data," and sees them instead as personally pointed *pro me*; the texts are meaningful only in the process of understanding, and understanding is identified with decision or appropriation./67/

Frei's entire program, in contrast, begins with the need to attend to the way in which the narratives, precisely as narratives, shape their meaning. Inquiring about the text's historical reference and the reader's appropriation of its meaning are logically separable enterprises. Frei thus wishes to maintain, on the hermeneutical level, a firm distinction between a text's meaning, referent, and significance. In parallel fashion, on the theological level, Frei insists on a sharp separation between the explication of the meaning of Christian beliefs in dogmatic theology, and all apologetic interpretations of Christian faith. Frei's concern for the integrity of the narratives as literary forms provokes him to insist that if these writings can in any sense be spoken of as vehicles for "revelation," it will not be because they contain a single and separable proposition which is the focal point for faith's decision. Instead, revelation must have something to do with the form and content of the narratives themselves.

In *Identity*, this argument is developed in terms of the identity (a particular man, Jesus) and presence (this man, Christians believe, lives now) of Jesus Christ. Frei's main contention is that Christ's identity and presence are known only together, and that one cannot begin with theological reflection on the latter and arrive at the former. This is the error of the tradition he criticizes, he argues, particularly in its existentialist form. One cannot, Frei maintains, know who Jesus is by starting with one's experience of Christ's presence. To begin by connecting Christ directly with the interior life of the Christian (the error of liberalism, in his view), turns the resurrection into a purely symbolic event, and Jesus becomes simply an archetypal man or the pattern for authentic humanity./68/ If we wish to insist on the total unity of Christ's presence and identity, says Frei, we must begin with his identity.

And for Christ's identity, we must turn to the Gospel stories themselves—leaving aside question of their historical referent or appropriation by the reader. Jesus' identity is to be found in the sense of the narrative in its own right. For Frei, the error of beginning theological reflection with Christ's presence has a parallel in the hermeneutics of understanding. As realistic narratives, perhaps unlike some other kinds of stories, Frei asserts, the biblical texts are "directly accessible":

> As I have said, they mean what they say, and that fact enables them to render depictively to the reader their own public world, which is the world one needs to understand them, even if it is not his own real world.

With this kind of narrative, the task of interpretation is to "look for the sense of the story," ask if we agree as to what we find there, and "discover its patterns to one another."/69/ Rather than hypothesizing an independently existing conceptuality to which the texts, once demythologized, must fit, we ought to consider the hermeneutical process in reverse fashion: we need the texts to have an existence independent of ourselves; we need a "Word" which can convey to us new realities, can generate in us new awareness, and can provide us with the questions the text would have us propose.

The hermeneutics of understanding is an inappropriate instrument for this task not only because it collapses the sense of the text (and thus Jesus' identity) into its significance for someone (into Christ's presence), but also because the specific understanding of human being it assumes makes it incapable of reading "realistic" narratives./70/ Frei proposes his own notion of identity and identity description to develop the latter point. One of the peculiarities of realistic narratives is the way in which character and social circumstance "fitly render" each other. As Henry James remarked: "What is character but the determination of incident? What is incident but the determination of character?"/71/ Identity, according to Frei, is "the specific uniqueness of a person, what really counts about him, quite apart from both comparison and contrast to others. . . . A person's identity is the total of all his physical and personality characteristics referred neither to other persons for comparison or contrast nor to a common ideal type called human, *but to himself.*"/72/

To describe the identity of a person (or a character in a realistic narrative) we can ask two purely formal questions: "What is a person like?" and "Who is he?" To answer the first question we look for those "typical state[s] or action[s] of a person that would properly and genuinely constitute or characterize him." We consider a person's actions as enactments of his intentions, or of others' intentions, or we view his response to external circumstances devolving upon him./73/

To answer the second, more elusive question, "Who is this person?" the question of a person's self-continuity from action to action, we look for the "manifestation" of a self's total being in a public medium (word, body, name, community) which both fitly *represents* and *is* the subject./74/ In both kinds of identity description, Frei stresses, there is a strong relation between the inward and the outward: intention is firmly linked with enactment, the subject self with manifestation.

What makes the existentialist anthropology unfit for realistic reading according to Frei is, first, that it describes identity in terms of comparative reference to the characteristics, conditions, or destinies of some other person or of all humankind, as it is viewed from a given cultural or social framework. This is to impose a material understanding of identity on a story's character. Second, it tends to view self-identity or self-understanding as separable from public circumstances and social contexts and structures.

Finally, this tradition not only places one's authentic, inner self at a distance from the forms in which it is externalized, but looks with suspicion on all manifestations, including social institutions, as distortions of the subject self. History, in this schema, becomes the "self-alienated quest of self for its true being through the cultural forms of its own distortedness," and myths, indirect communications, and forms of language other than the ordinary and public use of words become the only ways of pointing to what cannot be expressed directly./75/ Exegetically, this scheme tends to force all characters into a preconceived pattern—Jesus, for example, is conceived as manifesting a crucial choice against simple identification with the world, and as the occasion for our own decision for "authentic existence."/76/

If Bultmann's assumption that one's inner, existential self, the arena in which God meets us, is radically separate from public history, is joined to a consideration of literary form (as it is by Crossan, for example), it fits more readily with an analysis of metaphor and parable than of narrative. The separation and reversal of two levels of meaning on which metaphor depends can be easily juxtaposed with the existentialist self-world anthropology. The Bultmannian focus on faith as "event" and "decision" tends to view dialogue, address, and confrontation as the primary forms of the Christian message, with "justification by faith" the central theological model./77/ As Frei argues, there are theological consequences deriving from the narrative form for which the Bultmannian framework is ill-prepared. Frei notes, for example, that a theological model derived from attention to the narrative form of the Gospels will have less to do with "profound self grasp" than with moral obedience which, through struggle and action, moves toward a certain goal./78/

With these caveats and his own formal principles established, Frei offers a "realistic reading" of the Gospel story (Frei, for the most part, conflates the synoptic accounts). If we look carefully at the logic of the narratives themselves, Frei maintains, we find that Jesus' identity, as it is made known in the gathering action and passion, requires the climax of the resurrection. This particular "unsubstitutable" man, Jesus, could not *not* rise; his identity requires his presence. Frei reaches this conclusion by tracing four "intention-action" patterns in the narrative. Jesus' obedience to God's will, and the content of that obedience, Jesus' love for all humankind, is enacted in all that he does, but most fully in his obedience unto death. We see Jesus' obedience in the co-existence in him of power and powerlessness, and in the transition from one to the other. The crucial instance of this transition is the garden-arrest-trial sequence, where Jesus surrenders his own power to the authorities, or "historical forces." Yet this is at the same time to further enact his obedience to God, to place himself in God's power, since the power of Pilate and of the world is power given by God. Thus the more Pilate's power is exerted, the more God's action moves to its climax./79/

The climax of the narrative is not Jesus' death, but his resurrection. Here, startlingly, just where God's supplantation of Jesus' will and power is complete, for it is God's action alone which raises Jesus from the dead, it is not God but the crucified Jesus of Nazareth himself who marks the presence of that action ("See my hands and my feet; it is I and no other"). The narrative seems to say that Jesus somehow holds together his own identity in the transition from death to resurrection, and that the *enactment* of God's intention through the resurrection is at the same time the ultimate *manifestation* of who Jesus is.

Who Jesus is is manifest early in the narratives by means of "stylized" titles and symbols; Jesus is the promised king of Israel, then he who witnesses to the kingdom of God. As the narrative moves forward toward Jerusalem, Jesus becomes less a representative figure, and increasingly a unique individual in his own right. In the resurrection appearances, however, the pattern of self-manifestation becomes a circle. We see Jesus, now the unique individual, turn to reestablish his connection with the "stylized" titles, claiming them for himself in his "unadorned singularity" as Jesus of Nazareth, the crucified. In this circular pattern, Frei argues, Jesus "demythologizes" the savior myth and the other representations by making them his own.

The Gospel narratives, whether or not we take them to be historically true, thus, in Frei's view, render Jesus' identity and make it "accessible to us." In fact, while the passion-resurrection sequences may come closer to the actual historical events of Jesus' life than earlier parts of the story, it is these sequences which are most fiction-like in form, and place Jesus' identity most sharply before us. It is with the resurrection that the logic of the story itself merges fictional depiction with factual claim: with this climax the story says, in effect, that this Jesus of Nazareth *is*, is in fact, alive and present now./80/ To grasp who Jesus is is to believe that he has been raised from the dead. He *is* the resurrection and the life, so how can he not be conceived as resurrected?

Like a novel, Frei seems to be suggesting, the Gospels persuade us by the logic of their internal patterning, drawing us into the action and eliciting our consent, so that we come to recognize the resurrection as the only fit conclusion for the dramatic sequence. The narrative itself, as a cohesive whole, seeks to persuade us of its truth—but here, Frei argues, the truth of the conclusion is not only that of novelistic appropriateness, the truth of coherence, but also factual truth. It is up to the reader to accept or reject this factual claim, says Frei, and there is no argument from factual evidence or rational possibility to smooth the transition from literary to faith judgment./81/ For the nonbeliever, the Gospel will appear as a kind of "hyperfiction," claiming to be self-warranting fact./82/ For the believer, Frei seems to be saying, the referent of the narrative is not just a historical or imagined character, but one who is alive as the same person to confirm his identity; there is a closed circle between the accounts and the presence of Christ./83/ The logic of the story converges with the necessity for faith.

Frei's original and challenging studies obviously touch on a host of issues which lie beyond the direct concerns of my project. Of the three scholars under consideration here, Frei is most resolute in maintaining that the biblical texts, considered as literary works with their own integrity, should be the starting point for theological reflection. In his explication of what such a position entails Frei assumes many of the main tenets of the New Critics. Within the context of my study, it is this aspect of his proposal which merits the closest attention.

Like the New Critics, Frei tacitly defines the literary work as an autonomous, self-sufficient, non-referential organism; its meaning is located "in" the work itself; form and content are inseparable, so that a work cannot be translated into another sphere of meaning; the norms for criticizing and understanding a work are to be deduced from the work itself and not from any criteria extrinsic to it. By virtue of this autonomy, literature can stand over against culture, and demand to be heard on its own terms. Just how literature conveys truth or yields knowledge remained ambiguous in the New Critical program, however. As it was argued in Chapter II, the New Critics' stress on the literary work's discontinuity with the full range of human experience and value external to it made it difficult to describe how literature actually does, in fact, extend and transform our perceptions.

Frei's proposal is open to the same dangers. While many of his criticisms of the "hermeneutics of understanding" are justified, the starkness of many of his assertions concerning literary meaning—the text literally "means what it says," there is "no gap between representation and what is represented by it," the narratives are "directly accessible" and render their meaning *to* us—at least call for some qualification if Frei is not to assume the difficulties of the New Critical program.

One ambiguity in Frei's project is just how far he wishes to carry the analogy between the Gospel narratives and the realistic novel. Within limits, the analogy is clearly helpful, for it insists on the continuity between Jesus' ministry and death and his resurrection, and does not dissolve the resurrection into the disciples' response, in Bultmannian fashion. It is clear that Frei wishes to extricate the Gospels from the constraints modern historians must observe: the Gospels need not give up supernatural agency, nor obey the laws of accurate ostensive reference to be "realistic"; they need only depict a "common public world," even if it is not the "one we all inhabit." It is also clear that Frei refuses to surrender the narratives to demythologizing, which is to ask them to conform to a particular view of what is credible and of the universal structures of human existence. The human imagination makes demythologizing unnecessary, Frei implies, by enabling us to participate in the world depicted in the narratives.

Frei is correct, I think, to suggest that the "mythological world view" of the Gospels, as Bultmann spoke of it, need not be a barrier to our imaginative involvement in the stories, for we can participate in the Gospels as literary works, just as we can the diverse fictional worlds of other texts. But this does not mean that the Gospels resemble the realistic novel, for we can "participate" in the *Odessey* or Tolkien's *The Hobbit* in the same way./84/ In *Eclipse*, Frei laments the fact that biblical scholars did not turn to the developing tradition of literary realism, which might have provoked them to give "serious attention to narrative shape in its own right." While the definition of literary "realism" is as subject to debate among literary critics as most of its critical categories, it is at least clear that for the literary critics Frei has in mind, "realistic" fiction explicitly precludes all elements of supernatural agency, of the "mythical" or "marvelous."/85/ A realistic novel, in this view, must not only depict a "common public world" in which characters act and are acted upon, but the "common public world" to which we recognizably belong. This is more than a quibble over generic definitions, because it remains unclear in just what sense Frei means to say that the Gospels make Jesus' identity "accessible" to us, and how seriously he confronts the cultural distance between the first and twentieth centuries.

The resurrection, for Frei, is the point in the narratives which calls its readers to make a "transition from literary to faith judgment." New Testament scholars have reminded us, however, that the evangelists and the communities for which the Gospels were written did not see an intrinsic difference between the actions of Jesus of Nazareth, of the risen Lord, and of the Spirit, so that the post-resurrection appearances of Jesus are as much a mixture of narrative testimony and confession of faith as are the renderings of Jesus' identity in other portions of the Gospel stories. Furthermore, the resurrection is the *presupposition* of the form and content of the Gospel stories, and not simply the inevitable outcome of the movement of the narrative itself. While historical knowledge concerning the perspectives of the early Christian communities—and of other elements in the stories foreign to us, such as the titles ascribed to Jesus and the notion of the Kingdom of God—may enable us imaginatively to understand the "world" of the Gospels, Frei does not acknowledge the need for such efforts. This omission, together with the ambiguity of Frei's definition of realism, leaves the question of the alienness of the biblical texts unresolved.

A second ambiguity concerns Frei's suggestion that the texts' "meaning" is "in" the shape of the narratives themselves, and that there is no gap between representation and what it represents. As a corrective to the displacements of literary meaning by historical criticism and those who would extract moral or religious truths from the texts, this assertion of literary autonomy is helpful. But it is not at all clear what Frei really intends to assert here. Does Frei mean that the *representation* of Jesus in the Gospel stories *is*, ontologically, Jesus Christ? Clearly not. Or does he wish to say that the referent of the Gospels, like that of a novel, is a fictional or hypothetical referent? Does Frei really wish to carry the analogy that far? Or perhaps Frei means that the representation of Jesus in the Gospels is a true, or faithful, or trustworthy interpretation of the identity of Jesus Christ. But then there is a "gap" between representation and what it represents: there could, logically, be a false, or less adequate representation of Jesus' identity—as the exclusion of certain Gospels from the Christian canon demonstrates.

Frei seems to assume that his discussion of identity and identity description makes any further observations about literary meaning unnecessary. Frei's criticisms of the "idealist" or existentialist view that the self is alienated from its distorting objectifications are also, it appears, an implicit critique of the notion of language underlying Bultmann's demythologizing program. Language, in Bultmann's view, may distort, or conceal, or lead away from, its meaning as well as reveal it. But Frei's alternative understanding of identity does not help us very much with the problem of literary meaning. Frei's notion of the "fitness" between intention and action, self and public manifestation, is a valuable caution against seeking Jesus' inner self "behind" the Gospel stories. But also to assume, as Frei seems to do, that the meaning of a written text is directly and immediately given in the words and word sequences in the text is misleading: if the "letter" were perfectly congruent with the "spirit" of a text, no problems of interpretation would ever arise.

Frei's discussion of eighteenth and nineteenth-century biblical hermeneutics outlined the various interpretive errors entailed in seeking the meaning of the texts elsewhere than in the narratives themselves. Does Frei also imply, then, that if interpreters were to read the narratives as narratives, all interpretive difficulties would disappear? With the New Critics, Frei tacitly insists that linguistic form and content are inseparable: a text can never be adequately paraphrased, because a text's meaning is an affair of just this particular linguistic structure and no other; if the form changes, the meaning changes. Thus Frei argues that several modern novels that depict Christ figures do not render *Jesus Christ's* identity, because Christ's identity is given only in the particular linguistic patterns of the Gospels; a different literary rendering will give us a different Jesus Christ. /86/

If Frei does mean to assert that literary form directly compels meaning, so that there is no "gap" between representation and what is represented in this specific sense, then he must also argue that each of the four New Testament Gospels have a different meaning, and render a different Jesus—a conclusion Frei would certainly not wish to maintain. If a text "literally means what it says," furthermore, then all readers of the Gospels would interpret them the same way. This is not only empirically not the case, as the history of interpretation and of Protestant sectarianism demonstrates; it is also a dangerous position to maintain. By ruling out of hand the possibility of misinterpretation, such a position has no means to deal with the varieties of distortion of the Gospel narratives which do, in fact, occur.

In his desire to avoid what he perceives to be the errors of the Bultmannian hermeneutic—imposing a particular cultural perspective on the texts, and sundering the close relation between form and content in the narratives—Frei, like the New Critics, seems to exclude interpretive activity altogether. This position—if it is Frei's position—excludes too much. The reader must actively construe the meaning of a written work, and this is no less true for a literary text, where form and content, "representation" and what is "represented," are inextricably related. To discern the literary form, the work's patterns and structure, is itself an interpretive activity, for to "discover" the connecting shape of words and word sequences is to judge that they mean one thing rather than another. Irony is an extreme example of this general situation: a particular word sequence will mean something fundamentally different if irony is, or is not, present. /87/

Genre provides another example of the way in which the reader must actively construe the meaning of a text. /88/ The reader's notion of a text's genre governs his or her expectations concerning the particular meanings in a work—expectations including, for example, vocabulary and syntax, tone, the range of possible connotations of its words, its subject matter. These expectations will be readjusted, perhaps a number of times, as we become aware of the appropriateness or inappropriateness of our initial generic conception. As Frei's diagnosis of the "category error" of historical criticism demonstrates, a reader's generic expectations have much to do with discerning and explicating a work's meaning.

Furthermore, these expectations originate and are readjusted through a process of comparing and contrasting the "general" or "typical" properties a work shares with others. /89/ To declare a work absolutely unique is to pronounce it incomprehensible. Frei's comparisons of the Gospels with allegories, historical writing, and

fiction, and with "sub-genre" such as modern fictional representations of the Christ figure, or dying-and-rising redeemer figures,
demonstrate this point as well. While Frei seems to view these
exercises as entirely separate from his exegesis of the narratives,
they are in a sense part of the process of understanding and enriching the texts' meanings. To be concerned with genre in this way is
to say that pre-understanding is a prerequisite for understanding a
text's meaning, although in a quite different sense from the
romantic or idealist forms of the hermeneutical circle of which
Frei is critical. Genre is an objective property of the text, independent of a reader's immediate desires and needs. At the same time,
genre must be reconstructed through the reader's critical activity.

Frei's discussion of figural reading illustrates the way he blurs
the distinction between construing the meaning of a text and
imposing some alien perspective on it. Frei argues that figuration
was an act of "comprehension" rather than "creation," and in no
sense a "material contribution on the part of the interpreter."/90/
Frei is undoubtedly correct to note that pre-critical interpreters
understood themselves as standing within the historical sequence
depicted in the narratives, so that figuration was not perceived as
an anachronistic addition to the text's meaning. Nevertheless,
these interpreters did actively discover a pattern of meaning
which was not simply given in the word sequences themselves.
The energy pre-critical interpreters devoted to defining the literal,
historical and other senses of the biblical writings testifies to this
fact. Frei's suggestion that in figural reading the meaning, pattern
or theme "emerges solely as a function of the narrative itself" is as
ambiguous as his assertion that the meaning is "in" the shape of the
narrative itself. /91/

While some of Frei's implicit criticisms of Bultmann's
demythologizing program are pertinent, Bultmann did reckon
with the historical dimensions of the interpretive situation in a
way that the New Critics and Frei do not. If Frei maintains the
complete autonomy of the biblical narratives, we are left with a
puzzle as to how their meaning is actually discerned. If, on the
other hand, Frei accepts the active role of the reader in determining meaning, then he must address the problem of the historical situation of the reader, and the distance between past and
present—an undertaking he does not yet seem to have begun.

Dan Otto Via, Jr.:
Toward a "Literary-Existential" Hermeneutic

Dan Otto Via, Jr.'s 1967 study, *The Parables: Their Literary and Existential Dimension*, is an ambitious attempt to integrate a poetics based on the New Criticism with a Bultmannian existentialist hermeneutic./92/ While Via has also published many other works experimenting with other interpretive methods, this early study remains his most comprehensive theoretical statement.

With Frei and Crossan, Via maintains that hermeneutical inquiry should begin with a consideration of the biblical writings "in their own terms." For Via, this means an analysis of the biblical texts—specifically the parables—as "aesthetic objects." Via criticizes the "severely historical approach," as do Frei and the New Critics, for making a text's historical context the clue to its meaning—a procedure that turns the parables into allegories or reduces them to the status of illustrations for some pre-conceived idea. Via also criticizes this approach for threatening "to leave the parable in the past with nothing to say to the present."/93/ While Via maintains that it is important to seek a parable's meaning in its own setting, he argues that interpretation must also include a further step: "What is needed is a hermeneutical and literary methodology which can identify the permanently significant element in the parables and can elaborate a means of translating that element without distorting the original intention."/94/ As this formulation of the problem clearly indicates, Via turns to Bultmann for the means to carry out this second task.

Via has thus set himself a formidable agenda: he aims to begin with a New Critical theory of the "aesthetic object" which anathematizes the "heresy of paraphrase," and to then isolate and translate a "permanently significant element" into contemporary terms. How Via attempts to reconcile these apparently contradictory aims, and whether he succeeds in doing so, are the questions which direct this examination of Via's work.

The book is divided into two major parts; the first contains his constructive theoretical proposals, while the second, interpretive, section demonstrates the practical consequences of his theory with exegeses of eight parables. The divisions within the theoretical discussion represent the two poles of Via's agenda, the first part considering the problem within the context of biblical hermeneutics, the second developing his notion of the parable as aesthetic object. I will discuss the two aspects of Via's theory in reverse order.

Of our three case studies, Via by far makes the most systematic use of New Critical theory. His definition of the parable as aesthetic object includes most of the tenets of the New Critical program: the literary work is autonomous, and the critic's chief consideration is the internal meaning of the work itself./95/ The elements in a literary work do not in the first place refer to the world outside of it, but to each other, in a structure which is centripetally organized and tightly cohering. The parable is an "organic unity" in which form and content are inseparable; one cannot isolate a particular element in a work without breaking the unity of the whole. The literary form serves as a frame, providing "aesthetic distance" from the world, so that the work becomes what Eliseo Vivas calls a non-referential, "intransitive trap," keeping the reader's attention moving from part to part rather than to an extrinsic referent. Ruling out the "intentional" and "affective fallacies," Via calls upon the New Critics' incarnational principles to argue that poetic language, unlike propositional discourse, fuses form and content in such a way that the work can speak to human beings in their "psychosomatic wholeness." /96/

Via also astutely perceives the difficulties in the New Critical program. While arguing that the literary work is "an absolutely self-contained and discrete set of mutually interrelated references," "detached from sociological and psychological phenomena and from any independent and articulated system of thought," Via points out, they also wish to argue that "a literary work somehow contains a *Weltanschauung* which must confront the truth and knowledge of experience."/97/ Via argues that the New Critics need to clarify how literature can have meaning both "in itself" and "through itself," or, in Murray Krieger's terms, how it can be both a "mirror" and a "window."/98/

Drawing upon the work of Michael Polanyi, a number of literary critics, and his own Bultmannian perspective, Via proposes some modifications in the New which are, in my view, the most significant part of Via's study. In fact, I would argue that his brief discussion, were it to be developed more fully, could point the way to a successful integration of the strengths of both the New Critical and Bultmannian programs. Via does not pursue the implications of his suggestions, however, but instead introduces additional Bultmannian assumptions which are, from my perspective, both unnecessary and destructive of the integrity of the literary text.

Although Via only explicitly uses the term *pre-understanding* in his discussion of biblical hermeneutics, he implicitly introduces it in his criticism and modification of the New Criticism. Via's first criticism regards the literary work's autonomy. While the elements of a poem are indeed given a new context and new meaning by the poem's structure, Via argues, they retain their extrinsic, ordinary meanings as well. The new, particular meanings wrought by their placement in the poem are perceived as new precisely because they are seen in relation to their more general referents. A literary work could not "trap" our attention if its elements were completely discontinuous with our prior experience of the phenomenal world./99/ Understanding passes from something already grasped, however unarticulated that awareness might be, to something new which can be understood through it. Stated in more explicitly Bultmannian terms, understanding depends in part upon pre-understanding, on our prior "life relation" to the subject matter of the text./100/

Via adopts another Bultmannian term to present his second constructive proposal: a literary work, he argues, implicitly contains a "perspective on life or an understanding of existence." A literary text—or at least a narrative, which is Via's focus—depicts a segment of "happening existence" by creating a "hypothetical" world. Because it orders events and renders characters in a particular way, a literary work inevitably implies certain attitudes about the nature of reality and human being, so that "theological and philosophical views of how and why things happen as they do, if they are fused into the work's internal coherence, are not extra-aesthetic."/101/ Via is careful not to assert that literature directly states ideas, and he makes it clear that a work's "understanding of existence" is only implicit in the world it proposes. Nevertheless, in his view, it is part of the task of interpretation to bring this implied understanding to clarity./102/ As Via notes, literary critics inevitably use theological and philosophical terms in their analyses— characterizing Kafka's writing as "an oscillation between hope and despair" is his example—precisely because a good work demands that we attend to and evaluate all of the dimensions of its proposed world.

Drawing on Polanyi's notion of "subsidiary" and "focal awareness," Via develops a corresponding understanding of the reading experience. Literature has the capacity to test a reader, and "to move him into a new state of being or a new horizon," because a work engages us on both affective and cognitive levels./103/ While our attention may be divided as we participate in a work, so that we are "focally aware" of the particular narrative configuration, on a lower or "subsidiary" level of consciousness we attend to the referent of the work as a whole, to what it proposes to be the case./104/ By thus engaging us on several levels of our being, Via argues, literature can become a "language event" in a way that propositional discourse—including theological language—cannot.

This way of looking at the literary situation does, I think, contain the foundation for a hermeneutic which could successfully join New Critical and Bultmannian perspectives by modifying each. Because Via's suggestions are a potential contribution to biblical hermeneutics in general, and because the larger portion of Via's study is not consistent with what he proposes here, the implications of his discussion deserve further attention.

By introducing the notions of pre-understanding and "understanding of existence," Via provides the New Criticism with a means to describe what they do, indeed, wish to claim: that a work of art has cognitive content and yields new, experiential knowledge of human experience. By maintaining that the text presents a hypothetical world, Via can retain the New Critics' important insight that the work is a tightly ordered structure with its own intrinsic norms, while asserting at the same time that doing justice to that internal meaning entails a consideration of what it proposes about the way things are.

By the same token, Via significantly changes certain aspects of Bultmann's program. In contrast to Bultmann, Via suggests that a work implies an "understanding of existence" not in spite of, but precisely because of, its particular literary form. This implies, furthermore, that the work can indeed present a genuinely *new* way to understand life in the world; it can propose a new "possibility for self-understanding." While as readers we bring to the work our own implicit pre-understanding of the world to which we already belong, the literary text, as a unified, hypothetical "organism," genuinely enables us to see a new world, or the old world in a new way. To view the literary situation in this way is to avoid the problems in the Bultmannian hermeneutic of which Frei was justifiably critical. While Bultmann insisted that existentialist philosophy was simply the formal explication of the structure of existence, so that he did not impose a material understanding of existence on the texts, to assert that existentialist philosophy is *the* true description of reality is to limit what the text may propose in advance. By permitting the work to propose its own questions and answsers, so to speak, Via recognizes that a work may imply that existence is "structured" in a quite different way. Furthermore, to speak of reading as a participation in the text's own fictional world is to suggest that one's "decision" or "appropriation" of the content of that world is a process separate from, and subsequent to, our participation in its meaning. Our "assent" to the work, even as it engages us in our "psychosomatic wholeness," is also hypothetical. Only after a work's implications are clarified and assessed through critical reflection, a second aspect of understanding, Via seems to suggest, should one ask whether or not to make the text's "understanding of existence" one's own.

By retaining the New Critics' (now qualified) notion of textual autonomy, Via's proposal thus prevents the reader from imposing an extrinsic system of meaning on the text, and avoids collapsing the text's meaning into its significance. At the same time, Via's stress on the need to clarify what a work implies through critical reflection provides a place for the *Sachkritik* or "content criticism" which Bultmann recognized to be an inevitable consequence of our modernity.

Via does not pursue the implications of his proposals as far as I have done here./105/ Indeed, when we turn to the first part of Via's theoretical discussion, and when we examine his actual exegeses, we see that Via retains other Bultmannian assumptions as well. These segments of his study indicate that Via wishes to "translate" the meaning of the parables into the categories of existentialist philosophy. The second part of Via's theoretical discussion began with literary theory and implicitly introduced aspects of Bultmann's hermeneutic to modify it. The first part proceeds in reverse fashion: Via begins with Bultmannian assumptions and alters them to account for the aesthetic nature of the parables. The result is a lack of clarity and a conclusion at odds with the implications of his second section.

Via begins by noting that the normative status of the biblical texts makes the hermeneutical task especially urgent: the task is to relate the past to the reality that confronts us in the present./106/

Via accepts Krister Stendahl's distinction between what a text "meant," or "its original historical meaning," and what it "means" for a contemporary audience./107/ A contemporary interpretation of what a text means, furthermore, "must be tested by its faithfulness in rendering the text's original intention, what it meant," to prevent the text from becoming a sounding board for our own previously held ideas./108/ The task of interpretation is to identify and then to translate into contemporary terms the "subject matter," "original intention," or "translatable element" of the text. Its final goal is to enable the content of the texts to "come alive" again, to become a "language event" for audiences in the present.

Via's unstated assumption here is that the texts *cannot* engage a contemporary audience unless their meanings are restated in contemporary terms. This was, of course, the starting point for Bultmann's project of "demythologization": the mythological world view contained in the biblical writings was incomprehensible to modern thought and therefore prevented the true "scandal" of the texts' subject matter from "confronting" us in the present. Bultmann therefore proceeded to indeed "translate" the subject matter into the categories of existential philosophy, with the understanding that these interpretations were synonyms, and thus substitutes, for the subject matter of the texts.

While this premise is the basis for Via's discussion of biblical hermeneutics, it is not compatible with assumptions underlying his discussion of the parable as aesthetic object. Via's notion of the literary work assumed that both the literary text and the reader gain an "aesthetic distance" from their usual temporal situations: by virtue of its structure, a literary work assumes a life of its own. While Via demonstrated that the autonomous text is not absolutely discontinuous with the world and with human experience outside of it, he nevertheless viewed the work as a hypothetical world, situated in its own time and place, so to speak—a world in which one can temporarily participate. While the New Critics certainly recognized that historical knowledge about various elements within a work may be essential for that participation to occur, they assumed that the "gap" between past and present is bridged, or suspended, by virtue of the text's hypothetical status. Just as the work is aesthetically "distanced" from its origin and the ordinary world to which it indirectly refers, so as readers we distance ourselves from the ordinary present in which we live by giving our temporary, "as-if" assent to what the text proposes. As Via's delineation of the way a literary work addresses us in our "psychosomatic wholeness" presumes, a literary text *can* speak, or become a "language event," for the imagination in this way.

In his discussion of the parable as literary object, Via depicted the second step of interpretation as the "clarification" of a text's implied understanding of existence. Such clarification could, presumably, entail articulating the work's "implied metaphysic" in theological or philosophical terms, or weighing it against other views of what is the case—whether theological, philosophical, social scientific, or even literary. While this critical process is indeed a further and different way to make a text "come alive" and to inquire about what it might have to say to a contemporary audience, such interpretation is by no means a restatement, "translation," or synonymous substitute for the work's subject matter. Via does recognize that several aspects of Bultmann's program must be modified to account for the parables' status as aesthetic objects, but since he holds fast to his assumption that a text must be translated into contemporary terms, he cannot completely reconcile the two phases of his theoretical discussion.

It is not clear, for example, just what Via intends to say when he speaks of what a text "meant" as distinct from what it "means." He seems to mean "what the text meant for its author and original audience," as when he notes that we cannot ever be certain of our accuracy in this regard, since no interpreter is able to "leap over the expanse of time and to get completely inside the mind of an earlier author."/109/ At another point, however, he speaks of "spelling out what the New Testament meant in its own terms," an ambiguous phrase, and then suggests that our incapacity to view the text exactly as did its author may also be viewed positively:

> The language of the text itself may contain meanings that the author was not consciously aware of; and especially in the aesthetic use of language—hence in the parables—does the language itself empower the author to say more that he knows./110/

When Via then concludes this phase of his discussion with the assertion that "the texts offer possibilities for translation that are not altogether dependent on the conscious awareness of the author or original audience," it appears that what a text "meant" is now identified with its "possibilities for translation," which is at least a blurring, if not an eradication, of his original distinction./111/

A second difficulty appears when he discusses the process of translation itself. After outlining the hermeneutical task as that of translating what the text "meant" into contemporary terms, for example, Via offers the following qualifications. First, he notes, "Because the parables are aesthetic in nature, they are not as time conditioned as other biblical texts and the need for translation is not, therefore, as compelling."/112/ Second, because the parables are "linguistic aesthetic objects," it is impossible to translate them completely into any other terms. While "the need for clarity justifies the effort," "concomitant with the gain in clarity is the loss of the peculiarly aesthetic function."/113/ Therefore, Via recommends, "the interpretive translation should explicitly take into account the untranslatable dimension of the parables in order to make the loss as small as possible."/114/

Via does not say anything further about his first, potentially significant remark, although it seems seriously to challenge the basis of his entire program. Via does elaborate on his second qualification in an attempt to adapt the Bultmannian framework. The "translatable subject matter" of the text is its implied understanding of existence. Since this is to be found in the "pattern of connections" within the text, and since this structure itself shapes the text's meaning, any attempt to translate only the content of the work in the manner of Bultmann or the "New Hermeneutic" is impossible./115/ Instead, writes Via, "The meaning distilled from the form-and-content must be given a new form-and-content, a new pattern of connections which relates the original meaning to our time." Since this interpretation or translation of the parable will not itself be an aesthetic object, Via continues, "the relation of the form to content in the interpretation will not be the same as it is in the parable."/116/

This discussion is clearly compelled by Via's wish to preserve his initial assumptions. While he must admit that the translation cannot be a genuine "substitute," he nevertheless continues to perceive the hermeneutical task as one of providing a more or less adequate substitute meaning.

Via's exegeses of the parables reveal just how Bultmannian his program actually is, for they are indeed translations of the parables' meaning into existentialist categories. While Via's discussion of the literary work employed the term *understanding of existence* in a neutral way, so that the text could, in theory, imply any perspective at all, in Via's exegeses the term becomes explicitly existentialist.

Via turns to Northrop Frye's *Anatomy of Criticism* for assistance with what he now calls his "literary-existential analysis."/117/ Since a literary work's understanding of existence is implied by the "pattern of connections" and the "human encounters and their outcomes" depicted there, Via applies Frye's taxonomy of tragic and comic plot movements and his classification of protagonists' powers of action to the parables. The plots of the parables, Via finds, can be divided into tragic and comic types: "In comedy we have an upward movement toward well-being and the inclusion of the protagonist in a new or renewed society, while in tragedy we have a plot falling toward catastrophe and the isolation of the protagonist from society."/118/ The characters in the parables, Via suggests, are consistently those Frye calls "low mimetic": "a character superior neither to other men nor to his environment . . . rather like us."/119/

Although Via is certainly correct in his desire to pay close attention to the plot strategies and the interactions of the characters in the narratives, his preoccupation with taxonomy (in addition to the above distinctions, Via introduces the "ironic" and "picaresque" modes as well as a typology of the "recognition scene") sometimes threatens to become an end in itself, rather than a means for better understanding the parables. This suspicion receives further support when we see how Via's literary anatomy serves as a bridge to his existentialist framework. Via's agenda is clearly apparent in this summary statement:

> We may bring together our existential . . . and aesthetic concerns by stating that the ontological possibility—possibility in principle—of losing existence is aesthetically the tragic movement, and the ontological possibility of gaining existence is aesthetically the comic movement. How either one occurs ontically—actually or concretely—is seen in the nature of the connections between the events—as whether one episode follows another through the exercise of freedom or by being determined—and in the thought and self-understanding of the characters. Since a parable as an aesthetic object is within limits an autonomous world, the gain or loss of the one opportunity

which is presented in the parable suggests the gain or loss
of existence itself./120/

The results of Via's practical exegeses are thus pre-ordained.
In the "tragic" parable of The Talents (Matt 25:14–30), for
example, we find that the one-talent man would "not risk trying
to fulfill his own possibilities." His "refusal to be responsible" for
his actions is his "existential flaw," and "the very movement of
the plot to catastrophe means that one cannot think and act as
he did without losing his existence, that is, without being
inauthentic or existentially dead."/121/ The "comic" parable of
The Unjust Steward (Luke 16:1–9), in like manner, shows us that
"the image of man is that of a being who is capable of recognizing that he is in crisis and of laying hold of the situation in such
a way as to overcome the threat."/122/

One further question with which Via must deal is that of the
parables' religious referent. Since the parables are, in his view,
basically "secular" stories about ordinary persons in ordinary situations, what leads us to think that their implied understanding of
existence has any relation to God? To answer this, Via quite sensi-
bly appeals to their context: the parables are biblical texts, and
they are told by the Jesus depicted in the Gospels as the proclaimer
of the Kingdom of God. Furthermore, he notes, with Crossan, that
the "realism" of the parables is broken by the appearance of elements which are "extraordinary and improbable"—for example,
the behavior of both the prodigal's father and the vineyard owner
is surprising under the circumstances; the debt which the unfor-
giving servant owed was fantastic./123/ Unlike Crossan, for
whom the element of surprise became the basis for his analysis of
the metaphorical function of the parables, Via argues that the
presence of these elements in the narratives suggests "that everyday existence is crossed by the problematical, contingent, and
unpredictable." Stated in more explicitly existentialist terms, "The
parables' existential understanding is that existence is gained or
lost in the midst of ordinary life, that the eschatological occurs in
the everyday."/124/

While this is all that one can say about the parables' religious
referent on the level "literary-existential" analysis, Via argues that
this existential understanding can then be applied to the divine-
human relationship analogically, as a "definition of faith or unfaith."/125/ Following each of his "literary-existential" analyses,

Via therefore appends an "existential-theological" interpretation. When the understanding of existence implied in The Talents is thus viewed as a pointer to the divine-human relationship, for example, the one-talent man's refusal to risk and his concomitant inability to hold himself responsible become "unfaith":

> the man who so understands himself that he seeks to avoid risky action rather than trusting God for the well-being of his existence, though he may live long chrono-logically, will have no present. This time will be evacuated of content./126/

The neatness and predictability of Via's analyses indicate that he has not, after all, begun with the parables themselves, and with their own autonomous, hypothetical proposals, but with Bultmann. While Via's discussion of the parable as aesthetic object is a promising step toward a hermeneutic that combines the strengths of the New Critical and Bultmannian programs, he has finally, it seems to me, ignored the direction of his own best insights and demythologized the parables instead. Via's study is significant both for the potential fruitfulness of his understanding of the literary situation, and because his failure to fulfill that promise helps to bring into focus which aspects of Bultmann's hermeneutic are compatible with, and which destructive of, an approach which aims to begin with the texts as literary works of art.

NOTES

/1/   John Dominic Crossan, "Waking the Bible," *Interpretation* 32 (1978): 269–85.

/2/   John Dominic Crossan, *In Parables: The Challenge of the Historical Jesus* (New York: Harper & Row, 1973), p. 16. Among the poets and critics Crossan cites most often are: Cleanth Brooks, A. Tate, T. S. Eliot, Ezra Pound, W. H. Auden, and Yeats.

/3/   Ibid., p. 13. Crossan does not specify whether he is discussing metaphor as trope, or using metaphor as a metaphor for the literary work itself. The literary critics he cites are for the most part describing the literary work rather than the figure of speech.

/4/   Ibid., p. 16.

/5/   Ibid., p. 22. Crossan is here quoting Thomas Fawcett, *The Symbolic Language of Religion* (London: SCM Press, 1970), pp. 170–71.

/6/   Ibid., p. 21. Crossan's quotation is from Günther Bornkamm, *Jesus of Nazareth* (New York: Harper & Row, 1960), p. 69.

/7/   Ibid., p. 22.

/8/   Ibid.

/9/   Ibid., p. xiii.

/10/   Ibid., p. 22.

/11/   Ibid., p. 16. The story, that is, functions like "beliefs" or "ideas" in New Critical theory. As T. S. Eliot suggested, the conceptual framework in a poem is something like meat placed before a dog to divert its attention: the ideas are the "bait" which holds the reader's attention so that the full force of the poem can work upon its reader's consciousness independently.

/12/   Ibid., p. 10.

/13/   Cf. Cleanth Brooks' treatment of the problem of "belief" above.

/14/   Crossan, *In Parables*, pp. 31–32.

/15/   Ibid., pp. 26–27.

/16/   Ibid., pp. 65–66. Italics mine.

/17/   Crossan outlines the methodological principles of the New Quest, and explicitly affirms this framework as his own in *In Parables*, pp. 4–7. In addition, the New Testament scholars he most often cites are clearly part of this scholarly tradition: N. Perrin, G. Bornkamm, E. Käsemann, J. M. Robinson, R. Funk. The Bultmannian presuppositions noted in Crossan's work do not necessarily stem from Crossan's reading of Bultmann, then, but may derive from their continuing influence in this post-Bultmannian current in New Testament scholarship, as well as from Crossan's own reading of Heidegger.

/18/   Crossan often refers to the Bultmannian distinction between Proclaimer and Proclaimed, and proposes a more language-oriented formulation: the One who proclaimed God in parable (or paradox) became the Parable (or Paradox) of God. Bultmann certainly viewed this "reversal" as only one aspect of metanoia: the disorientation of eschatological advent is to result in a new reorientation of life and action. Whether or not Crossan also intends to include both negative and positive moments in his discussion is at this point not clear.

/19/   John Dominic Crossan, *The Dark Interval: Towards a Theology of Story* (Niles, IL: Argus Communications, 1975), p. 121.

/20/   Ibid., p. 17.

/21/   Ibid., p. 9.

/22/   Ibid., p. 26.

/23/   Ibid., pp. 53–54.

/24/   Ibid., p. 57.

/25/   Ibid., pp. 37–39.

/26/   Ibid., pp. 40–41.

/27/   John Dominic Crossan, *Raid on the Articulate: Comic Eschatology in Jesus and Borges* (New York: Harper & Row, 1976), p. 60.

/28/   Crossan distinguishes between "religious" and "theological" language at several points, but the basis for this distinction is never clarified.

/29/   Crossan draws on Ricoeur's writings extensively. See Ricoeur's own analysis of the parable as religious discourse in *Semeia* 4 (1975): 29–148. See also David Tracy, *Blessed Rage for Order* (New York: Seabury Press, 1975), pp. 91–131.

/30/   Crossan, *Raid*, p. 34. Crossan is quoting Derrida's "Structure, Sign, and Play in the Discourse of the Human Sciences," in *The Languages of Criticism and the Sciences of Man*, ed. R. Macksey and E. Donato (Baltimore: Johns Hopkins University Press, 1970), p. 260.

/31/   John Dominic Crossan, *Cliffs of Fall: Paradox and Polyvalence in the Parables of Jesus* (New York: Seabury Press, 1980), p. 87.

/32/   Ibid., p. 94.

/33/   Stanley E. Fish, *Self-Consuming Artifacts* (Berkeley and Los Angeles: University of California Press, 1972).

/34/   John Dominic Crossan, *Finding Is the First Act: Trove Folktales and Jesus' Treasure Parable*, Semeia Supplements, no. 9 (Missoula, Montana: Scholars Press and Philadelphia: Fortress Press, 1979), p. 120. In this and the following analysis of the parable of The Sower, Crossan never makes plain whether he is claiming that this particular parable, all of Jesus' parables, or all parables, function in this way.

TER

/35/ Crossan, *Raid*, p. 127. This analysis is worked out in detail in Crossan, *Cliffs*, pp. 25–64.

/36/ Crossan, *Raid*, p. 44.

/37/ Ibid., p. 49. See William A. Beardslee's perceptive reading of Crossan in relation to the Desert Fathers and Zen Buddhism, "Parable, Proverb, Koan," in *Semeia* 12, part 1 (1978): 151–77.

/38/ "Indeed it is a very great pity that Judaism gave Jesus up so early to Christianity," Crossan continues. "It is a great pity for Christianity." *Raid*, p. 179. While Crossan's Jesus may represent "an iconoclasm on all the major forms of his spiritual tradition" (*Raid*, p. 77), Crossan himself here stands squarely in the tradition of nineteenth-century liberal New Testament scholarship, seeking the "religion of Jesus" behind the corrupting overlay of primitive Christianity.

/39/ Meyer H. Abrams, "How to Do Things with Texts," *Partisan Review* 46 (1979): 574.

/40/ Crossan, *Cliffs*, pp. 9–10.

/41/ Jacques Derrida, *Writing and Difference*, trans. Alan Bass (Chicago: University of Chicago Press, 1978), p. 297. Quoted in *Cliffs*, p. 10. It is obvious that Crossan's desire to fix the historical Jesus as the author of these "metaparables" is another such hypostatization, and a clear departure from Derrida.

/42/ Franz Kafka, *Parables and Paradoxes*, bilingual ed. (New York: Schocken Press, 1961), pp. 92–93. My interpretation of the parable is indebted to Geoffrey Hartman, *Beyond Formalism*, pp. 22–23.

/43/ Frei, *Eclipse*, p. 10.

/44/ Hans W. Frei, *The Identity of Jesus Christ* (Philadelphia: Fortress Press, 1975). A major portion of this study was previously published as "The Mystery and Presence of Christ" in *Crossroads* (January–March 1967). See also Frei's essay "Theological Reflections on the Accounts of Jesus' Death and Resurrection," *Christian Scholar* 49 (Winter 1966): 263–306.

/45/ *Eclipse*, p. 13.

/46/ Ibid., p. 14. Cf. Erich Auerbach, *Mimesis* (Princeton: Princeton University Press, 1968), p. 44.

/47/ Eclipse, p. 15.

/48/ Ibid., p. 14.

/49/   Ibid., pp. 280–81; 13.

/50/   Ibid., p. 3.

/51/   Ibid., p. 3. Cf. *Mimesis*, pp. 13–15.

/52/   *Eclipse*, pp. 28–29. Cf. *Mimesis*, pp. 73, 555.

/53/   *Eclipse*, p. 29.

/54/   Ibid., p. 36. Cf. *Mimesis*, p. 48.

/55/   *Eclipse*, pp. 4–5.

/56/   Ibid., pp. 127–28.

/57/   Ibid., p. viii.

/58/   Ibid.

/59/   Hans W. Frei, "The Availability of Karl Barth," review of *Karl Barth: His Life from Letters and Autobiographical Texts*, by Eberhard Busch, in *The New Review of Books and Religion* 1 (December 1976): 8.

/60/   Ibid.

/61/   *Identity*, p. xi.

/62/   *Eclipse*, pp. 283–84.

/63/   Ibid., p. 293.

/64/   Ibid., p. 290.

/65/   Ibid, p. 304.

/66/   Ibid., p. 306.

/67/   *Identity*, pp. xvi, xii.

/68/   Ibid., pp. 29–33.

/69/   Ibid., p. xv.

/70/   Ibid., pp. xvi–xvii.

/71/   Ibid., p. 88.

/72/   Ibid., pp. 37–38.

/73/   Ibid., pp. 91–93.

/74/   Ibid., pp. 94–101.

/75/   Ibid., p. 100.

/76/   Ibid., p. 101.

/77/   On this point see Beardslee, *Literary Criticism of the New Testament*, pp. 80–81.

/78/   *Identity*, pp. 107–8.

/79/   Cf. Karl Barth's exegeses of the passion-resurrection sequence in *Church Dogmatics*, 13 vols. (Edinburgh: T & T Clark, 1957–1969), 4/1, p. 224; 4/2, p. 219. See also the following essays on Barth's hermeneutics which adopt a perspective similar to that of Frei: David H. Kelsey, *The Uses of Scripture in Recent Thrology*, pp. 39–50, and D. F. Ford, "Barth's Interpretation of the Bible," in *Karl Barth: Studies of His Theological Method*, ed. by S. W. Sykes (Oxford: Clarendon Press, 1979), pp. 55–87. An excellent study of Barth's hermeneutics is that of Rudolf Smend, "Nachkritische Schriftauslegung," in *Parrhesia, Karl Barth zum 80. Geburstag*, ed. Eberhard Busch (Zurich: EVZ Verlag, 1966), pp. 215–37.

/80/   *Identity*, pp. 145–46.

/81/   Ibid., p. 151.

/82/   Ibid., p. 143.

/83/   Cf. Ford, "Barth's Interpretation," pp. 81–82.

/84/   See John E. Zuck's critique of Frei's notion of myth, "Tales of Wonder: Biblical Narrative, Myth, and Fairy Stories," *Journal of the American Academy of Religion* 44 (1976): 299–308.

/85/   A helpful survey of the history of literary criticism is that of Wimsatt and Brooks. See esp. pp. 313–38, on Samuel Johnson and English Neo-Classicism.

/86/   Frei simply assumes here that modern novelists *intend* to render Jesus' identity. That the Christ-figure phenomenon is more complex than this is amply demonstrated by Theodore Ziolkowski's study, *Fictional Transfigurations of Jesus* (Princeton: Princeton University Press, 1972).

/87/   Compare Hirsch's criticisms of stylistics in this regard in *Aims*, pp. 50–73.

/88/   For an excellent assessment of the importance of genre in literary criticism, see Mary Gerhart, "Generic Studies: Their Renewed Importance in Religious and Literary Interpretation," *Journal of the American Academy of Religion* 45 (1977): 309–25.

/89/   See Wellek and Warren, *Theory of Literature*, pp. 5–8.

/90/   *Eclipse*, pp. 36, 34.

/91/   Ibid., p. 35.

/92/   Dan Otto Via, Jr., *The Parables: Their Literary and Existential Dimension* (Philadelphia: Fortress Press, 1967) (hereafter this work will be cited as P). Via refers extensively to the writings of the New Critics, as well as to their critics. Among those he cites most frequently are: Murray Krieger, Elizabeth Sewall, Eliseo Vivas, Wimsatt and Beardsley, Northrop Frye, and Wellek and Warren.

/93/   P, pp. 24, 22.

/94/   P, pp. 23–24.

/95/   P, p. 77.

/96/   P, pp. 77, 76.

/97/   P, pp. 70–71, 79.

/98/   P, p. 84. Via thus shares the analysis of the New Criticism spelled out in greater detail in Chapter II.

/99/   P, p. 82.

/100/   P, p. 45.

/101/   P, p. 87.

/102/   P, p. 94. This view has been put forward by a number of scholars who have argued for the pertinence, and even the necessity, of theology for literary criticism. Via has found the writings of Nathan A. Scott, Jr. most helpful in this regard. See, for example, Scott's *The Climate of Faith in Modern Literature* (New York: Seabury Press, 1964), and *Modern Literature and the Religious Frontier* (New York: Harper & Row, 1958).

/103/   P, p. 56.

/104/   Cf. Philip Wheelright's analysis of the varying "assertorial weights" found in literary art, in *The Burning Fountain*, Rev. ed. (Bloomington: Indiana University Press, 1968), pp. 92–96, 193–94, 200, 241.

/105/ Two scholars who have developed similar views of the literary work and its interpretation are Giles B. Gunn and Paul Ricoeur. See Gunn's introduction to his *Literature and Religion*, and his *The Interpretation of Otherness* (New York: Oxford University Press, 1979). Ricoeur's views are outlined in the following chapter.

/106/ P, p. 27.

/107/ Via does disagree with several of Stendahl's conclusions in a note, p. 29, but that dialogue does not pertain to this discussion.

/108/ P, p. 29.

/109/ P, pp. 31–32.

/110/ P, p. 30, 32.

/111/ P, p. 32.

/112/ P, p. 32.

/113/ P, p. 33.

/114/ P, p. 33.

/115/ P, pp. 43–44.

/116/ P, p. 44.

/117/ Northrop Frye, *Anatomy of Criticism* (Princeton: Princeton University Press, 1957).

/118/ P, p. 96.

/119/ P, p. 98.

/120/ P, p. 101.

/121/ Via discusses the parable of The Talents on pp. 113–22.

/122/ The analysis of this parable appears on pp. 155–62.

/123/ P, p. 105.

/124/ P, p. 106. Via's discussion of the religious referent of the parables includes a lengthy "detour" in which he cites the philosophical debates concerning religious language among Flew, MacIntyre, Ramsey, Crombie, and others. Via relates Ramsey's notion of the "qualifier" to the "extraordinary" elements in the parables, and makes use of Crombie's description of the "parabolic" nature of theological discourse.

The detour, though interesting in itself, does not advance Via's argument in any significant way. See pp. 57–69.

/125/ P, p. 95.

/126/ P, p. 122.

CHAPTER IV
RETHINKING BIBLICAL HERMENEUTICS

The desire to canonize secular literature, to see it as a kind of continuing Bible, marks much modern literary criticism. As Robert Langbaum has observed, modern literary criticism rests on the assumption that literature "is the only continuing source of revelation, the only value-making, as opposed to value-remembering or value-describing, force in the modern world."/1/ Behind this assumption lie not only the imperious march of secularization and the increasing tendencies toward scientism in the modern period, but also the elevation of the productive imagination to a central place. As we have seen, the New Criticism, along with other formalist modes of literary theory, shifted the Romantics' psychological elaboration of the special capacities of the imagination in the artistic personality to poetic language. The special "logic" of the imagination is now the peculiar logic, and illogic, of poetic discourse, with metaphor as the primary principle of poetry. The literary work viewed as an autonomous, aesthetic organism distinct from all other forms of discourse and modes of thought, becomes a serious vehicle of knowledge which can rival science in its capacity to disclose truth, rescue the "world's body" from abstractions, and create and reveal the values that console and sustain us.

The ironies in this development with regard to both literary and biblical interpretation have been explored in previous chapters. While secular literary critics increasingly turned to literature as the source for cultural redemption, they also tended to describe the nature and understanding of literature in exclusively formalist terms, making it difficult to account for their assertion of literary art's revelatory and transformative potential. Furthermore, the same secularizing forces which provoked artists and critics to look to the languages of the imagination prompted biblical scholars to treat the biblical writings as one collection of secular texts among others. Since modern biblical scholars for the most part viewed the biblical writings as historical documents, with historical criticism the paradigmatic method of study, the question of how these texts could be spoken of as the source or vehicle of revelation became a central problem.

While the nineteenth-century liberals could still assert that what was of ultimate importance for Christians were the life and teachings of the historical Jesus to be discovered in, or at least "behind," the biblical documents, subsequent scholarship made it impossible to view the biblical texts as reliable biographical sources—,and thus undercut their solution to the problem of revelation as well. Bultmann's radical modernity lay in the way he shifted the question of revelation away from Scripture to an "event" in the believer's existential self-understanding. For both pre-critical interpreters and the nineteenth-century liberals, in different ways, Scripture was the locus of revelation. Bultmann, in contrast, extended the insights of both Luther and Schleiermacher to argue that revelation concerns the Word of God which is only "hidden" in, or "paradoxically related" to both historical events and the biblical texts themselves. The biblical writings can be studied as texts among other texts, for Bultmann, because revelation is no longer primarily a property of the writings, but instead a transformation of the existential awareness of the faithful individual.

In both modern literary criticism and liberal and neo-orthodox Christian theologies, the term 'revelation' thus assumed a central role. For the former, however, revelation concerned both the imagination and literary *texts*. Among the theologians, in contrast, reflection on revelation was conducted in primarily epistemological terms, focusing on the need for an appropriate second-order conceptual language for a radically historical revelation. The complex relation between the first order religious discourse of the Scriptures, as expressions of the actual originating experience of revelation, received little attention, and the role of the imagination in the experience and expression of revelation was generally ignored./2/

The question of how the biblical texts are to be studied is therefore inextricably related to the problem of the locus of revelation. When the Reformers rejected pre-critical allegory for grammatical-historical study, they laid the basis for secular literary criticism as well: in contrast to the presupposition of the allegorists that literary form does not necessarily, or directly, express the whole of the meaning of the biblical texts, the Reformers (and the modern New Critics) assumed that if one can describe the formal language of a text, its meaning is grasped as well.

Bultmann's hermeneutical program, as we have seen, is in one sense a return to certain pre-critical assumptions. He could address the problem of the foreignness of the biblical texts by arguing that their content is not bound to the original forms in which they were expressed. This assumption, together with the distinctively modern awareness that an interpreter's pre-understanding of the content or "subject matter" of a text is a condition for the appropriation of its meaning, sets his program apart from both the Reformers and the modern New Critics in this regard— grammatical-historical exegesis is insufficient for the full task of interpretation. While Bultmann could in this way argue that it is possible to recover the meaningfulness of the biblical writings for the present, the question of their relation to revelation was not explored adequately. His efforts toward a notion of analogical language outline a direction for further inquiry, by pointing to the question of how the texts themselves may be expressions of and vehicles for the experience of revelation.

Appropriation of the theories and practices of modern literary theory has potential significance for both biblical studies and Christian theology at precisely this point. Attention to the way particular literary forms in the biblical texts shape and disclose their meaning not only opens the way for an enriched understanding of these confessional documents, but introduces a new source for reflection on the relation between the languages of the imagination and the experience and expression of revelation. The promise of this kind of inquiry lies partly in the possibilities it offers for returning the locus of revelation to the scriptural texts themselves.

The case studies considered above indicate not only the promise, but also the difficulties, entailed by such a shift in critical assumptions, however. The specific limitations of formalist literary theory for the larger task of biblical interpretation are, I hope, now clear. The central difficulty, to restate it briefly, is that the centripetal focus of New Critical theory—its stress on the autonomy, self-sufficiency, and objectivity of the literary work of art—tends to prevent literature from exercising those cognitive and thus transformative powers which this theory also wishes to claim for it. To describe adequately literature as a vehicle for transformative knowledge, the New Critics must provide a better account of the way literature is, in fact, experienced, understood, and appropriated by readers who stand within particular, ambiguous and shifting historical horizons. Without further elaboration of the interpretive dimensions of the literary situation the New Critics' notions of the meaning and the experience of literature remain unclear.

When New Critical theory is employed in the analysis of the New Testament texts, a variety of difficulties emerge. Since New Critical theory is itself unclear about how a literary text is related to contexts of meaning outside of it, biblical scholars appropriating these critical assumptions may repeat these ambiguities in their own work. Crossan's studies of the parables illustrated one form of this difficulty: his attempt to move from an analysis of the parables to a recovery of the "experience" of the historical Jesus contained some confusion about the relation between the parable as linguistic artifact and some reality outside of language. Frei's stress on the objectivity, uniqueness and closure of the Gospel narratives, on the other hand, left us with a number of questions about how one comes to understand and to be changed by a text whose autonomy is defended so resolutely.

A difficulty of another kind appears in the way these critical assumptions and specifically theological presuppositions can become intertwined. The limits of formalist theory are such that other interpretive assumptions are indeed required to complete the full task of biblical interpretation. This Via perceives and attempts to remedy, by correlating an "objective" moment of literary analysis with a Bultmannian hermeneutic designed to render the texts meaningful for the present. As both Via's and Crossan's studies demonstrate, however, Bultmann's theological and hermeneutical program, with its own specific strengths and weaknesses, is an uneasy ally of literary criticism. Via's project shows us how Bultmann's perceptions of the historical character of understanding, of the way certain texts imply an understanding of existence, and of the need to attend to the specifically religious referent of the biblical texts are important supplements to the New Critical program. At the same time, Via's inability to disentangle the positive aspects of Bultmann's theories from those in tension with the presuppositions of literary analysis—his desire to reduce or translate New Testament discourse into philosophical categories, for example—also demonstrates that further systematic reflection on the critical assumptions of both programs is required.

A final source of the difficulties which this kind of literary theory can provoke lies in the underlying affinities between the New Criticism and modern Protestant neo-orthodox theologies, specifically that of Bultmann. Reflecting the concerns of the same cultural period, these literary critics and theologians both tended to stress the ambiguities, conflicts, and sometimes even meaninglessness in the modern historical situation, while seeking a norm and agency for human redemption in the autonomous, paradoxical Otherness of the literary or kerygmatic word. This affinity, together with the difficulties which these programs share—the need to specify more adequately how this radically discontinuous word which must be "experienced" or "participated in" to be effective is related to our reflective awareness of the historical situation in which we already stand—can result in an exaggeration of the tendencies of both. Crossan's radicalization of the event character of revelation well beyond Bultmann, and his intensification of the paradoxical quality of metaphorical language to the point that it becomes the "self-consuming" vehicle for a purely negative experience of transcendence is an example of this possibility.

A conclusion to be drawn from this study, therefore, is that if one wishes to include a formalist program for literary analysis within the larger aim of biblical interpretation, further reflection on the critical assumptions underlying both aspects of the task is required. Nevertheless, the representatives of each program examined here, the New Criticism as an example of formalism, and Bultmann as a model of biblical hermeneutics, remain, in my view, valuable starting points for constructive efforts of this kind.

In this context, the work of the philosopher Paul Ricoeur is of exemplary significance. Ricoeur has developed an interpretation theory which provides a place for formalist literary analysis, as a moment of explanation, within a comprehensive model for the process of textual understanding which acknowledges the existential and historical dimensions of interpretation. Ricoeur has also reflected on the distinctive problems of interpreting biblical texts, on the relation between general and theological hermeneutics, and on specific theological concepts—revelation and testimony in particular—as they are related to the concerns of biblical interpretation. As we shall see, Ricoeur argues that revelation is a characteristic of the "world" the biblical texts themselves disclose through their linguistic forms. While Ricoeur argues, with Bultmann and the pre-critical allegorists, that a purely formal analysis of the texts is inadequate to grasp their meaning, he also maintains, in keeping with the formalist axioms of the New Critics, that the form and content of a text are generated and understood together. While Ricoeur's position does not represent the only way a biblical hermeneutic might be constructed, an analysis of his interpretation theory is an appropriate and helpful way to set out the basic issues which any constructive position must resolve./3/ This chapter therefore aims to delineate those aspects of Ricoeur's thought which in my view are of significance for rethinking biblical hermeneutics.

Ricoeur's Interpretation Theory

For the purposes of this study, it is not necessary to outline the development of Ricoeur's thought, and excellent discussions of the larger context of Ricoeur's reflections on interpretation are available elsewhere./4/ Don Ihde, for example, has shown how the "hermeneutical turn" first explicitly announced in Ricoeur's *The Symbolism of Evil* is anticipated in his earlier writings on the philosophy of the will, *Freedom and Nature* and *Finitude and Guilt*./5/ In *The Symbolism of Evil*, part two of the latter study, Ricoeur turned to a hermeneutic of the symbols of defilement, sin and guilt, and of the myths which interpret these symbols, because he discovered that direct reflection on the problems of guilt and evil was impossible. While we can use direct language to speak of purpose and motive, Ricoeur found, human fallibility can only be expressed in symbolic language. Thus reflection on the self can only proceed indirectly, through the detour of a hermeneutic of symbols. In both this study and *Freud and Philosophy*, his next major publication, Ricoeur "wagers" that a hermeneutics of symbol will lead "to a better understanding of man and of the bond between the being of man and the being of all beings."/6/

While these two projects initiate Ricoeur's investigations of the problems of language and interpretation, in both works hermeneutics is limited to the problem of interpreting symbolic language, and the task is undertaken to advance his larger philosophical project. *Freud and Philosophy*, however, goes beyond the earlier work's concern with specific symbols to explore the question of symbolic language in general and the cosmic, oneiric, and poetic dimensions of experience in which symbols appear. Here Ricoeur

also confronted what he calls "the conflictual structure of the hermeneutical task," or "the conflict of interpretations." Freud,
together with Marx, Nietzsche and Feurbach, are each in their
own way exponents of a "hermeneutics of suspicion," a theory of
reductive explanation and demystification. While Ricoeur's aim,
in contrast, is not to reduce but to retrieve or recollect the meaning
of symbols through a "hermeneutics of restoration," he recognizes
that the claims of the former must be acknowledged. Ricoeur is
therefore compelled to develop a broader comprehension of interpretation theory, one which can include both hermeneutical
demands while recognizing the proper limits of each./7/

The need to situate both critical and recollective moments
within the interpretive process, together with Ricoeur's continuing interest in the developing structuralist philosophies in
France, in the theologies of the Word of the post-Bultmannian
school, and in Anglo-American philosophies of ordinary language, have provoked Ricoeur to develop, or at least to begin to
construct, a general theory of interpretation, a theory for the
interpretation of written texts in particular./8/ While Ricoeur's
reflections on interpretation are undertaken within the general
context of a philosophy of language rather than of a philosophy
of the will, the final aim of his theory of the interpretation of
texts remains consistent with that of his initial philosophical
project—to understand human selfhood in the world. If reflection on the self can proceed only indirectly, by deciphering the
expressions in which life objectifies itself, nevertheless, Ricoeur
maintains, interpetation is a detour which will give rise to new
self-understanding. As he writes:

> It is the task of this hermeneutics to show that existence
> arrives at expression, at meaning, and at reflection only
> through the continual exegesis of all the significations
> that come to light in the world of culture. Existence
> becomes a self—human and adult—only by appropri-
> ating this meaning, which first resides 'outside' in works,
> institutions, and cultural monuments in which the life of
> the spirit is objectified./9/

Ricoeur's interpretation theory is developed in dialogue with
two partners, the linguistic sciences and the hermeneutic tradition
of Schleiermacher, Dilthey, Heidegger and Gadamer./10/ In
Ricoeur's view, the dual heritage of the latter in critical and
romantic philosophies has given rise to a persistent problem. From

Kant's Copernican revolution, which gave epistemology priority over ontology, and the subsequent growth of positivism, which made the empirical methods of the natural sciences the model for intelligibility, came the impulse which prompted Dilthey to seek for the human sciences a methodology for understanding which could rival the explanatory methods of the natural sciences. From romantic philosophy, however, came the fundamentally psychological aim for hermeneutics: to understand human "life" in its subjectivity and individuality, to understand the author of a text as well as, or better than, he understood himself.

Dilthey's antimony between explanation and understanding was displaced, but did not disappear, with Heidegger's second Copernican revolution, which reconceived the hermeneutical problem as one for a fundamental ontology. For Heidegger the proper question is not "how do we know?" but "what is that mode of being who only exists through understanding?" With this transfer of the problem of method to the problem of Being went another shift: the question of understanding no longer first concerns the psychic life of another, but rather one's being in the world, that tie to reality which is more fundamental than the subject-object relation that governs knowledge. With Heidegger, understanding becomes the "project" of unfolding the possibilities that inhere in the situation into which one is already "thrown." While Ricoeur will remain faithful to Heidegger in conceiving of understanding as concerned with the question of one's being in the world, rather than with communion with another psyche, he argues that Heidegger retains the antimony between explanation and understanding as well: the dichotomy now appears between ontology and epistemology taken as wholes, rather than between two modes of knowledge. In Ricoeur's view, Heidegger therefore cannot deal with vital methodological questions regarding the status of the human sciences, or with that "conflict of interpretations" with which Ricoeur is vitally concerned.

A central aim of Ricoeur's interpretation theory is to reconceive the relation between existential understanding and critical explanation, so that they appear in dialectical relation rather than opposition. Understanding calls for explanation, Ricoeur will argue, because the nature of discourse itself involves the objectification of meaning. Structuralist and other modes of explanation, on the other hand, are insufficient by themselves:

explanation is only a mediating moment between naive and critical phases of understanding.

One detour is appropriate before examining Ricoeur's proposals. Between Heidegger's ontological hermeneutic and Ricoeur's interpretation theory stands the monumental work of the German philosopher Hans Georg Gadamer, *Truth and Method*. While Ricoeur will provide his own corrections and extensions of Gadamer's hermeneutic theory, the latter's contributions to hermeneutic philosophy and to Ricoeur's own reflections deserve brief consideration here.

As many interpreters of Gadamer have noted, the title of his work might more appropriately read "truth *or* method," for Gadamer's study opposes a Heideggarian notion of truth as disclosure to the "alienating distanciation" which, in his view, grounds the objectivity of the human sciences. The alienation between subject and object implicit in the methods of these sciences, Gadamer argues, destroys the primordial relation of "participation" that characterizes our situation as historical beings.

Gadamer first turns to the work of art as the primary place to address the question of truth, because in his view the kind of truth resident in the experience of a work of art implies a fundamental connection between subject and object, between the work and one's experience of it. Gadamer therefore opposes all "aesthetic differentiation" which, in directing itself to the work alone, dissolves the connections between art and the world, abstracts what is aesthetically intended from all conditions which make the work accessible, and ignores the elements of its content that would induce one to take up an attitude toward it./11/ By insisting that the true mode of being of a work of art is its capacity to affect, to transform the one who experiences it, Gadamer counters the Enlightenment "prejudice against prejudices," and emphasizes the actual finitude and historicity of the experiencing subject.

The work of art has two ontological components, in Gadamer's analysis: it is a "transformation into structure" and it exists as a "self-representation." By the latter, Gadamer indicates that it is part of the work's nature to be a representation *for* someone. The one for whom a work is a representation, the one who experiences the work, thus has a share in its meaning.

The work's potentiality for significance (its "ideality of meaning") exists because the work is a "transformation into structure." Transformation refers to the total change of something into a new thing. In art, finite reality, which is always incomplete, standing in a horizon of still undecided possibilities, is transformed into a completed, meaningful whole. In this sense, the transformation of an aspect of reality into a work is a transformation of reality into the true; art raises up the infinite potentiality of meaning to truth. A work is essentially revelatory, for in it the essence of something is brought forth from all the chance and variable circumstances in everyday reality which condition and hide it. In Heideggerian language, in art "Being is brought to stand."/12/

This essence remains in the work as potential truth until it is "recognized." What one experiences in a work and what one is directed toward is how true it is, i.e., to what extent one knows and recognizes something there. Since a work is both a work and a self-representation, dependent for its truth on being recognized by an experiencer, it exists, in a sense, to always be different. But however much it is changed in each experience of it, the work still remains itself; it is like a game, which is essentially always itself and yet is always some particular persons playing. The recognition of a work's truth involves a tension between strangeness and familiarity, of discontinuity in continuity. The experiencer makes the work "contemporaneous" by entering the world of the work in "self-forgetfulness," and yet what is recognized there is the truth of one's own familiar world.

Gadamer extends this model to the understanding of texts, developing the anticipatory structure of understanding in terms of the "principle of effective history." Human beings always already belong to a particular history. In Heidegger's terms, we are a "thrown projection"; our experience of events and our attempts to grasp the meaning of a text are grounded, pre-reflectively, in the context and fabric of relations of our tradition, the "horizon" in which we think./13/ Gadamer speaks of the dialectic of strangeness and familiarity involved in the experience of art as the dialectic of the dialogue or conversation in relation to a text. We project our pre-understanding, our horizon, onto the text as an anticipation of the text's meaning; this is our response to the work's claim to possible truth. Only what stands under anticipation can be understood. There is a structure of question and answer to this dialogue: understanding is possible only as the self is also "self-forgetful," willing to seek out the subject matter of the text and to ask its proper question. Genuine dialogue occurs only when the subject matter of the text assumes primacy over the subjectivity of the reader: to question implies a not-knowing, which is to make the content of the work fluid, the possibility of its truth unsettled. Understanding requires, then, that one be both anticipatory and self-forgetful, knowing and not knowing. In this way the subject matter of the text can put the interpreter's projected horizon into question as well.

Texts, then, are dynamic, rather than static. They are "occasions" where the horizon of the text as intentional object meets and interacts with the horizon of the interpreter in dialogue. Understanding, which is always a happening, an event, is a consequence of this "fusion of horizons." What Gadamer is concerned to demonstrate here is that through this kind of dialectical process, *new* meaning emerges. As he writes: "It is enough to say that we understand in a different way if we understand at all."/14/ The interpretation of texts is always both a mediation of the past and a production of new meaning for the present in the light of the future. Tradition, our "effective history," is thus not a substance, but a moving fabric of inexhaustible possibility, made concrete in each particular, finite disclosure of meaning.

While Ricoeur's interpretation theory builds on the central insights of Gadamer's analysis of understanding, in Ricoeur's view Gadamer's model also gives rise to an untenable opposition between explanation and understanding, "alienating distanciation" and "participation."/15/ Gadamer forces us to choose between a methodological attitude that loses the ontological density of the reality under study, and the attitude of truth, which surrenders the objectivity of the human sciences. By positing a dialectical relation between explanation and understanding, Ricoeur intends to introduce a productive, non-alienating notion of distanciation, which in his view more adequately describes the tension between self and other, near and far, that occurs when historical understanding passes through the interpretation of the signs, works, and texts in which our traditions are inscribed.

Ricoeur's interpretation theory, then, attempts to be responsible to both the explanatory methods of the human and linguistic sciences—particularly those of structuralism—and the wider existential and ontological concerns reflected in Heidegger's and Gadamer's notions of understanding. While it would therefore be incorrect to suggest that Ricoeur's theory directly sets out to relate this study's specific examples of formalist method and hermeneutics, the New Critics and Bultmann, it will be possible to view

Ricoeur's work as an indirect clarification, extension, and integration of these programs. Once Ricoeur's proposals have been examined more closely, the relation between his interpretation theory and our examples can be considered.

Structuralism, with which Ricoeur is directly concerned, can be viewed as a radicalization of the specifically formalist traits of New Critical theory./16/ When the Swiss linguist, Ferdinard de Saussure, distinguished *langue*, language considered as a synchronic system or code, from *parole*, the message a particular speaker produces, he laid the foundation for linguistics as a scientific method of investigation. Bracketing the temporal, contingent, intentional and referential characteristics of language, as language is actualized in speech, the linguistic model was extended beyond phonological systems and the lexicon of natural languages to linguistic entities larger than the sentence, as in the treatment of folktales by the Russian formalists, or in Lévi-Strauss's structural analyses of myth.

The New Critics' stress on the "objective" character of poetry and criticism, and their focus on the linguistic medium of poetry become, with structuralism, the objectivity of scientific study, with the semiotic system the object of investigation. For the New Critics, the literary work is a closed, autonomous whole, existing in a timeless literary universe, the meaning of each of its elements derived from its relation to the whole. For the structuralists, more radically, it is the code that is viewed as an atemporal, self-sufficient system, the meaning of any entity within the system a result of its opposition to other entities within the same system. Where the New Critics minimized the importance of the author's intention, and insisted, with their dictum against the heresy of paraphrase, that the meaning of a work is inseparable from its formal structure, the structuralists maintain that the semiotic system is anonymous, and that there is no meaning or message distinct from the code itself.

In Ricoeur's view, the price which linguistics must pay to constitute itself as a science is high./17/ It must suppress what is for Ricoeur the essential aspect of language: its capacity to produce new enunciations, and thus to generate and mediate that living tradition by which a cultural community is constituted and by means of which it interprets itself. In contrast to the principles of the linguistic sciences, Ricoeur insists that language appears as what it essentially is only when it is *used*. As discourse, Ricoeur maintains, language is essentially a mediation—that through which, and by means of which, we express ourselves and express things. The experience we have of language, both in ordinary speech and in literature, shows us that language is not a world of its own; rather, because we are already in the world, we have experience to bring to language. Language, in other words, is related to our ontological condition of being in the world: because we are in the world, we not only have something to say, but we have something to speak about. Discourse, in Ricoeur's view, is fundamentally referential; it intends to say something about the world.

Ricoeur's critique of Lévi-Strauss illustrates his insistence on the ontological foundation and destiny of discourse./18/ For Lévi-Strauss, myth, like the rest of language as it is conceived by linguistic study, is made up of constituent units, "mythemes," which can be analyzed according to the rules that apply to smaller linguistic units such as phonemes, morphemes, or sememes. Just as the latter entities have "meaning" only as oppositive values within the system, so mythemes have "meaning" only as they are related to other mythemes within a "bundle of relations." Analyzed this way, myth appears as a kind of logical instrument that draws together contradictions in order to overcome them.

Ricoeur's main criticism of Lévi-Strauss is that his kind of formal analysis presupposes the real existential conflicts within human experience which the immanent "logic" of myth attempts to solve. Unless birth and death, blindness and lucidity, for example, were already meaningful oppositions, having their source and ultimate referent in the boundary situations of humankind, then myth would have no contradictions to overcome; it would have no logical function. In Ricoeur's view, Lévi-Strauss's structural analyses of myth, like all analyses based on the theoretical postulates of linguistics, is an abstraction from, and depends upon, the fact that myths, stories, and indeed all discourse, arise from and are directed toward human experience in and of the world. Ricoeur thus shares the non-formalist aim of the New Critics: to describe how poetry arises from and addresses that "recalcitrant and contradictory context" which is our situation./19/

Ricoeur's insistence on the ontological foundation of language, it should be noted, not only sets his program in opposition to that of structuralism, but to the presuppositions of both "deconstructionist" and "reader response" criticism as well. Ricoeur argues against Derrida and others, as he does against Lévi-Strauss, that there *is* an "outside-the-text" to which language refers. Ricoeur's investigations in *The Symbolism of Evil* and *Freud and Philosophy* examine the way in which symbolic language both arises from and is always already incipiently embedded in human experience. These studies are the indirect foundation for Ricoeur's disagreement with Derrida. In the latter's view, of course, Ricoeur's argument here is another form of the nostalgic quest for "presence" that marks the western philosophical tradition. Derrida's deconstruction of this nostalgia rests on his contention that metaphoricity pervades language to such an extent that there is no escape from the "free-play" of intersignification; it is impossible to give a non-metaphorical account of the real. Ricoeur argues that Derrida overlooks the distinction between "live" and "dead" metaphors, and that Derrida's thesis of the infinite circularity of language relies on an analysis of the latter alone. In Ricoeur's view, dead, worn out metaphors are no longer metaphors—they language. *Live* metaphors can, and do, generate new insights with genuinely new cognitive content, without being caught in the infinite regress of circularity, because metaphors emerge from a contrast with the literal, or usual, meaning of words in a specific time and culture. Metaphor—and new insight—is born from the collapse of literal meaning; all language is not, as Derrida maintains, wholly metaphorical./20/

Nevertheless, Ricoeur accepts structuralism and other formalist modes of literary criticism as both possible and legitimate approaches to a text. From the perspective of the production of discourse, as it is actualized in ordinary conversation, as it is inscribed in writing, and finally as it is composed as a literary work, we see that there is an objective character to meaning which makes communication possible, and which is the condition for both the possibility and necessity of explanatory methods such as structuralism. As will become clear below, Ricoeur's insistence on the objective dimension of literary meaning—and here he stands with the New Critics—distinguishes his program from all critical orientations which define meaning wholly in terms of the reader's consciousness or response—from those recent advocates of a *Rezeptionsaesthetik* as well as from the dangers to which Bultmann's demythologizing program is prone./21/

Even in spoken discourse, Ricoeur argues, we find a dialectic of "event" and "meaning." By the "event" character of discourse Ricoeur means all of those qualities that distinguish language as it is actualized in communication from its merely virtual existence as a semiotic system: discourse is the event of saying something by someone to another. This event is not merely transitory, however, because it has a meaning, a propositional content, that remains and can be identified and reidentified as the same when the "saying" itself has been completed. "If discourse is actualized as event," Ricoeur asserts, "it is understood as meaning."/22/

Meaning, for Ricoeur, includes, after Frege, both "sense"—the "what" is said immanent in the sentence—and "reference"—the "about what" of discourse—where reference relates language both back to the speaker and to the world. The meaning, or sense and reference, of discourse thus fixes and preserves the *event* of saying. Ricoeur speaks of this process of fixation and preservation of the event of saying as its "exteriorizaton" or "distanciation." Because the intention to speak about something is exteriorized in a fixed meaning, communication is possible.

This dialectic of event and meaning becomes more explicit when discourse is written. Here, the semantic autonomy of meaning merely implicit in the dialogical situation of oral speech makes possible the communication of meaning across temporal and cultural distance. In Ricoeur's words, "writing is the full manifestation of discourse."/23/ The changes which writing introduces in the discourse situation are especially apparent if we consider writing as a direct form of discourse, rather than as a transcription of previously spoken language. When the speaker-hearer relationship is replaced by that of writer-reader, the meaning fixed in the text transcends and escapes the intentions of the author and its original audience and situation. The semantic autonomy of the text also opens it to be recontextualized by new readers in widely divergent socio-cultural contexts.

The most complex changes brought by the exteriorization of discourse in writing concern the question of reference. Partners in dialogue belong to a present and common situation, so that the referent of discourse can be pointed to, or indicated with grammatical devices such as the demonstratives, adverbs of time and place, and the verb tenses. When the spatial and temporal distance between writer and reader replaces the shared situation of speaker and hearer, however, the referent of a text is freed from the limits of ostensive reference. Ricoeur proposes that the referent of a text be thought of not as "behind it," in its author's intention or its genetic context, nor simply immanent "within" its sense, but rather as the kind of world the text displays or projects "in front" of it./24/ Thanks to writing, Ricoeur suggests, human beings, and only human beings, have a world and not just a situation. This world, he writes, "is the ensemble of references opened up by every kind of text, descriptive or poetic, that I have read, understood, and loved."/25/

The distance between event and meaning entailed by the passage from speaking to writing ("distanciation") becomes yet more complex when written discourse is composed as a work./26/ As Ricoeur notes, the term *work*, and the distinctive traits it possesses as a structured, closed totality—composition, belonging to a genre, and individual style—are categories of production and labor; in a work, language becomes material to be shaped and formed. With Kant and the New Critics, Ricoeur compares the structure of a work of art to a living organism, a teleological system of whole and parts, composed in a hierarchy of ordered relationships. Ricoeur stresses the importance of the role of genre in producing discourse as a work, when genre is viewed not as a set of classificatory devices for mastering the chaos of individual works already in existence, but as the generative "rules" of codification according to which discourse is produced as a poem, essay, narrative, or other form. The generative rather than the taxonomic function of literary genres is the key, for Ricoeur, in explaining what the New Critics described as the inseparability of form and content in a literary work. Content and form are generated together; the dynamics of form is at the same time a dynamics of thought.

A second important function of genre is its role in mediating the meaning of a work to its readers. As the meaning of discourse is fixed and preserved in writing, and then in a work, in increasingly complex ways, the problem of understanding the meaning becomes correspondingly greater. Even in oral discourse, we are already confronted with a need for interpretation, since language is, by nature, polysemous./27/ The plurality of possible meanings for any word in a lexical system can be partially limited by its use within a sentence, and by the context of the situation in which it is spoken. While some ambiguity remains even here, the dialogical situation of oral discourse makes it possible for partners to clarify their meanings through conversation. Even at this level, however, it is important to note that for Ricoeur, and in contrast to the psychological formulation of romantic hermeneutics, what is to be understood is the meaning (both as sense and reference) of the discourse, not the mental intention of the speaker. Because the event of intending to say is embodied in the "said," understanding takes place in a properly semantic space, not a psychological one./28/

New levels of ambiguity are introduced when writing frees discourse from the context of its author and original situation. From the perspective of the act of reading, genre becomes an important instrument of distanciation for both writer and reader. By virtue of its generic form, a work does not perish with the loss of its original situation, but is preserved from distortion and is available to be understood in new situations. The decontextualization necessary for the preservation of meaning at the same time creates both the need for, and the possibility of new interpretations, as the text is subsequently recontextualized in new situations by new readers. The event character of discourse does not disappear even with the further distanciation made possible by formal composition, however. The author's presence is conveyed by the distinctive style inscribed in the individual formal structure of the work, so that the author becomes, in Wayne Booth's terms, the author "implied" by the work itself./29/

The distanciaton of the speech event in the production of meaning through semantics, syntax, genre and style thus corresponds, in Ricoeur's view, to the dialectic of explanation and understanding in the act of reading. Because, as Ricoeur astutely perceives, a text is a structured totality rather than a linear succession of sentences, and because the author's intention is beyond our reach, we must reconstruct the text's architecture by relating parts to whole and whole to parts./30/ In this procedure, as in the process of constructing the meaning of a metaphor, we must rely on the clues contained in the semantic, syntactical, generic and stylistic structures of the work./31/ Here explanatory methods such as structuralism or the formal analyses of the New Critics have their necessary and proper function. "Explanation," as Ricoeur writes, "is henceforth the required path to understanding."/32/

Nevertheless, as Ricoeur's criticisms of structuralism indicate, explanation remains a mediating moment corresponding to the distanciation of meaning in writing, between a naive understanding and a critical one. Understanding "envelops" the process of explanation, so that the "hermeneutical arc" as Ricoeur conceives it is one of understanding-explanation-understanding. For what is finally understood in a text is not only the immanent sense that formal analysis reconstructs, but its referent, the world the text displays through its sense. "To understand a text," Ricoeur argues, "is to follow its movement from sense to referent: from what it says, to what it talks about."/33/

This is so in an especially complex way with fictional and poetic literature, which seem to abolish all reference to ordinary reality. Even here, Ricoeur maintains, fiction refers to the real at a more fundamental level. The abolition of a "first-order" reference accomplished by fiction and poetry is the condition of the possibility for the liberation of a "second order" reference at the level of what Husserl called the *Lebenswelt* and Heidegger "being in the world." Poetic and fictional texts make possible a distanciation of the real from itself: they intend Being, but do so in the "mode of possibility" rather than of givenness. Like both a metaphor and the theoretical models of science, a literary text works a special kind of poetic *mimesis*. It does not duplicate reality, but recreates it according to its own particular *mythos*—that immanent sense through which it reaches the deepest essence of the real./34/

The methodological dialectic of explanation and understanding is thus also an existential one: the text is a mediation by which we understand ourselves. Here Ricoeur rejoins the ontological concerns of Heidegger and Gadamer and the over-arching non-formalist aim of the New Criticism. To understand is to rescue the cultural heritages of the past from the alienation of distance, to make one's own what is other by actualizing the meaning of the text in the present. Ricoeur has not outlined the details of this process in the way that he has for the dialectic of event and meaning in the production of discourse, and his model is perhaps best seen as an extension and modification of Gadamer's theory at this point. For both, the interpreter already stands within a horizon of meanings, an effective history: one belongs to history before one belongs to oneself. For both, understanding therefore has an anticipatory structure; to experience or participate in a text means that I enter the work with some pre-understanding of its subject matter, and submit to its claim to be a truth addressed to me personally, here and now. To interpret is not to leave history but to be radically conscious of it, and in this consciousness to "wager" that a particular text, rooted in its own historical time, has something to say to me now as I come to it with my own questions and attempt to interpret its questions and responses. As will be seen in more detail below, this way of recovering meaning for the present does not fall prey to the dangers of Bultmann's program of demythologizing because for Ricoeur form and meaning are both generated and understood together. One's pre-understanding is itself subjected to a moment of distanciation and explanation, corresponding to the objectification of meaning in the text, as one's understanding passes through the explication of the text's formal structure.

For both philosophers, finally, the ultimate aim of interpretation is an appropriation of the text which gives rise to a new self-understanding. As Ricoeur writes: "Interpretation is completed as appropriation when reading yields something like an event . . . which is an event in the present moment."/35/ Thanks to the kind of dispossession of the self which explanation requires, however, to interpret is not to read one's prior self-understanding into the text, but to discover, as one is challenged and provoked by the text's proposed world, a new possible way of understanding oneself in the world. At this final level, to understand is to understand oneself before the text, to expose oneself to the text in order to receive from it a self. As Ricoeur writes:

> This implies that the reader does not submit the meaning of the text to his own finite capacity for understanding, but that he lets himself be exposed to the text, in order to receive from it a *Self*. I mean a non-egoistic, non-narcissistic, non-imperialistic mode of subjectivity which responds and corresponds to the power of the work to display a *world*. The *Self* is the correlate of the 'thing' of the text./36/

The hermeneutical circle of the romantic hermeneutic tradition is not denied, but displaced, from a subjective to an ontological level. As Ricoeur explains: "The circle is between my way . . . of being—beyond the knowledge which I may have of it—and the mode . . . of being disclosed by the text as the work's world."/37/ This Ricoeur asserts in full awareness of the opposing claims of those original masters of suspicion, Freud, Nietzsche and Marx, and over against the more recent claims of Derrida and other deconstructionists. For, to repeat, in Ricoeur's view such appropriation is only the final stage of an interpretive process which has passed through a *critical* moment of explanation. In contrast to Gadamer, Ricoeur emphasizes that interpretation of the past is always communication through a distance which is not simply alienating, but productive as well. Because a text is a formal, structured whole, autonomous with respect to its author and original situation, it involves potential horizons of meaning which may be actualized, or constructed, in different ways. This process, Ricoeur insists, is a critical process, involving both discernment and judgment about the nature of the intention of the text as a whole, and of the relative importance of each of the work's partial meanings within it. Explanatory methods such as structuralism and the formalist analyses of the New Criticism serve to "develop," or explicate, the various possible ways the text may be construed.

Explanation must involve more than this, however, if Ricoeur is to deal adequately with the possible "conflict of interpretations" operative in both the interpreters' pre-understandings and in the various methods of explanation applied to a text. While the particular "prejudices" of one's pre-understanding will be exposed and challenged by the distanciating process of critical explanation, these methods are themselves always informed by particular value judgments, which become explicit when one examines the different interpretations of a text's subject matter, or world, to which they give rise./38/ The New Critics, for example, found that those literary works deserving the most positive evaluation were "about" the complexities, conflicts, and ambiguities of human experience, rendered through formal strategies such as irony, paradox, and "dramatic structure." Ricoeur's theory of interpretation thus makes room not only for explanatory methods, but for a plurality of complementary and conflicting accounts of a text's sense, and through that sense, the referent that the work displays in front of it.

There are two points to be noted here, each deserving further reflection than Ricoeur has given them thus far. First, it is clear that Ricoeur's central interest in the problem of the "conflict of interpretations" in his earlier writings enters his theory of the text at this point: the polysemous nature of a work, whose sense and referent can be construed in various ways, seems to demand that a genuine *pluralism* of explanations be part of the interpretive process. Just as the meaning of a metaphor emerges out of the "clash" of literal meanings, so, Ricoeur seems to suggest, an interpreter's construction of the meaning of a text will be richer when it emerges from, and indeed is earned by, a wrestling with the various contents and conflicting contexts that different methods provide./39/ Furthermore, Ricoeur's stress on the interpreter as always already situated in a culture, a history, a community, would also seem to encourage an interpreter to enter into conversation with the wider community of readers whose varying pre-understandings may conflict with, complement, challenge, and thus transform, her own.

A second question concerns the problem E. D. Hirsch calls "validity" in interpretation: while a text is open to a number of possible constructions, not all readings will be probable, and some will be more probable than others. Ricoeur has given only a few hints about the criteria necessary for judging the adequacy of one's interpretation of a text. With Hirsch, he agrees that the procedures for validation are closer to a logic of probability than to a logic of empirical verification. The role of falsification in the former, Ricoeur further notes, will be played by the conflict between competing interpretations—one will argue for or against an interpretation, confront alternative interpretations, and attempt to arbitrate between them and to seek agreement, even if agreement remains beyond immediate reach. Of the "criteria of relative superiority" on which such arguments could be based, Ricoeur suggests only that that interpretation is most probable which "accounts for the greatest number of facts provided by the text, including potential connotations," and "offers a better qualitative convergence between the traits which it takes into account: a poor explication may be said to be narrow or far-fetched." A good explication will also satisfy the principle of "plenitude": "all the connotations that can fit are to be attached; the poem means all that it can mean."/40/

This last principle also points to a final and crucial way in which critical explanation is part of the interpretive process. When (and only when) the possible meanings of a text have been construed through explanation, we return to the final phase of interpretation: understanding as appropriation of the text's proposed world. Here we meet again the text's proposal as a claim to truth: is this possible way of being in the world one I wish to adopt as my own? While we may interpret a work's sense and referent, and reconstruct the model of reality it creates and reveals in a mode of "as-if," to actualize the text as an event in the present is to risk moving from the status of aesthetic spectator to decision. At this point the task of criticism becomes properly ethical, philosophical, and, at the limit, theological. As it was suggested in the analysis of the New Criticism in Chapter II, as Dan Via argued in his critique of formalism, and as Bultmann recognized with his insistence on the need for "content criticism," so Ricoeur maintains that genuine understanding finally requires that we reckon with the text as an understanding of existence, or a vision of the whole, by placing it in conversation with the understandings of existence set out by ethicists, philosophers and theologians. Ricoeur thus suggests that the appropriation of the meaning of a text will not be "authentic" unless understanding has allowed itself to pass through a process of interpretation which involves the comparison and conflict of possible ways to construe the text's meaning. With regard to the biblical writings, this clearly implies that no appropriation is earned if it has not been engaged with possible reductive explanations of the text. Beyond the question of appropriation lies the question of truth—can the respective understandings of existence of Shakespeare, Melville and Auden all be true? The question of truth at this level, Ricoeur seems to suggest, lies beyond the task of interpretation; it is the province of philosophical thought./41/

Ricoeur and the New Critics

Insofar as Ricoeur's hermeneutic is a theory for the interpretation of literary texts, it has striking affinities with the New Critics' proposals. As a philosophical hermeneutic, it seems to me, Ricoeur's interpretation theory offers a conceptual foundation for the New Critical program as a whole, while providing a clarification and extension of those aspects of their theory which remained inadequately formulated. Ricoeur and the New Critics share a general orientation and intention. Both uphold the distinctive capacity of poetic texts to provide a kind of knowledge beyond that available to direct reflection, and inexpressible in ordinary or scientific language. Literature, for both, confounds our modern tendency to construe the world in terms of the Cartesian dichotomy between sovereign consciousness and an objectivized, manipulable nature. The language with which the New Critics describe literature's disclosive power is various and often imprecise: literature embodies an "ontological insight," it provides knowledge of a "mythical order," it reveals a "more original world" than the one we commonly inhabit. Ricoeur clearly shares this aim, and articulates it in philosophical terms. As we have seen, literary texts, in Ricoeur's view, refer to the world at a level more fundamental than that of manipulable objects—they disclose what Husserl spoke of as the *Lebenswelt*, and Heidegger as "being-in-the-world." As he writes:

> My deepest conviction is that poetic language alone restores to us that participation or belonging-to an order of things which precedes our capacity to oppose ourselves to things taken as objects opposed to a subject./42/

For both, this claim has several corollaries: literature has cognitive value, and is to be defended against all positivistic attempts to reduce it to "emotion" or "nonsense." Literature also has transformative power—it can challenge, complicate, and extend our visions of the world and our perceptions of what it means to be human.

With the New Critics (and with the Kantian-Coleridgean tradition behind them), Ricoeur sees literature as a paradigmatic expression of the productive imagination. For both, however, the stress is not on the author's creative capacities, but on language: a poem is an artifact made of words./43/ As the analogies between metaphor and literature which both propose indicate, the "momentous creation" effected by metaphor and poem alike is a properly semantic, rather than a psychological, event. Ricoeur and these literary theorists, in short, each intend to displace both the romantic tradition's psychological emphases, and the historicist's presupposition that a literary work receives its intelligibility from its relation to its original situation. Both philosopher and literary critic therefore insist on the semantic autonomy of a work. Meaning is not an idea or experience in an individual psyche, but an ideal, objective property of a text. A work's form and content are therefore inextricably related.

As outlined above, the central difficulty in the New Critical program is that the two aims of their theory, each resolutely defended, tend to work against each other. On the one hand, they argue that literature provides knowledge, and knowledge of the real. On the other, they uphold literature's autonomy by asserting that literature is "non-referential" and unrelated to contexts of meaning outside of it. To defend the semantic autonomy of literature against the claims of romanticism and historicism, they stress the self-sufficiency of art, and refuse to refer the structure of a work to extrinsic dimensions through paraphrase. To uphold the poem's cognitive value against the claims of positivism, however, they assert that a literary work does disclose and transform human experience in the world outside of it.

A consequence of this dichotomy is that many of the New Critics' formulations are vague or confusing. As Chapter II discussed in detail, these critics are particularly unclear about the relation between "experience" and reflection, the problem of "belief," and about how the poem is related to extra-linguistic reality. While they insist that a poem must be "experienced" to be understood—that it is only through "participation in the drama of the poem" that literature gives knowledge—they never explain how one moves from experiencing a work to understanding or assessing its content. "Experience" becomes an ambiguous notion applied alternately to a reader's involvement in a work, to the work's structure (the poem "is" an experience), and to its content (a work contains and resolves the conflicting "experiences" which characterize human existence). The New Critics are therefore also unclear about whether and how a poem refers to reality: they argue that it is not a "mimesis" of the real, but an "analogy" or "similacrum." Since this notion also does double duty—it intends to relate literature to reality while also claiming that a work is a closed, non-referential totality—the notion itself remains ambiguous. Finally, the New Critics are most unclear about how we assess the truth claims of a work. As Brooks' treatment of the problem of belief indicated, these critics tend to bar all reflection from the participatory process of understanding, for fear that it will place the poem "in unreal competition with philosophy or theology."/44/ We are therefore left wondering just how a literary work, whose truth is entirely an affair of "coherence," can be said to disclose the real and transform our self-understanding.

Seen from the perspective of Ricoeur's formulations, the central antimony in the New Critical program is another version of the dichotomy between explanation and understanding that Ricoeur's theory is designed to overcome. Insofar as Ricoeur succeeds in placing these poles in dialectical relation, by demonstrating that both are essential parts of the ontological structure of discourse, he indirectly provides a more adequate conceptualization of the New Critics' own intentions. Rather than representing the general outline of Ricoeur's argument again here, it will be more helpful to point to specific elements in his theory that clarify several of the New Critics' formulations.

One of the most helpful aspects of Ricoeur's program in this regard is his definition of meaning as inclusive of both sense and reference. From the first, inchoate exteriorization of the speech event in meaning in oral discourse, through the increasingly complex ways in which meaning is distanciated in writing and text, Ricoeur demonstrates that language as it is used has an extralinguistic, ontological foundation and destiny. Language refers both back to the speaker and to the experience to which it gives expression, and toward the world it speaks about. Because Ricoeur grounds this referential trait in the structure of discourse itself, he can explain how texts refer without sacrificing the semantic autonomy both he and the New Critics wish to preserve. Because he explains how author and world are inscribed in and implied by the structural "sense" of a text, Ricoeur can assert with conceptual force, rather than with the New Critics' ambiguity, that a literary work is both "closed" and "open." The work is closed, as the New Critics claim, because it is a complex, structured totality, its partial meanings dependent upon their organization within the architecture of the whole. As closed, the work transcends its author and original situation; it is, as the New Critics insist, atemporal, objective, self-sufficient, and "decontextualized." But the literary work is also open—and here Ricoeur provides a decisive extension of the New Critical program. While the interpreter must "participate" in the structure of the poem, construing its immanent or intrinsic meaning by relating part to whole and whole to part, one moves through the dynamics of the work's sense to its referent—to the world it opens up or projects in front of it.

This understanding of sense and reference both satisfies the New Critics' insistence on the formal integrity of a literary text and clarifies what they seem to intend with their notion of the work as an analogy or similacrum of the world. For Ricoeur, with the New Critics, a literary work does not refer directly to given reality. Unlike the first-order reference of ordinary language, literature refers to the real by recreating it. The "world" the text displays is, in this sense, an analogy of the world—or, in Ricoeur's terms, a model which asks us to see the real *as* the text redescribes it. Because this "possible world" is created by the work's syntactic, semantic, generic, and stylistic structures, the immanent "sense" of the poem, it is not a content that can be abstracted from its formal embodiment. It is, nevertheless, a subject matter, a "proposition," which makes a claim to truth in the mode of imaginative possibility.

This notion, in turn, helps to untangle the most crucial problem in New Critical theory—the relation between experience and reflection, and the question of "belief." Ricoeur does share the New Critics' insistence that a literary work can never be adequately paraphrased. In Ricoeur's terms, a text has a "surplus of meaning," irreducible to any single statement of its content. Nevertheless, in Ricoeur's suggestive phrase, "the symbol gives rise to thought": while a work always speaks of more than we can know through direct reflection, it does demand that we reflectively wrestle with the full dimensions of what it proposes to be the case./45/ Ricoeur's arguments for the necessity of critical explanation at the various levels outlined above illumines what the New Critics have actually done, and often done brilliantly, in their practical criticism. Their detailed analyses of the way a poem means through its formal strategies demonstrates their discernment and judgment; their participation in or "experience" of the poem clearly entails a critical reconstruction of its meaning. Most importantly, their evaluations of the "depth," "sensitivity," "richness," and indeed "truth" of the vision, "total meaning," or world the poem discloses demonstrates that they do measure the adequacy of a poem by bringing it into dialogue with ethical, philosophical, and theological reflection, as well as with the proposals of other literary works.

By arguing that interpretation includes moments of both explanation and understanding, Ricoeur can account for the way experience and reflection are both necessary phases of the interpretive process without reducing a literary work to propositional statement. To reflect on a text's vision of what might be the case by placing it in conversation with the questions and responses provided by other contexts of meaning is not to measure a work against "some abstract philosophical yardstick," as Brooks feared, but to "participate" in the work in a fuller, because both emotive and cognitive, sense.

The role of "belief" in understanding, in turn, can now be more clearly formulated./46/ In Ricoeur's terms, the distanciation provided by the structure of a work includes a distanciation of the reader from his or her self. One gives one's as-if assent to the "partial meanings" in a work, as Brooks argued, postponing the question of belief until what he called the work's "total meaning" has been construed. Lacking a clear notion of the referential character of literature and of the role of reflection in interpretation, however, Brooks was unable to specify how this total meaning can address, transform, or elicit our consent. Ricoeur's understanding of reference as the work's proposed world, and his description of the final phase of interpretation as a (now critical) appropriation of that world, makes it clear that the problem of belief is best conceived as that final process by which one evaluates and accepts or rejects a work's proposal as one's own. To "believe" in a work is thus to move from a "willing suspension of disbelief," or a merely aesthetic participation, to consent to see the world *as* the work redescribes it.

Ricoeur, Bultmann, and the Task of Biblical Interpretation

While Ricoeur's theory can thus lend coherence and cogency to the New Critical program, it remains to be seen how his text-centered hermeneutic can contribute to the specific concerns of biblical interpretation. Here an examination of Ricoeur's reflections on the relation between general and theological hermeneutics, and of the relation between Ricoeur's program and that of Bultmann, will be the central focus.

In a key essay, "Philosophical Hermeneutics and Theological Hermeneutics," Ricoeur wrestles with a central question for biblical exegesis in the modern period: whether the interpretation of biblical texts should be considered as a province within a broader field of textual hermeneutics, or whether, conversely, the specificity of the task of interpreting biblical texts demands that theological hermeneutics be viewed as a "special hermeneutics," albeit one which makes use of a general interpretation theory./47/ While the biblical texts are primarily texts, texts among other texts, and are therefore subject to the conditions applying to all literature, Ricoeur argues, the particularity of the biblical writings—both as texts with a distinctive content, and as scriptural texts bound to the community of faith—makes the latter alternative the proper perspective.

Ricoeur stands here with the Bultmann of *Kerygma and Myth* and *Theology of the New Testament*, for whom the general principles of interpretation became the organon for a specifically theological task: to recover the kerygma as an address and event for the present. Ricoeur also argues, however, that it is only by first treating the biblical texts like other texts, applying to them the principles of a general hermeneutic, that the specificity of their content, and the response appropriate to that content, become clear. Ricoeur argues that the subject matter of the biblical texts becomes an "issue" to be appropriated in the present only through interpretation: "Faith in what the text is concerned with," he writes, "must be deciphered in the text that speaks of it and in the confession of faith of the primitive church which is expressed in the text."/48/

What appears to us today as a central and distinctive modern problem for biblical hermeneutics—what Bultmann spoke of as the scandalous foreignness of these ancient documents for contemporary interpreters—can also, in Ricoeur's view, hermeneutic situation that have actually been present since its origin. "The meaning and function of our modernity," he writes, "is to unveil, by means of the distance which today separates our culture from ancient culture, what has been unique and extraordinary in this situation from the beginning."/49/ These unique and extraordinary dimensions appear, Ricoeur maintains, when one examines the hermeneutical situation through the central categories of his interpretation theory: the relation between speech and writing, the text as a structured work, the referent of the text as its projected "world," and the text as a mediation of self-understanding.

Protestant theologies of the Word have stressed its oral and event character. The kerygma of Christ as act and word of God, they maintain, is above all a preached word, experienced as a radical word of address to the self in the present. The origin, object, and expression of faith together constitute a unique "word-event." Ricoeur's understanding of the speech-writing relation points to other dimensions of this situation, however. As he notes, the newness of the Christ event and the proclamation of that event are from the beginning transmitted by means of an interpretation of available and written signs: Jesus himself interpreted the Torah, Paul interprets Christ in light of the prophets and the old covenant, the christological titles in the Gospels reinterpret figures received from the written Hebraic and Hellenistic cultures. And while in this sense "Christianity is, from the beginning, an exegesis," it in turn becomes a new writing, a New Testament, to be interpreted./50/

The chain speech-writing-speech, or writing-speech-writing thus, in Ricoeur's view, *constitutes* what we call proclamation, preaching, or kerygma, speech sometimes mediating between two forms of writing, as Jesus' speech does between the two testaments, and writing sometimes mediating between two forms of speech, as the Gospel texts do between the first preaching of the Christ event and all contemporary preaching. Only because the Christ event is an interpreted event, exteriorized or distanciated in writing, is it freed from its original speaker and situation and able to speak to us in the present. In this sense, our distance from the texts reveals an original distance at the heart of Christianity—as a writing, the New Testament already expresses a difference and a distance, however minimal, from the event that it proclaims. We are related to the object of faith, Ricoeur insists, only through the apostolic community's inscribed confession of faith./51/

The clear and radical implication of Ricoeur's notion of distanciation for the question of revelation is that we can come to hear the living Word only through interpretation. In contrast to the existentialist emphases of neo-orthodox theologies stressing revelation as "event of encounter," Ricoeur contends that revelation, the Word, is not only related to written discourse in a fundamental way, but also experienced as "event" only indirectly, as the event of understanding inscribed texts.

This perception is, of course, the basis for Bultmann's principle of demythologization. As Ricoeur observes, on the one hand, Bultmann's program represents the discovery of the distance which separates our culture from that of the early Christian communities. To demythologize in this sense is to abandon or deconstruct the "mythic wrapping" in which these confessions are expressed. In another sense, however, to demythologize is to discover that distance between witness and event, writing and speech, constitutive of primitive Christian faith. Demythologizing here becomes the inverse side of the grasp of the kerygma; it is moved by the will to better comprehend, and to re-experience, the text's own intention to speak of God's act in Christ.

Ricoeur credits Bultmann for revising the psychological emphases of the romantic tradition. Bultmann perceives that the interpretive task is not to understand the author, but to submit to the subject matter. The hermeneutical circle, Bultmann recognizes, is not a psychological, but a methodological one: it is not immediately between believing and understanding, since, as Ricoeur writes:

> Behind believing there is the primacy of the object of
> faith over faith, and behind understanding there is the
> primacy of exegesis and its method over the naive read-
> ing of the text. . . . It is the circle constituted by the
> object that regulates faith and the method that regulates
> understanding./52/

In Ricoeur's view, however, Bultmann is still trapped by the
opposition between explanation and understanding he inherits
from Dilthey, and by an antimony between the 'objective' and
the 'existential' he acquires from (an overly anthropological
reading of) Heidegger./53/ While Bultmann does perceive that
the kerygma is grasped only through interpretation, Ricoeur
argues, he has not sufficiently thought through this objective,
explanatory phase of interpretation, and moves too quickly to
the moment of "decision." The source of this problem, in turn, is
that Bultmann has not adequately thought through the signifi-
cations of both mythological and non-mythological elements in
the New Testament writings.

Bultmann argues that non-mythological notions such as "act
of God," "word of God," and "future of God," along with
"wholly other," "transcendent," and other expressions, are statements of pure faith that derive their meaning from the event in
which we surrender our will in faith. Only in the event of faith
does one experience what "act of God" signifies. In Ricoeur's
view, this is to avoid the question of the content of these non-
mythological expressions. Bultmann's too exclusive preoccupation with the opposition between the "objectifying" language of
myth and the kerygma prevents him from exploring the languages of faith which replace those of myth and which call for a
new kind of interpretation. Ricoeur argues that the meaning of
the kerygma must be objective in a sense other than the "objectifying" representations of mythological statements, since the
kerygma must be both "event" *and* "meaning." When it comes
to deciphering the meaning of the non-mythological core of
the New Testament, Bultmann's hermeneutical circle is not
adequately methodological. As Ricoeur's interpretation theory
makes clear, the moment of exegesis is not that of existential
decision, but first of all that of construing a text's meaning:
"there is no exegesis without a 'bearer [*teneur*] of meaning'
which belongs to the text and not to the author of the text."/54/
For Ricoeur the semantic moment, the moment of objective

meaning, must precede the existential moment, the moment of
personal decision, if a hermeneutic is to do justice to both the
objectivity of meaning and the historicality of understanding:

> If there is no objectivity of meaning, then the text no
> longer says anything at all; without existential appropri-
> ation, what the text says is no longer living speech./55/

Finally, and most importantly, Ricoeur argues that it is as theologian as well as exegete that Bultmann must reformulate the
relation between the meaning of the biblical texts and existential
decision. For if the New Testament writings are to be in any sense
a vehicle for the coming of God's word to us, rather than one
which proceeds from us, Ricoeur maintains, then the texts must
have a non-physical and non-psychological objective meaning./56/ If the meaning of the text does not already confront the
reader, Ricoeur asks, how shall the act it announces not be reduced
to a simple symbol of inner conversion, of the passage of the old
self to the new? The expression 'word of God' presupposes that the
word of the text itself belongs to God—to "the being who addresses
himself to my existence." If Bultmann's enterprise is not to collapse
into fideism at this point, if the expression 'word of God' is to be
meaningful, Ricoeur argues, then a complete ontology of language
is required. While Bultmann adopts the Heideggerian anthropology in order to furnish the proper conceptuality for interpreting
the cosmological and mythological statements in the biblical writings, he has, in Ricoeur's view, ignored the inquiry about Being to
which Heidegger's anthropology is attached, and thus the question
of how the language we speak is related to the coming of being
into language.

    With regard to biblical interpretation, then, Ricoeur shares
with Bultmann the view that the New Testament writings are
most appropriately viewed as texts that witness to that event of
God's self-disclosure in Jesus Christ which the kerygma proclaims. He agrees with Bultmann that, as witnesses, the New
Testament writings may may be more or less adequate expressions of the kerygma; demythologization as content criticism is
demanded by the character of the texts themselves. With Bultmann, furthermore, Ricoeur agrees that the reader's existential
involvement with the text is an essential element of
interpretation—both as the particular pre-understanding with
which we approach the texts, and as our existential response to

the text's claim upon us. We come to the biblical texts with our own questions concerning the meaning of existence, and with our own, however tentative, experiences of God's act in Christ. We come with the anticipation that here, as Bultmann phrased it, the truth of our existence is at stake. Beyond Bultmann, however, Ricoeur insists on a better understanding of the content of the New Testament's languages of faith. Ricoeur's notions of the structure and world of a work, and his description of the way a text mediates self-understanding, suggest how a better understanding of this problem may be achieved.

Ricoeur's general interpretation theory has demonstrated the need and appropriate place for explanatory methods such as structuralism or other formalist literary analyses: the objectification of discourse as a work, composed as a finite and closed whole, codified according to the rules of genre, and marked as a unique configuration by its style, means that explanation is the unavoidable road to understanding. Form and content are generated together; one comes to understand a text's referent, its world or subject matter, through a critical reconstruction of its sense. With regard to biblical interpretation, this analysis implies that the "confessions of faith" which are expressed in the biblical documents are inseparable from the forms of discourse there, be they literary genres such as narrative, parable, hymn, or prophecy, or symbol, image, or doctrine./57/ In this way Ricoeur's recent writings have confirmed in a more systematic and rigorous manner the pioneering insights of interpreters such as Amos Wilder in *The Language of the Gospel*./58/

This perception is, of course, one shared with the three scholars considered in Chapter III, and with other biblical scholars who have applied various literary critical methods to the biblical writings. Ricoeur has explored the relation between the narrative form and its theological content in several essays, since it is with narrative forms and structures that structural analysis has been most successful. As Ricoeur notes, this example shows us that one cannot construct a biblical theology without acknowledging that something distinctive is said about Yahweh and about his relations with his people, Israel, because it is said in narrative form: "Not just any theology whatsoever can be tied to the narrative form, but only a theology which proclaims Yahweh to be the grand Actor in a history of deliverance."/59/ The value of Ricoeur's proposals here is not the uniqueness of this particular insight, nor his own experiments in exegesis, with which other scholars may disagree, but the way such formal analyses are situated within a comprehensive interpretation theory.

Of decisive importance is Ricoeur's insistence that it is not the structure of a work, but the referent, or world, the text projects through its structure, that is the object of understanding. The hermeneutical and theological implications here are considerable. First of all, it makes it clear that a purely formal analysis of the way a text is structured is only one part of the interpretive task. In addition, it cautions against those who, like Via, would too quickly introduce existential categories to counterbalance a formalist analysis of the text's structure. Between structural explanation and self-understanding lies the task of unfolding the world of the text: it is this which finally forms and transforms the self of the reader according to its intention. The new being projected by the text thus has a kind of objectivity which, while certainly *pro me*, begins with the text itself.

Herein lies its capacity to confront us with a power that is not of our own making, that comes to us from beyond ourselves, and that can create in us an awareness of the realities it conveys. Both Bultmann and the New Critics, it was suggested, each in their own way insisted on this quality of "otherness": Bultmann, as a trait of the kerygma, the New Critics, as a characteristic of the autonomous literary work. For the New Criticism, Ricoeur's program provides a way to explain how the objective or autonomous text gives rise to a referent. For Bultmann, it cuts through his strict opposition between kerygma as event and mythological statements, by showing how the non-mythological forms of expression in the New Testament writings, by disclosing a possible mode of being in the world, have an irreducible content which confronts us as a claim demanding decision. The event which the kerygma proclaims is available to us now only through the mediation of the "world" both inscribed in and displayed by the biblical testimonies.

A second implication concerns the plurality of forms of expression the biblical writings contain. If we take seriously the notion that literary form and theological content are mutually related, then Ricoeur's theory encourages us to consider the tensions and interactions among the multiple forms and contents within the biblical canon./60/ Investigations of the tensions between various structures and the contents they shape permits us to recognize, for example, that God appears differently throughout these discourses—sometimes as the hero of the saving act, sometimes as wrathful or compassionate, sometimes as He to whom we can speak in an I-Thou relation, or sometimes as He whom I meet only in a cosmic order which ignores me./61/ While this perception is, again, not new, Ricoeur's program provides a systematic conceptual foundation for this enterprise.

Biblical hermeneutics here has implications for a number of theological issues, the questions of the status of the canon, and of the canon within the canon in particular. While Ricoeur is cautious about prescribing an answer for either of these concerns, his analysis invites us to consider the closed canon as a limited space for interpretation within which the multiple forms of discourse constitute a circular system, and in which the theological content of each of them receives its meaning from the total constellation of forms of discourse. To speak of the biblical "world," Ricoeur's analysis suggests, is to speak of the contrast and convergence of all the forms of discourse taken together. Because Ricoeur's focus is on the world of the text in the sense of a global horizon and of a totality of meanings, his proposal implies that one should be cautious about giving priority to any single form of discourse. In contrast to Bultmann and the post-Bultmannians' stress on the mode of personal address, Ricoeur's consideration of the biblical world as a whole points to aspects which are cosmic and communitarian, historical and worldly, anthropological, ethical, doctrinal and personalistic./62/ Whether or not one wishes to accept the kind of necessity Ricoeur's hypothesis confers on the closing of the canon, his theory provides a hermeneutic foundation for reconsidering the question of the relative priority of the various canonical writings, by insisting that it is no longer possible to consider their content without making a detour through the explication of their forms of expression./63/

Ricoeur's   most   important   contribution   to   biblical hermeneutics—and the point at which it becomes most appropriate to say that Ricoeur indirectly extends and integrates the New Critical and Bultmannian programs—lies in his application of his analysis of the redescriptive and revelatory power of poetic texts to the biblical writings. If we place the biblical confessions under the sign of the poetic function of language, Ricoeur suggests, then we can think of the concept of biblical revelation as that concerned with what the text says, with the new being it unfolds before us, rather than with some psychologistic interpretation of biblical inspiration. He writes:

> I would go so far as to say that the Bible is revealed to the extent that the new being unfolded there is itself revelatory with respect to the world, to all reality, including my existence and my history. In other words, revelation, if the expression is meaningful, is a trait of the biblical *world*./64/

As this statement indicates, the truth of the biblical writings is, in Ricoeur's view, best thought of as that truth of disclosure which poetic texts exhibit. Here truth means neither verification nor adequation, but manifestation, letting what shows itself be. The texts reveal more than science or reason can know directly, and they elicit our participation and consent not by immediately confronting our will or our reason, but by proposing to our imaginations that we see the world *as* it is redescribed there. The "participation" in a work of which the New Critics spoke, or the model of "play" which Gadamer applied to the act of reading, are both pertinent here: if a work opens up a new vision of possibility through its heuristic fictions, the act of reading which corresponds to this revelation is that process of risk and self-forgetfulness by which the self is opened to the possibility of metamorphosis. As Ricoeur applies this to the biblical texts:

> Imaginative variation, play, metamorphosis—all of these expressions seek to discern a fundamental phenomenon, namely, that it is in the *imagination* that the new being is first formed in me. . . . The power of letting oneself be grasped by new possibilities precedes the power of deciding and choosing. Imagination is that dimension of subjectivity which responds to the text as *poem*. . . .
> The distanciation of imagination responds to the distanciation which the "issue" of the text unfolds in the heart of reality./65/

It is with this understanding of imaginative redescription that the question of the relation between general and biblical hermeneutics can most appropriately be addressed. If, as Ricoeur's modifications of the New Critical program permit us to recognize, the biblical texts open up a new being, a new reality of the possible within the world of ordinary experience, is it the case that they are simply another instance of poetic language? This is Bultmann's question with a distinct shift. For Bultmann, the "scandal" which the mythological elements in the biblical texts posed for modern consciousness served to conceal the true scandal to which these writings intend to point. Ricoeur has insisted, in contrast, that the true "scandal" is not concealed by the biblical forms of discourse, but displayed through them, in the new being which all of the forms of discourse taken together project. What, then, makes the possible reality referred to by the biblical texts a religious and not simply a poetic reality?

Ricoeur argues that in at least some forms of biblical expression, religious discourse *modifies* poetic language by means of what the philosopher Ian Ramsey speaks of as "qualifiers."/66/ Unlike other discourse, Ricoeur suggests, religious language redescribes those human experiences which can be spoken of as "limit-experiences"—those experiences, both positive (intense joy, reassurance, creation) and negative (guilt, anxiety, sickness, recognition of death as one's personal destiny), in which we recognize that the final dimension of our situation is neither one of our own making nor one under our control./67/ These experiences of the "limits-to" our experience, in the language Ricoeur shares with David Tracy, may in turn become disclosive of a reality which, as Tracy writes, "functions as a final, now gracious, now frightening, now trustworthy, now absurd, always uncontrollable *limit-of* the very meaning of existence itself."/68/

No form of discourse, even poetic or religious discourse, can express such experience without remainder. Religious language points to that sense of a limit-of our existence, to the Wholly Other or the transcendent, Ricoeur argues, by radicalizing poetic language still further. In the biblical writings, we see this process of "intensification" occur in different ways. As William Beardslee has analyzed this process in the New Testament proverbs, as Norman Perrin interprets it in the proclamatory sayings of Jesus, as Crossan, Via and Ricoeur have demonstrated its function in the parables, in each case the forms are subject to a kind of "abuse" or transgression of their ordinary use./69/ This intensification brings the listener to a sense of the limits to and of human possibility, and to a sense of the limit dimensions within everyday existence itself. Ordinary life is ruptured; the unexpected occurs; a strange world of meaning appears which disorients our everyday perception by showing us the limits to the ordinary and by projecting a sense of the whole that grounds our existence.

Religious language is thus not one kind of "fiction" among

others, just as religious experience is not a region of experience separate from the rest of our existence. Religious language, which both emerges from and is addressed to religious-as-limit experience, breaks open and limits our demand for conceptual knowledge. By intensifying, by "carrying to the limit" ordinary and poetic discourse, it points to the basic horizon which is the limit of all of our activities. The referent of the biblical language is in one sense, then, human reality in its wholeness: religious experience does not have to do with a supernatural world separate from or added to human existence in the world, but with authentically human experience, to use Bultmann's existentialist language. Religious discourse involves what Ramsey calls "total commitment" and "universal significance" in the sense that it intends to speak of the whole of reality and of personal lives within it, and in the sense that it engages the auditor's whole being./70/

In another sense the ultimate referent of the biblical texts is God, or the Kingdom of God. For as *religious* poetic fictions, the world projected by the biblical texts is an intensified, extravagant, "impossible possible" mode of being in the world./71/ It is a disclosure of possibilities for human existence which are beyond the limit our ordinary experience can imagine. The limit which grounds our existence is both opened up by the vision of possibility the texts project and escapes them, for as limit it is beyond all signification. In this sense, Ricoeur describes the significance of the word 'God' as the point of convergence that gathers together all the referents which issue from the many partial discourses in the biblical canon: it is at once "the coordinator of these varied discourses and the index of their incompleteness, the point at which something escapes them."/72/

The biblical text only finds this referent when it has been appropriated: "when ordinary experience has recognized itself as *signified*, in its breadth, its height, its depth, by the 'said' of the text."/73/ The event in which the biblical world is appropriated in faith, is, as Bultmann also insisted, both the limit of all hermeneutics and the non-hermeneutical origin of all interpretation, for interpretation begins and ends in the risk of a response which is neither engendered nor exhausted by commentary. But Ricoeur's model of understanding-explanation-understanding reminds us that interpretation is necessary nevertheless. Like all poetic texts, not only must the "sense" of the biblical writings be reconstructed, but the possible mode of being which they project as their referent must be tested, through reflection, and in conversation with other contexts of meaning. Insofar as the biblical texts claim to redescribe the "whole experience of man and the experience of all men,"/74/ interpretation must include that "conflict of interpretations" by which these testimonies are explored and tried./75/

At the same time, the distanciation which constitutes the hermeneutical situation, including the distanciation or dispossession of the self before the text, means that our own pre-judgments, including our skepticisms and suspicions, will be challenged, even demythologized, in the interpretive process. In this way criticism of both text and reader is an integral and internal part of all appropriation of meaning. If the response of faith is not created nor exhausted by interpretation, it is in another sense *constituted* by the new being which is the "issue" of the text: "Ultimate concern," Ricoeur notes, "would remain *mute* if it did not receive the power of a word ceaselessly renewed by its interpretation in signs and symbols which have, we might say, educated and formed the concern over the centuries."/76/ Faith, hope, and unconditional trust would all remain empty if they were not a response *to* the proposition of a new being which opens up new possibilities of existence—possibilities discovered through a constantly renewed interpretation of the biblical texts.

If it can be said that Ricoeur's general interpretation theory indirectly provides coherency and conceptual force for the New Critical program, it is his application of this program to biblical hermeneutics that renders his model an indirect clarification and modification of Bultmann's program as well. Ricoeur's model of understanding-explanation-understanding provides a more adequate conceptual foundation for Bultmann's insistence that the hermeneutical circle is a properly methodological, rather than a psychological, one. By arguing that it is the referent of the biblical writings generated and projected through their sense which is the issue of the texts, and by articulating this referent in terms of the poetic function of language, Ricoeur preserves Bultmann's stress on the texts' subject matter while postponing both the moment of decision or appropriation, and the necessity for "translation" into philosophical or theological categories.

All figurative language, Ricoeur has argued, calls for interpretation—for "a new speech-act which would paraphrase the first one without exhausting its meaningful resources."/77/ This need not, however, be an extrinsic encounter between religious language and concepts appropriate to our present cultural and philosophical situation, as Bultmann's existentialist hermeneutic seemed to suggest. Ricoeur's investigaton of the variety of forms of discourse in the biblical canon, and of their interaction, permits us to think of the problem as an internal inquiry into the conceptual potentialities of religious language. The "dynamism" thanks to which symbolic language calls for interpretation is the primary condition for any move from figurative to conceptual expression, and different forms of religious discourse—parable, proverb, image, for example—will call for interpretation in a different way. "Translation," if we use this term at all, thus remains under the control of the hermeneutic potential of the discourse itself.

Ricoeur's sensitivity to the variety of forms of discourse also allows him to extend Bultmann's view that the New Testament has already begun the work of demythologization itself. In addition to observing that Paul and John, as Bultmann argued, demythologize certain mythological concepts, we can see that the New Testament contains a plurality of symbolic and semi-conceptual modes of discourse. Ricoeur calls the latter "translation language," a language which mediates between the original language and a language more capable of dealing with other religions, foreign cultures, and with philosophy itself, by picking up new metaphors, rhetorical strategies, and new conceptual dimensions./78/ By beginning with the forms of discourse themselves rather than with conceptual categories, Ricoeur can explore the similarities and differences between the kinds of "logic" in forms of poetic-religious discourse such as the parable and the "logic" of semi-conceptual notions such as "justification by faith."

Most importantly, perhaps, Ricoeur's investigation of the revelatory power and ontological foundation of religious-as-poetic discourse permits us to think of demythologization in a different way. Bultmann saw that one must come to the biblical texts with a pre-understanding that includes questions concerning one's existence as created, lost or saved, condemned or justified, in order to hear its message. For Ricoeur, it is not so much the false scandal constituted by the cultural categories of the ancient message which is the fundamental hermeneutical problem, but the loss of this pre-understanding, the forgetting of these questions, which marks our present cultural situation. The distance is not only between us and the culture in which the kerygma was expressed, but between us and what is at stake in the kerygma. For Ricoeur, the biblical writings, by awakening new possibilities for existence in our imaginations, can activate the questions in us anew./79/ To return the locus of revelation to the scriptural texts themselves thus, in Ricoeur's view, is the fundamental basis for their recovery in the present.

The main task of hermeneutics is thus not to break the cultural framework of myth, although Ricoeur agrees with Bultmann that to demythologize myth's explicative pretensions is appropriate. But in Ricoeur's view, the question of myth properly belongs within a larger inquiry into the poetic, redescriptive function of all imaginative discourse, so that the fundamental hermeneutical task is the liberation of the revelatory capacity of this discourse to awaken, within the heart of our culture, the imagination of the possible. "Is not The Good News the instigation of the *possibility* of man by a creative word?"/80/

Ricoeur's reflections on the task of biblical interpretation, like his general theory of interpretation, are not offered as a complete and systematic program, and there are a number of issues which both literary critics and biblical interpreters would wish to see developed further. From the side of literary theory, it was noted, Ricoeur's position can be challenged by structuralist and deconstructionist critics on the one side, and by a *Rezeptionsaesthetik* on the other. With regard to biblical interpretation, Ricoeur has said little, for example, about the place of historical, form and redaction criticism in the interpretive process, and his own exegetical studies are certainly subject to discussion among biblical scholars. Furthermore, his reflections on the kind of philosophical and theological criteria appropriate to the cognitive uses of religious language, his emphasis on a "return to Kant through Hegel," and his analysis of the category of hope may be contested by theologians./81/ Neither Ricoeur's exegetical nor theological studies have been discussed in detail here, because they are not integral to his hermeneutical program itself. It is the latter which merits acknowledgement as one exemplary model for a biblical hermeneutic that provides a place for literary analysis while remaining faithful to the traditional aim of interpretation—to make the texts speak *hodie usque ad nos*, "even to us today."

NOTES

/1/   Langbaum, *The Modern Spirit*, p. 5.

/2/   On this point see David Tracy, "The Particularity and Universality of Christian Revelation," in *Revelation and Experience*, ed. Edward Schillebeeckx, Concilium, vol. 113 (New York: Seabury Press, 1979), pp. 106–15, and his observations in *The Analogical Imagination*, pp. 139–40, n. 36.

/3/   For an alternate model which seeks to combine Dilthey's hermeneutic with structuralism see McKnight, *Meaning in Texts*.

/4/   See esp. Patrick L. Bourgeois, *Extension of Ricoeur's Hermeneutic* (The Hague: Martinus Nijhoff, 1975), and Don Ihde, *Hermeneutical Phenomenology: The Philosphy of Paul Ricoeur* (Evanston: Northwestern University Press, 1971).

/5/   Paul Ricoeur, *Freedom and Nature: The Voluntary and the Involuntary* (Evanston: Northwestern University Press, 1966). The study of fault, *Finitude and Guilt*, appears in two volumes, *Fallible Man* (Chicago: Henry Regnery Co., 1965), and *The Symbolism of Evil* (Boston: Beacon Press, 1967). For a nearly exhaustive bibliography of Ricoeur's writings through 1974, see "Bibliographie de Paul Ricoeur," ed. Frans D. Vansina in *Revue Philosophique de Louvain* 60 (1962): 394–413; 66 (1968): 85–101; 72 (1974): 156–81. This bibliography is extended through 1976 in *Studies in the Philosophy of Paul Ricoeur*, ed. Charles E. Reagan (Athens, OH: Ohio University Press, 1979), pp. 180–94.

/6/   Ricoeur, *The Symbolism of Evil*, p. 355, and *Freud and Philosophy* (New Haven: Yale University Press, 1970). See Ricoeur's own account of the development of his thought in "From Existentialism to the Philosophy of Language," pp. 86–93.

/7/   See Ricoeur, *Freud*, pp. 17, 27, 277, and "The Critique of Religion," in *Philosophy*, pp. 213–22.

/8/   See Ricoeur, "From Existentialism to the Philosophy of Language," p. 88, and "Preface to Bultmann," pp. 381–401.

/9/   Paul Ricoeur, "Existence and Hermeneutics," in *Philosophy*, p. 106.

/10/   Ricoeur's interpretation theory is developed in numerous essays. The most important are: the collection *Interpretation Theory: Discourse and the Surplus of Meaning* (Fort Worth: Texas Christian University Press, 1976) (hereafter cited as IT); "The Hermeneutical Function of

Distanciation," *Philosophy Today* 17 (1973): 129–41 (hereafter cited as "Distanciation"); "Metaphor and the Main Problem of Hermeneutics," in *Philosophy*, pp. 134–48; and "Explanation and Understanding," in *Philosophy*, pp. 149–66. For Ricoeur's discussion of Schleiermacher, et al., see also "The Task of Hermeneutics," *Philosophy Today* 17 (1973): 113–28.

/11/ Gadamer's critique of aesthetic consciousness is thus indirectly a critique of certain aspects of New Critical theory as well. His critique appears in *Truth and Method*, Part One, on the mode of being of a work of art, pp. 5–150. See esp. pp. 39–73. Part Two extends this discussion to the historical sciences, and Part Three to an ontology of language.

/12/ See esp. Martin Heidegger, *Poetry, Language and Thought* (New York: Harper & Row, 1971).

/13/ Martin Heidegger, *Being and Time* (London: SCM Press, 1962), pp. 349–83, and Gadamer, *Truth and Method*, pp. 225–41.

/14/ Gadamer, *Truth and Method*, p. 484.

/15/ For Ricoeur's critique of Gadamer, see "The Task of Hermeneutics," pp. 125–28, and "Ethics and Culture," a discussion of the Gadamer-Habermas debate, in *Philosophy Today* 17 (1973): 153–66.

/16/ Among the literary scholars who have reflected on the relationship between the New Criticism, structuralism, and other modes of formalist criticism, several excellent studies are those cited above in the Introduction, n. 10.

/17/ For Ricoeur's critique of structuralism, see "Structure, Word, Event," in *Philosophy*, pp. 109–19. Ricoeur speaks of language as it is used as "discourse," whose primary unit is not the code, or linguistic units smaller than the sentence, but the sentence. For the following discussion, see also IT, pp. 1–23; 81–88.

/18/ In addition to the essay cited immediately above, see "Structure and Hermeneutics," in *Conflict*, pp. 27–61, and "Biblical Hermeneutics," *Semeia* 4 (1975): 51–73. For Lévi-Strauss see *Structural Anthropology* (Garden City, NY: Anchor Books, 1967).

/19/ The phrase is that of Robert Penn Warren, from "Pure and Impure Poetry," in Adams, ed., *Critical Theory*, p. 983.

/20/ See Derrida, "Structure, Sign and Play in the Discourse of the Human Sciences," and *Of Grammatology*, trans. Gayatri Spivak (Baltimore: Johns Hopkins University Press, 1967). For Ricoeur's responses to Derrida, see *The Rule of Metaphor*, trans. Robert Czerny with Kathleen

McLaughlin and John Costello (Toronto: University of Toronto Press, 1977), esp. pp. 216–556.

/21/ For references to reader-response criticism see above, Chapter II, n. 80.

/22/ IT, p. 12. Cf. Ricoeur, "Distanciation," p. 131.

/23/ See IT, pp. 25–44.

/24/ For Ricoeur's discussion of referent as "world" see ibid., pp. 34–37, and "Distanciation," pp. 139–41.

/25/ IT, p. 37.

/26/ Ricoeur discusses discourse as "work" in "Distanciation," pp. 134–39.

/27/ See "Creativity in Language," *Philosophy Today* 17 (1973): 97–111.

/28/ For the following discussion, see IT, pp. 71–88, and "Explanation and Understanding," pp. 149–55.

/29/ Wayne Booth, *The Rhetoric of Fiction* (Chicago: University of Chicago Press, 1961).

/30/ This is a point that reader-response criticism tends to overlook. This problem appears, for example, in Stanley Fish, *Is There a Text in This Class? The Authority of Interpretive Communities* (Cambridge: Harvard University Press, 1980).

/31/ Ricoeur's major, and most recent, work on metaphor is *The Rule of Metaphor*. See also "Metaphor and the Main a Problem of Hermeneutics," and IT, pp. 45–69.

/32/ "Distanciation," p. 139.

/33/ IT, pp. 87–88.

/34/ Ricoeur also compares the world displayed by poetic texts to the theoretical models of science. For his discussion of mimesis, see "Distanciation," pp. 140–41. For mimesis and models, see "Metaphor and the Main Problem of Hermeneutics"; "Biblical Hermeneutics," pp. 75–88; and IT, p. 92.

/35/ For Ricoeur's analysis of appropriation, see IT, pp. 89–95, and "Distanciation," p. 141.

/36/   "Philosophical Hermeneutics and Theological Hermeneutics," *Studies in Religion. Sciences Religieuses* 5 (1975): 30.

/37/   "Metaphor and the Main Problem of Hermeneutics," pp. 145–46.

/38/   Cf. David Tracy's extension and application of Ricoeur's model in his argument for the need for a critical pluralism in theology, in *The Analogical Imagination*, esp. pp. 154–78. See also Wayne Booth, *Critical Understanding* (Chicago: University of Chicago Press, 1979).

/39/   The key essay for Ricoeur's discussion of pluralism is "Metaphor and the Main Problem of Hermeneutics." See Mary Gerhart's interpretation and adaptation of Ricoeur's notion of "diagnostics" in this regard, "Paul Ricoeur's Notion of 'Diagnostics': Its Function in Literary Interpretation," *Journal of Religion* 56 (1976): 137–56. Both Wayne Booth and David Tracy provide important extensions of Ricoeur's theory on this point.

/40/   Ricoeur discusses these criteria in IT, pp. 78–79, and "Metaphor and the Main Problem of Hermeneutics," pp. 142–43. Ricoeur draws upon E. D. Hirsch's outline of the procedures for validation in *Validity in Interpretation*. Ricoeur's criticisms of Hirsch appear in IT, pp. 99–100, n. 50. In Ricoeur's view, Hirsch's attempt to retrieve the author's intention as normative for interpretation is mistaken.

/41/   For examples of Ricoeur's engagement with the question of truth on a philosophical level, see his argument for the relative adequacy of the Adamic myth in *The Symbolism of Evil*. See also Ricoeur's essays in *The Religious Significance of Atheism*, by Paul Ricoeur and Alasdair MacIntyre (New York: Columbia University Press, 1969), pp. 57–98.

/42/   Paul Ricoeur, "Toward a Hermeneutic of the Idea of Revelation," *Harvard Theological Review* 70 (1977): 24. From Derrida's perspective, this argument, again, would be an illusory longing for a philosophic Eden.

/43/   Ricoeur presented his theory of the imagination, together with analyses of the positions of other major Western philosophers, in a seminar offered at the University of Chicago Divinity School, "The Imagination as a Philosophical Problem," Autumn 1975. As his analysis of poetic redescription suggests, Ricoeur argues that the imagination is a productive, rather than simply a reproductive, faculty. In addition, and against a purely romanticist understanding of the imagination, Ricoeur insists that the imagination is rule-governed, and thus demands an explanatory account.

/44/   Brooks, *The Well Wrought Urn*, p. 186.

/45/ Ricoeur first uses this term in *The Symbolism of Evil*, where it is the title of his concluding chapter, pp. 347–57.

/46/ For an excellent discussion of Ricoeur's contribution to this issue, see Mary Gerhart, *The Question of Belief in Literary Criticism: An Introduction to the Hermeneutic Theory of Paul Ricoeur* (Stuttgart: Verlag Hans-Dieter Heinz, 1979).

/47/ "Philosophical Hermeneutics and Theological Hermeneutics," (hereafter cited as "Philosophical").

/48/ "Preface to Bultmann," p. 390.

/49/ Ibid., p. 388.

/50/ "Philosophical," pp. 19–20.

/51/ "Preface to Bultmann," p. 388.

/52/ Ibid., p. 389.

/53/ Ibid., p. 396. The critique of Bultmann which follows is presented in this essay.

/54/ Ibid., p. 397.

/55/ Ibid., p. 398.

/56/ While this is indeed Ricoeur's most important criticism of Bultmann, it should be noted that it is also the point at which he is most open to challenge. Ricoeur's insistence on the objective character of meaning is subject to opposition from both reader-response criticism and theologies stressing truth as "encounter," while Ricoeur's assertion of the ontological foundation of language can be challenged by the structuralists and deconstructionists.

/57/ "Philosophical," pp. 22–24.

/58/ Amos Wilder, *The Language of the Gospel* (New York: Harper & Row and London: SCM Press, 1964). Published in England under the title *Early Christian Rhetoric*.

/59/ "Philosophical," p. 23. It should be noted that Ricoeur's analyses of the forms of discourse in the Hebrew canon are significantly influenced by von Rad. See the latter's *Old Testament Theology*, trans. D. M. G. Stalker, 2 vols. (New York: Harper & Row, 1962, 1965). For Ricoeur's exegeses of narrative see "Toward a Hermeneutic of the Idea of Revelation"; "Biblical Hermeneutics"; and "The Hermeneutics of Testimony," *Anglican Theological Review* 61 (1979): 435–61.

/60/ See esp. "Toward a Hermeneutic . . . Revelation." Cf. David Tracy's analysis of the interrelations of proclamation, narrative, apocalyptic, doctrine, and symbol, in *The Analogical Imagination*, pp. 248–304.

/61/ "Philosophical," p. 24.

/62/ Ibid., p. 27.

/63/ For Ricoeur's discussion of the canon, see ibid., pp. 24–25. That the use of genre theory and literary history can enhance even as venerable an enterprise as writing a biblical commentary is apparent in Hans Dieter Betz's *Galatians: A Commentary on Paul's Letter to the Churches in Galatia, Hermenia—A Critical and Historical* Commentary on the Bible (Philadelphia: Fortress Press, 1979).

/64/ Ibid., p. 27.

/65/ Ibid., p. 33.

/66/ Ricoeur's use of "limit" as an indicator of the religious character of poetic discourse appears in his discussion of the parables in "Biblical Hermeneutics." How adequate the criterion is for other forms of biblical discourse—the pastorals, for example—needs further consideration if "limit" language is not to become another kind of canon within the canon. For Ricoeur's use (and critique) of Ramsey, see "Biblical Hermeneutics," pp. 107–35.

/67/ Ricoeur here draws upon Karl Jaspers' notion of "boundary experiences" and David Tracy's discussion of religious-as-limit. See Karl Jaspers, *Philosophy*, 2 vols. (Chicago: University of Chicago Press, 1970), 2:177–218; and Tracy, *Blessed Rage for Order*, pp. 105–9 and passim.

/68/ Tracy, *Blessed Rage*, p. 108.

/69/ See, for example, William A. Beardslee, "The Uses of the Proverbs in the Synoptic Tradition," *Interpretation* 24 (1970): 61–76, and *Literary Criticism of the New Testament*, pp. 30–42; Norman Perrin, *Rediscovering the Teachings of Jesus* (New York: Harper & Row, 1967), and *A Modern Pilgrimage in New Testament Christology* (Philadelphia: Fortress Press, 1974), pp. 1–10, 41–57, 104–22. Ricoeur's "Biblical Hermeneutics" is an analysis of the parables. See also his "Listening to the Parables of Jesus," in *Philosophy*, pp. 239–45.

/70/ Ricoeur, "Biblical Hermeneutics," p. 124.

/71/ The phrase is that of David Tracy in *The Analogical Imagination*, p. 176 and passim.

/72/ "Philosophical," p. 28; cf. "Biblical Hermeneutics," pp. 129–30.

/73/ Ibid., p. 128.

/74/ Ibid., pp. 130–31.

/75/ On the notion of "trial," see "The Hermeneutics of Testimony."

/76/ "Philosophical," p. 32. Cf. "Toward a Hermeneutic of the Idea of Revelation," pp. 21–27.

/77/ "Biblical Hermeneutics," p. 133. For the following discussion see pp. 129–45.

/78/ Ibid., p. 135. See Ricoeur's remarks on the "New Hermeneutic" on pp. 136–37.

/79/ For this discussion of demythologizing see "The Language of Faith," pp. 223–38.

/80/ Ibid., p. 238.

/81/ Ricoeur discusses historical criticism in "Biblical Hermeneutics," pp. 133–35. For his discussion of the need for "limit-concepts" appropriate to the limit-language of the biblical texts, see pp. 129–45. For one theologian's criticism of Ricoeur on this issue see Tracy, *Blessed Rage for Order*, p. 111, n. 11; 142–43, n. 67. For Ricoeur's discussion of the philosophical and theological dimensions of "hope," see "Freedom in the Light of Hope," in *Conflict*, pp. 402–24.

SELECTED BIBLIOGRAPHY

Rudolf Bultmann

Glauben und Verstehen. Gesammelte Aufsätze. 3 vols. Tübingen: J. C. B. Mohr (Paul Siebeck), 1933–1959.

Theology of the New Testament. Translated by Kendrik Grobel. 2 vols. New York: Charles Scribner's Sons, 1951–1955.

Essays Philosophical and Theological. Translated by James C. G. Grieg. London: SCM Press, 1955.

Introduction to *What Is Christianity?* by Adolf von Harnack. New York: Harper & Row, Harper Torchbooks, 1957.

Jesus and the Word. Translated by L. C. Smith and E. H. Lantero. New York: Charles Scribner's Sons, 1958.

Jesus Christ and Mythology. New York: Charles Scribner's Sons, 1958.

"Preaching: Genuine and Secularized." In *Religion and Culture: Essays in Honor of Paul Tillich,* pp. 236–42. Edited by W. Leibrecht. New York: Harper and Bros., 1959.

Existence and Faith: The Shorter Writings of Rudolf Bultmann. Edited and translated by Schubert Ogden. New York: Living Age Books, 1960.

"New Testament and Mythology." In *Kerygma and Myth,* pp. 1–44. Edited by Hans Werner Bartsch. Translated by R. H. Fuller. New York: Harper & Row, 1961.

History and Eschatology: The Presence of Eternity. New York: Harper & Row, Harper Torchbooks, 1962.

"On the Problem of Demythologizing." *Journal of Religion* 42 (1962): 96–102.

History of the Synoptic Tradition. Translated by John Marsh. Rev. ed. New York: Harper & Row, 1963.

Review of *Epistle to the Romans,* by Karl Barth. 2d ed. In *The Beginnings of Dialectical Theology,* pp. 100–120. Edited by James M. Robinson. Richmond: John Knox Press, 1968.

"Religion and Culture." In *The Beginnings of Dialectical Theology,* pp. 205–20.

206   Literary Criticism and Biblical Hermeneutics

"The Problem of a Theological Exegesis of the New Testament."
    In *The Beginnings of Dialectical Theology*, pp. 236–56.
Faith and Understanding. Edited by Robert W. Funk. Trans-
    lated by Louise Pettibone Smith. New York: Harper & Row,
    1969.

John Dominic Crossan

In Parables: The Challenge of the Historical Jesus. New York:
    Harper & Row, 1973.
The Dark Interval: Towards a Theology of Story. Niles, IL.:
    Argus Communications, 1975.
Raid on the Articulate: Comic Eschatology in Jesus and Borges.
    New York: Harper & Row, 1976.
"Waking the Bible." *Interpretation* 32 (1978): 269–85.
*Finding Is the First Act: Trove Folktales and Jesus' Treasure
    Parable*. Semeia Supplements, no. 9. Missoula, MT: Scholars
    Press and Philadelphia: Fortress Press, 1979.
Cliffs of Fall: Paradox and Polyvalence in the Parables of Jesus.
    New York: Seabury Press, 1980.

Hans W. Frei

"Theological Reflections on the Accounts of Jesus' Death and
    Resurrection." *Christian Scholar* 49 (1966): 263–306.
"The Availability of Karl Barth." Review of *Karl Barth: His Life
    from Letters and Autobiographical Texts* by Eberhard
    Busch. *The New Review of Books and Religion* 1 (1976):
    6–8.
The Eclipse of Biblical Narrative. New Haven: Yale University
    Press, 1974.
The Identity of Jesus Christ. Philadelphia: Fortress Press, 1975.

Dan Otto Via, Jr.

The Parables: Their Literary and Existential Dimension. Phila-
    delphia: Fortress Press, 1967.
Kerygma and Comedy in the New Testament. Philadelphia:
    Fortress Press, 1975.
"Parable of the Unjust Judge: A Metaphor of the Unrealized
    Self." In *Semiology and the Parables*, pp. 1–32. Edited by
    Daniel Patte. Pittsburgh: Pickwick Press, 1976.

"Religion and Story: Of Time and Reality." Review of *The Dark
Interval*, by Dominic Crossan; *Religion as Story*, ed. by James
B. Wiggins; and *Narrative Elements and Religious Meaning*,
by Wesley A. Kort. *Journal of Religion* 56 (1976): 392–99.

Paul Ricoeur

Fallible Man. Chicago: Henry Regnery Co., 1965.
Freedom and Nature: The Voluntary and the Involuntary.
Evanston: Northwestern University Press, 1966.
Symbolism of Evil. Boston: Beacon Press, 1967.
"The Problem of the Double-Sense as Hermeneutical Problem
and as Semantic Problem." In *Myths and Symbols*,
pp. 63–79. Edited by J. M. Kitagawa and C. H. Long. Chi-
cago: University of Chicago Press, 1969.
Freud and Philosophy: An Essay on Interpretation. Translated
by Denis Savage. New Haven: Yale University Press, 1970.
"The Model of the Text: Meaningful Action Considered as Text."
Social Research 38 (1971): 529–62.
"Sur l'exégèse de Genèse 1, 1–2.4a." In *Exégèse et hermeneu-
tique: Parole de Dieu*, pp. 67–84. Edited by Roland Barthes.
Paris: Editions de Seuill, 1971.
Philosophy Today 17 (1973). Special number on Paul Ricoeur.
The Conflict of Interpretations: Essays on Hermeneutics.
Edited by Don Ihde. Evanston: Northwestern University
Press, 1974.
"Philosophy and Religious Language." *Journal of Religion* 54
(1974): 71–85.
"Biblical Hermeneutics." *Semeia* 4 (1975): 29–148.
*The Rule of Metaphor: Multidisciplinary Studies of the Crea-
tion of Meaning in Language*. Translated by Robert Czerny
with Kathleen McLaughlin and John Costello. Toronto: Uni-
versity of Toronto Press, 1975.
"Philosophical Hermeneutics and Theological Hermeneutics."
Studies in Religion: Sciences religieuses 5 (1975): 14–33.
Interpretation Theory: Discourse and the Surplus of Meaning.
Fort Worth: Texas Christian University Press, 1976.
"Toward a Hermeneutic of the Idea of Revelation." *Harvard
Theological Review* 70 (1977): 1–37.
"Manifestation and Proclamation." *Blaisdell Institute Journal* 12
(1978): 13–35.

"The Narrative Function." *Semeia* 13, part 2 (1978): 177–202.
"The Metaphorical Process as Cognition, Imagination, Feeling."
　　Critical Inquiry 5 (1978): 143–59.
The Philosophy of Paul Ricoeur: An Anthology of His Work.
　　Edited by Charles E. Reagan and David Stewart. Boston:
　　Beacon Press, 1978.
"The Hermeneutics of Testimony." *Anglican Theological
　　Review* 6 (1979): 435–46.

Biblical and Theological Studies

Achtemeier, Paul J. *An Introduction to the New Hermeneutic.*
　　Philadelphia: Fortress, 1969.
Alter, Robert. *The Art of Biblical Narrative.* New York: Basic
　　Books, 1981.
Augustine, Saint. *On Christian Doctrine.* Translated by
　　D. W. Robertson, Jr.
Barr, James. *Old and New in Interpretation.* London: SCM
　　Press and New York: Harper & Row, 1966.
—————. *The Bible in the Modern World.* London: SCM
　　Press and New York: Harper & Row, 1973.
—————. *The Scope and Authority of the Bible.* Philadelphia:
　　Westminster Press, 1980.
Barth, Karl. *Church Dogmatics.* 13 vols. Edinburgh: T & T
　　Clark, 1957–1969.
Beardslee, William A. *Literary Criticism of the New Testa-
　　ment.* Philadelphia: Fortress Press, 1970.
—————. "Parable, Proverb, and Koan." *Semeia* 12 (1978):
　　151–71.
Betz, Hans Dieter. *Galatians: A Commentary on Paul's Letter
　　to the Churches in Galatia.* Hermenia: A Critical Commen-
　　tary on the Bible. Philadelphia: Fortress Press, 1979.
Black, Max. *Models and Metaphors: Studies in Language and
　　Philosophy.* Ithaca, NY: Cornell University Press, 1962.
Bornkamm, Günther. *Jesus of Nazareth.* Translated by Irene
　　and Fraser McLuskey with James M. Robinson. New York:
　　Harper & Row, 1960.
—————. *Paul.* Translated by D. M. G. Stalker. New York:
　　Harper & Row, 1971.
Braaten, Carl E., and Harrisville, Roy A., eds. *Kerygma and
　　History.* New York: Abingdon Press, 1962.

Brown, Raymond E. "Parable and Allegory Reconsidered." *Novum Testamentum* 5 (1962): 36–45.

Calloud, Jean. *Structural Analysis of Narrative.* Translated by Daniel Patte. Semeia Supplements, no. 4. Missoula, MT: Scholars Press and Philadelphia: Fortress Press, 1976.

Cambridge History of the Bible. 3 vols. Cambridge: Cambridge University Press, 1963–1970. Vol. 1: *From the Beginnings to Jerome,* edited by P. R. Ackroyd and C. F. Evans. Vol. 2: *The West from the Fathers to the Reformation,* edited by G. W. H. Lampe. Vol. 3: *The West from the Reformation to the Present Day,* edited by S. I. Greenslade.

Campenhausen, Hans von. *The Formation of the Christian Bible.* Translated by J. A. Baker. Philadelphia: Fortress, 1972.

Carlston, Charles E. *The Parables of the Triple Tradition.* Philadelphia: Fortress Press, 1975.

Childs, Brevard. *Biblical Theology in Crisis.* Philadelphia: Westminster Press, 1970.

_____. "The Old Testament as Scripture of the Church." *Concordia Monthly Quarterly* 43 (1972): 709–22.

Cobb, John B. *Living Options in Protestant Theology.* Philadelphia: Westminster Press, 1962.

_____. "A Theology of Story: Crossan and Beardslee." In *Orientation by Disorientation: Studies in Literary Criticism and Biblical Literary Criticism,* pp. 151–64. Edited by Richard A. Spencer. Pittsburgh Theological Monograph Series, no. 35. Pittsburgh: Pickwick Press, 1980.

Daniélou, Jean. *From Shadows to Reality.* Translated by Wulstan Hibberd. Westminster, MD: Newman Press, 1960

Dodd, Charles Harold. *The Parables of the Kingdom.* Rev. ed. New York: Charles Scribner's Sons, 1961.

Ebeling, Gerhard. *Word and Faith.* Philadelphia: Fortress Press, 1960.

_____. *Luther: An Introduction to His Thought.* Philadelphia: Fortress Press, 1970.

Flew, Anthony and MacIntyre, Alasdair, eds. *New Essays in Philosophical Theology.* London: SCM Press, 1963.

Ford, D. F. "Barth's Interpretation of the Bible." In *Karl Barth: Studies of His Theological Method,* pp. 55–87. Edited by S. W. Sykes. Oxford: Clarendon Press, 1979.

Frye, Roland Mushat. "Literary Criticism and Gospel Criticism." *Theology Today* 36 (1979): 207–19.

_____. "Metaphors, Equations and the Faith." *Theology Today* 37 (1980): 59–67.

Fuchs, Ernst. *Studies of the Historical Jesus.* Translated by A. Scobie. Studies in Biblical Theology, no. 42. London: SCM Press, 1964.

Funk, Robert W. *Language, Hermeneutic and the Word of God.* New York: Harper & Row, 1966.

_____. *Jesus as Precursor.* Semeia Supplements, no. 2. Missoula, MT: Scholars Press and Philadelphia: Fortress Press, 1975.

Gilkey, Langdon. *Naming the Whirlwind.* Indianapolis: Bobbs-Merrill Co., 1969.

_____. *Reaping the Whirlwind: A Christian Interpretation of History.* New York: Seabury Press, 1976.

Grant, Robert M. *The Bible in the Church.* New York: Macmillan Co., 1948.

_____. *The Letter and the Spirit.* London: Oxford University Press, 1957.

Hanson, R. P. C. *Allegory and Event.* London: SCM Press, 1959.

Hartt, Julian. *Theological Method and Imagination.* New York: Seabury Press, 1977.

Harvey, Van. *The Historian and the Believer.* New York: Macmillan Co., 1966.

Henderson, Ian. *Myth and the New Testament.* London: SCM Press, 1952.

Hyatt, James Philip, ed. *The Bible in Modern Scholarship: Papers Read at the 100th Meeting of the Society for Biblical Literature, Dec. 28–30, 1964.* Nashville: Abingdon Press, 1965.

Interpreter's Dictionary of the Bible. Rev. ed. (1962). S.v. "Biblical Criticism, History of," by S. J deVries; s.v. "Interpretation, History and Principles of," by K. Grobel.

Jeremias, Joachim. *The Parables of Jesus.* Rev. ed. New York: Charles Scribner's Sons, 1963.

Juel, Donald, with Ackerman, James S. and Warshaw, Thayer S. *An Introduction to New Testament Literature.* Nashville: Abingdon Press, 1978.

Käsemann, Ernst. *Essays on New Testament Themes.* London: SCM Press, 1964.

Kähler, Martin. *The So-Called Historical Jesus and the Historic, Biblical Christ.* Translated by Carl E. Braaten. Philadelphia: Fortress Press, 1964.

Kegley, Charles, ed. *The Theology of Bultmann*. New York: Harper & Row, 1966.

Kelsey, David. *The Uses of Scripture in Recent Theology*. Philadelphia: Fortress Press, 1975.

Kümmel, Werner Georg. *The New Testament: A History of the Investigation of Its Problems*. Translated by S. MacLean and Howard C. Kee. Nashville: Abingdon Press, 1972.

Lubac, Henri de. *Exégèse médiévale: les quatre sens de l'Ecriture*. 4 vols. Paris: Aubier, 1959–1964.

Luther, Martin. *Luther's Works*. Edited by Jaroslav Pelikan. American ed. 55 vols. St. Louis: Concordia Publishing House, 1958–1976.

McFague, Sallie. *Speaking in Parables: A Study in Metaphor and Theology*. Philadelphia: Fortress Press, 1975.

McKnight, Edgar V. *Meaning in Texts*. Philadelphia: Fortress Press, 1978.

Maier, John and Tollers, Vincent, eds. *The Bible in Its Literary Milieu*. Grand Rapids: William B. Eerdmans Co., 1979.

Marxsen, Willi. *The New Testament as the Church's Book*. Translated by James E. Mignard. Philadelphia: Fortress Press, 1972.

Metz, Johann Baptist and Jossua, Jean-Pierre, eds. *The Crisis of Religious Language*. New York: Herder and Herder, 1973.

Niebuhr, H. Richard. *The Meaning of Revelation*. New York: Macmillan Co., 1960.

Ogden, Schubert M. *Christ Without Myth*. New York: Harper & Row, 1961.

_____. *The Reality of God*. San Francisco: Harper & Row, 1963.

_____. "The Authority of Scripture for Theology." *Interpretation* 30: 242–61.

Origen. *On First Principles*. Translated by G. W. Butterworth.

Pannenberg, Wolfhart. *Basic Questions in Theology: Collected Essays*. Vol. 1. Translated by George H. Kehm. Philadelphia: Fortress Press, 1970.

Patte, Daniel. *What Is Structural Exegesis?* Philadelphia: Fortress Press, 1976.

Perrin, Norman. *Rediscovering the Teachings of Jesus*. New York: Harper & Row, 1976.

_____. *Jesus and the Language of the Kingdom*. Philadelphia: Fortress Press, 1976.

_____. *The Promise of Bultmann*. The Promise of Theology Series. Philadelphia: Lippincott Co., 1969; reprint ed., Philadelphia: Fortress Press, 1979.

Peters, Ted. "Sola Scriptura and the Second Naivete." *Dialog* 16 (1977): 268–80.

Petersen, Norman. *Literary Criticism for New Testament Critics*. Philadelphia: Fortress Press, 1978.

Polzin, Robert M. *Biblical Structuralism: Method and Subjectivity in the Study of Ancient Texts*. Philadelphia: Fortress Press and Missoula, MT: Scholars Press, 1977.

Preus, J. Samuel. *From Shadow to Promise: Old Testament Interpretation from Augustine to the Young Luther*. Cambridge: Harvard University Press, The Belknap Press, 1969.

Ramsey, Ian. *Religious Language: An Empirical Placing of Theological Phrases*. New York: Macmillan Co., 1963.

Religion in Geschichte und Gegenwart. 3d ed. (1959). S.v. "Hermeneutik," by Gerhard Ebeling.

Robinson, James M. *A New Quest of the Historical Jesus*. Naperville, IL: Alec R. Allenson, 1959.

_____ed. *The Bultmann School of Biblical Interpretation: New Directions?* Journal for Theology and the Church, no. 1. New York: Harper & Row, 1967.

Robinson, James M. and Cobb, John B., eds. *The New Hermeneutic*. New Frontiers in Theology, no. 2. New York: Harper & Row, 1964.

Sanders, James. *Torah and Canon*. Philadelphia: Fortress Press, 1972.

Schleiermacher, F. D. E. *On Religion*. Translated by John Oman. New York: Harper & Row, Harper Torchbooks, 1958.

Schleiermacher, F. D. E. *Hermeneutics: The Handwritten Manuscripts*. Translated by James Duke and Jack Forstman. AAR Texts and Translations Series, no. 1. Missoula, MT: Scholars Press, 1977.

Schmithals, Walter. *An Introduction to the Theology of Rudolf Bultmann*. Translated by John Bowden. Minneapolis: Augsburg Publishing House, 1968.

Schneidau, Herbert N. *Sacred Discontent: The Bible and Western Tradition*. Berkeley: University of California Press, 1976.

Schweitzer, Albert. *The Quest of the Historical Jesus*. Translated by W. Montgomery. New York: Macmillan Co., 1964.

Smalley, Beryl. *The Study of the Bible in the Middle Ages.* 2d ed. Notre Dame: Notre Dame University Press, 1964.

Smart, James D. *The Interpretation of Scripture.* Philadelphia: Fortress Press, 1963.

_____. *The Divided Mind of Modern Theology: Karl Barth and Rudolf Bultmann, 1908–1933.* Philadelphia: Westminster Press, 1967.

Smend, Rudolf. "Nachkritische Schriftauslegung." In *Parrhesia: Karl Barth zum 80. Geburtstag,* pp. 215–37. Edited by Eberhard Busch. Zurich: EVZ Verlag, 1966.

Steinmetz, David. "The Superiority of Pre-Critical Exegesis." *Theology Today* 37 (1980): 27–38.

Stroup, George III. "A Bibliographic Critique." *Theology Today* 32 (1975): 133–243.

Tannehill, Robert C. *The Sword of His Mouth.* Semeia Supplements, no. 1. Missoula, MT: Scholars Press and Philadelphia: Fortress Press, 1975.

Tolbert, Mary Ann. *Perspectives on the Parables: An Approach to Multiple Interpretations.* Philadelphia: Fortress Press, 1979.

Tracy, David. *Blessed Rage for Order.* New York: Seabury Press, 1975.

_____. "Metaphor and Religion: The Test Case of Christian Texts." *Critical Inquiry* 5 (1978): 91–106.

_____. "The Particularity and Universality of Christian Revelation." In *Revelation and Experience,* pp. 106–15. Edited by Edward Schillebeeckx. Concilium, no. 113. New York: Seabury Press, 1979.

_____. *The Analogical Imagination.* New York: Crossroad, 1981.

Von Rad, Gerhard. *Old Testament Theology.* Translated by D. M. G. Stalker. 2 vols. New York: Harper & Row, 1962–1965.

Wilder, Amos. "Mythology and the New Testament." Review of *Kerygma und Mythos,* edited by Hans Werner Bartsch. *Journal of Biblical Literature* 69 (1950): 113–27.

_____. "Scholars, Theologians, and Ancient Rhetoric." *Journal of Biblical Literature* 75 (1956): 1–11.

_____. "New Testament Hermeneutics Today." In *Current Issues in New Testament Interpretation,* pp. 38–52. Edited by William Klassen and Graydon F. Snyder. New York: Harper and Bros., 1962.

_____. *Language of the Gospel: Early Christian Rhetoric.* New York: Harper & Row and London: SCM Press, 1964. Published in Britain as *Early Christian Rhetoric.*

_____. *Theopoetic.* Philadelphia: Fortress Press, 1976.

Yu, Anthony C. "Recovering the Sense of Story." Review of *The Eclipse of Biblical Narrative*, by Hans W. Frei. *Journal of Religion* 58 (1978): 198–203.

Zuck, John E. "Tales of Wonder: Biblical Myth, Narrative and Fairy Stories." *Journal of the American Academy of Religion* 44 (1976): 299–308.

Literary Criticism, Interpretation Theory, and Related Studies

Abrams, Meyer H. *The Mirror and the Lamp.* New York: Oxford University Press, 1953.

_____. "Poetry, Theories of." In *Princeton Encyclopedia of Poetry and Poetics*, pp. 639–48. Edited by Alex Preminger. Enlarged ed. Princeton: Princeton University Press, 1974.

_____. "The Limits of Pluralism: The Deconstructive Angel." *Critical Inquiry* 3 (1977): 425–38.

_____. "How to do Things with Texts." *Partisan Review* 46 (1979): 565–88.

_____., ed. *Literature and Belief: English Institute Essays, 1957.* New York: Columbia University Press, 1958.

Adams, Hazard, ed. *Critical Theory since Plato.* New York: Harcourt, Brace, Jovanovitch, 1971.

Aristotle. *Rhetoric.* Translated by J. A. Smith and W. D. Ross.

_____. *Poetics.* Translated by S. H. Butcher.

Arnold, Matthew. *Selected Poetry and Prose.* Edited by Frederick L. Mulhauser. New York: Holt, Rinehart and Winston, Rinehart Editions, 1953.

Auden, W. H. *The Dyer's Hand.* New York: Random House, Vintage Books, 1968.

Auerbach, Erich. *Mimesis: The Representation of Reality in Western Literature.* Translated by W. R. Trask. Princeton: Princeton University Press, 1953.

Barthes, Roland. *S/Z.* Translated by Richard Howard. New York: Hill and Wang, 1974.

Bate, Walter Jackson, ed. *Criticism: The Major Texts.* Enlarged ed. New York: Harcourt, Brace, Jovanovitch, 1970.

Beneviste, Emile. *Problems in General Linguistics*. Translated by Mary Elizabeth Meek. Coral Gables, FL: University of Miami Press, 1971.

Blackmur, R. P. *Language as Gesture*. New York: Harcourt, Brace, Jovanovitch, 1952.

Bleich, David. *Subjective Criticism*. Baltimore: Johns Hopkins University Press, 1978.

Bloom, Harold. *A Map of Misreading*. New York: Oxford University Press, 1975.

Bloom, Harold; Miller, J. Hillis; and deMan, Paul, eds. *Deconstruction and Criticism*. New York: Seabury Press, 1979.

Bloomfield, Morton. "Allegory as Interpretation." *New Literary History* 3 (1972): 301–17.

Booth, Wayne. *The Rhetoric of Fiction*. Chicago: University of Chicago Press, 1961.

_____. *The Rhetoric of Irony*. Chicago: University of Chicago Press, 1974.

_____. *Critical Understanding: The Powers and Limits of Pluralism*. Chicago: University of Chicago Press, 1979.

Bourgeois, Patrick L. *Extension of Ricoeur's Hermeneutic*. The Hague: Martinus Nijhoff, 1975.

Brooks, Cleanth. *Modern Poetry and the Tradition*. Chapel Hill: University of North Carolina Press, 1939.

_____. *The Well Wrought Urn*. New York: Reynal and Hitchcock, 1947.

Brooks, Cleanth and Warren, Robert Penn. *Understanding Poetry*. New York: Harcourt, Brace, and World, 1960.

Burke, Kenneth. *The Rhetoric of Religion*. Berkeley: University of California Press, 1970.

Calinescu, Matei. "Hermeneutics or Poetics." *Journal of Religion* 59 (1979): 1–17.

Chatman, Seymour, ed. *Literary Style: A Symposium*. New York: Oxford University Press, 1970.

Crane, Ronald S. *The Languages of Criticism and the Structures of Poetry*. Toronto: University of Toronto Press, 1953.

Culler, Jonathan. *Structuralist Poetics: Structuralism, Linguistics, and the Study of Literature*. Ithaca, NY: Cornell University Press, 1975.

Davis, Walter A. *The Act of Interpretation: A Critique of Literary Reason*. Chicago: University of Chicago Press, 1978.

deMan, Paul. "The Crisis of Contemporary Criticism." *Arion* 6 (1967): 38–57.

――――――. *Blindness and Insight*. New York: Oxford University Press, 1971.

Derrida, Jacques. *Of Grammatology*. Translated by Gayatri Chakravorty Spivak. Baltimore: Johns Hopkins University Press, 1967.

――――――. "Structure, Sign and Play in the Discourse of the Human Sciences." In *The Languages of Criticism and the Sciences of Man*, pp. 278–93. Edited by R. Macksey and E. Donato. Baltimore: Johns Hopkins University Press, 1970.

――――――. "White Mythology: Metaphor in the Text of Philosophy." *New Literary History* 6 (1971): 5–74.

――――――. *Writing and Difference*. Translated by Alan Bass. Chicago: University of Chicago Press, 1978.

Dilthey, Wilhelm. *Pattern and Meaning in History*. Translated and edited by H. P. Rickman. New York: Harper & Row, Harper Torchbooks, 1962.

――――――. *Wilhelm Dilthey: Selected Writings*. Translated by H. P. Rickman. Cambridge: Cambridge University Press, 1976.

Eliot, T. S. *The Sacred Wood*. London: Methuen and Co., University Paperbacks, 1960.

――――――. *Selected Essays*. New York: Harcourt, Brace and World, 1964.

Fish, Stanley. *Self-Consuming Artifacts*. Berkeley: University of California Press, 1972.

――――――. *Is There a Text in This Class? The Authority of Interpretive Communities*. Cambridge: Harvard University Press, 1980.

Fletcher, Angus. *Allegory: The Theory of a Symbolic Mode*. Ithaca, NY: Cornell University Press, 1964.

Foster, Richard. *The New Romantics*. Bloomington: Indiana University Press, 1962.

Frye, Northrop. *Anatomy of Criticism*. Princeton: Princeton University Press, 1957.

――――――. *The Secular Scripture: A Study of the Structure of Romance*. Cambridge: Harvard University Press, 1976.

――――――. *Spiritus Mundi: Essays on Literature, Myth, and Society*. Bloomington: Indiana University Press, 1976.

Gadamer, Hans Georg. *Truth and Method.* Translated by G. Barden and J. Cumming. New York: Seabury Press, 1975.

_____. *Philosophical Hermeneutics.* Translated by David Linge. Berkeley: University of California Press, 1976.

Gallie, W. B. *Philosophy and Historical Understanding.* 2d ed. New York: Schocken Books, 1964.

Gardner, Helen Louise. *Religion and Literature.* New York: Oxford University Press, 1971.

Geertz, Clifford. *The Interpretation of Cultures.* New York: Basic Books, 1973.

Gerhart, Mary J. *The Question of Belief in Literary Criticism: An Introduction to the Hermeneutical Theory of Paul Ricoeur.* Stuttgart: Verlag Hans-Dieter Heinz, 1970.

_____. "Paul Ricoeur's Notion of 'Diagnostics': Its Function in Literary Interpretation." *Journal of Religion* 56 (1976): 137–56.

_____. "Generic Studies: Their Renewed Importance in Religion and Literary Interpretation." *Journal of the American Academy of Religion* 45 (1977): 309–25.

Gombrich, E. H. *Art and Illusion.* The A. W. Mellon Lectures in Fine Arts, 1956. Bollingen Series, XXXV/5. Princeton: Princeton University Press, 1961.

Graff, Gerald. *Poetic Statement and Critical Dogma.* Evanston: Northwestern University Press, 1970.

_____. *Literature Against Itself.* Chicago: University of Chicago Press, 1979.

Gunn, Giles B. *The Interpretation of Otherness.* New York: Oxford University Press, 1979.

_____., ed. *Literature and Religion.* New York: Harper & Row, Harper Forum Books, 1971.

Hartman, Geoffrey. *Beyond Formalism: Literary Essays, 1958–1970.* New Haven: Yale University Press, 1970.

_____. *The Fate of Reading.* Chicago: University of Chicago Press, Phoenix Books, 1975.

_____. *Criticism in the Wilderness.* New Haven: Yale University Press, 1980.

_____. *Saving the Text.* Baltimore: Johns Hopkins University Press, 1981.

Heidegger, Martin. *Being and Time.* Translated by John Macquarrie and Edward Robinson. New York: Harper & Row, 1962.

_____. *Poetry, Language, Thought*. Translated and introduction by Albert Hofstadter. New York: Harper & Row, 1971.

Hirsch, E. D. *Validity in Interpretation*. New Haven: Yale University Press, 1967.

_____. *The Aims of Interpretation*. Chicago: University of Chicago Press, 1976.

Honig, Edwin. *Dark Conceit: The Making of Allegory*. Cambridge, MA: Walker deBerry, 1960.

Hopper, Stanley Romaine and Miller, David, eds. *Interpretation: The Poetry of Meaning*. New York: Harcourt, Brace and World, 1967.

Hoy, David Couzens. *The Critical Circle*. Berkeley: University of California Press, 1978.

Ihde, Don. *Hermeneutical Phenomenology: The Philosophy of Paul Ricoeur*. Evanston: Northwestern University Press, 1971.

Iser, Wolfgang. *The Implied Reader*. Baltimore: Johns Hopkins University Press, 1974.

Jameson, Fredric. *The Prison-House of Language*. Princeton: Princeton University Press, 1972.

Kant, Immanuel. *Critique of Judgement*. Translated by J. H. Bernard. 2d ed. New York: Hafner Publishing Co., 1931.

Kermode, Frank. *The Sense of an Ending*. London: Oxford University Press, 1966.

_____. *The Classic*. New York: Viking Press, 1975.

_____. *Genesis of Secrecy: On the Interpretation of Narrative*. Cambridge: Harvard University Press, 1979.

Kirk, G. S. *Myth: Its Meaning and Function in Ancient and Other Cultures*. Cambridge: Harvard University Press, 1970.

Krieger, Murray. *The New Apologists for Poetry*. Minneapolis: University of Minnesota Press, 1956.

_____. *A Window to Criticism*. Princeton: Princeton University Press, 1964.

Langbaum, Robert. *The Modern Spirit*. New York: Oxford University Press, 1970.

Lévi-Strauss, Claude. *Structural Anthropology*. Garden City, NY: Anchor Books, 1967.

Lynch, William F., S.J. *Christ and Apollo*. New York: Sheed and Ward, 1960.

Mazzeo, Joseph. *Varieties of Interpretation*. Notre Dame: University of Notre Dame Press, 1978.

Miller, J. Hillis, ed. *Aspects of Narrative.* Selected Papers from the English Institute. New York: Columbia University Press, 1971.

Murrin, Michael. *The Veil of Allegory.* Chicago: University of Chicago Press, 1969.

Nietzsche, Friedrich. *The Birth of Tragedy and The Genealogy of Morals.* Translated by Francis Golffing. Garden City, NY: Doubleday and Co., 1956.

Palmer, Richard E. *Hermeneutics.* Evanston: Northwestern University Press, 1969.

Pearce, Roy Harvey. "Historicism Once More." *Kenyon Review* 20 (1958): 555–91.

Plato. *Republic.* Translated by Benjamin Jowett.

_____. *Timaeus.* Translated by Benjamin Jowett.

Ransom, John Crowe. *The World's Body.* New York: Charles Scribner's Sons, 1938.

_____. "Criticism as Pure Speculation." In *The Intent of the Critic,* pp. 92–124. Edited by D. A. Stauffer. Princeton: Princeton University Press, 1969.

Reagan, Charles E., ed. *Studies in the Philosophy of Paul Ricoeur.* Athens, OH: Ohio University Press, 1979.

Richards, Ivor Armstrong. *Science and Poetry.* New York: W. W. Norton Co., 1926.

_____. *The Philosophy of Rhetoric.* New York: Oxford University Press, 1936.

_____. *Principles of Literary Criticism.* New York: Harcourt, Brace and World, Harvest Books, 1965.

Saussure, Ferdinand de. *Course in General Linguistics.* New York: McGraw-Hill, 1966.

Scholes, Robert. *Structuralism in Literature: An Introduction.* New Haven: Yale University Press, 1974.

Scholes, Robert and Kellog, Robert. *The Nature of Narrative.* New York: Oxford University Press, 1966.

Singleton, Charles S., ed. *Interpretation: Theory and Practice.* Baltimore: Johns Hopkins University Press, 1969.

Smith, Barbara Herrnstein. *On the Margins of Discourse.* Chicago: University of Chicago Press, 1978.

Stallman, Robert Wooster, ed. *Critiques and Essays in Criticism: 1920–1948.* New York: Ronald Press, 1949.

Steiner, George. *After Babel: Aspects of Language and Translation.* New York: Oxford University Press, 1975.

Suleiman, Susan R. and Crossman, Inge, eds. *The Reader in the Text*. Princeton: Princeton University Press, 1980.

Tate, Allen. *On the Limits of Poetry: Selected Essays 1928–1948*. New York: Swallow Press, 1948.

_____. *The Man of Letters in the Modern World*. New York: Meridian Books,1955.

Trilling, Lionel. *Sincerity and Authenticity*. Cambridge: Harvard University Press, 1972.

Turner, Victor W. *Dramas, Fields, and Metaphors*. Ithaca: Cornell University Press, 1974.

Warren, Robert Penn. *Selected Essays*. New York: Random House, 1958.

Wellek, René. *Concepts of Criticism*. Edited by Stephen G. Nichols, Jr. New Haven: Yale University Press, 1963.

Wellek, René and Warren, Austin. *Theory of Literature*. New York: Harcourt, Brace and World, Harvest Books, 1942.

Wheelright, Philip. *Metaphor and Reality*. Bloomington: Indiana University Press, 1962.

_____. *The Burning Fountain*. Rev. ed. Bloomington: Indiana University Press, 1968.

White, Hayden. *Metahistory*. Baltimore: Johns Hopkins University Press, 1973.

Wimsatt, William K. and Beardsley, Monroe C. *The Verbal Icon*. Lexington: University of Kentucky Press, 1954.

Wimsatt, William K. and Brooks, Cleanth. *Literary Criticism: A Short History*. New York: Random House and Alfred Knopf, Vintage Books, 1957.